access to history

The Unification of
Germany 1815–1919
THIRD EDITION

Alan Farmer and Andrina Stiles

HODDER
EDUCATION
AN HACHETTE UK COMPANY

Study guides updated, 2008, by Sally Waller (AQA) and Angela Leonard (Edexcel).

The publishers would like to thank the following individuals, institutions and companies for permission to reproduce copyright illustrations in this book: AKG-images, page 94; © Bettmann/CORBIS, pages 11, 53, 68, 95, 131, 163, 187; © Bibliotheque des Arts Decoratifs, Paris, France/Archives Charmet/The Bridgeman Art Library, page 60; © BPK, pages 8, 44; © Christel Gerstenberg/CORBIS, page 141; © Historisches Museum, Frankfurt, Germany/Archives Charmet/The Bridgeman Art Library, page 31; Hulton Archive/Stringer, pages 78, 154; © Hulton-Deutsch Collection/CORBIS, pages 20, 156, 199, 207; Mary Evans Picture Library, pages 105, 167; Mary Evans/Weimar Archive, page 203; © Michael Nicholson/CORBIS, page 57; © Private Collection/Archives Charmet/The Bridgeman Art Library, page 39; © Private Collection/The Bridgeman Art Library, page 55; Reproduced with permission of Punch Ltd., www.punch.co.uk, page 119; Oscar Gustav Rejlander/Stringer, page 84; Time Life Pictures, page 133.
The publishers would like to thank the following for permission to reproduce material in this book: Edexcel Limited for extracts used on pages 81, 137.
The publishers would like to acknowledge use of the following extracts: Addison Wesley Publishing for an extract from *Germany 1815–1939* by F. McKichan, 1992; Ariel Publications for an extract from *Bismarck* by B. Waller, 1985; Blackwell Publishers for an extract from *The Long Nineteenth Century* by D. Blackbourn, 1997; Cambridge University Press for an extract from *The Austro-Prussian War* by Geoffrey Wawro, 1996; Frank Cass for an extract from *The Zollverein* by W.O. Pankhurst, 1939; Clarendon Press for an extract from *Germany After the First World War* by R. Bessel, 1993; Clarendon Press for an extract from *German History 1770–1866* by James Sheehan, 1993; Hodder Arnold for an extract from *Bismarck and Modern Germany* by W.N. Medlicott, 1965; Oxford University Press for an extract from *The Foundation of the German Empire* by H. Bohme, 1967; Taylor and Francis, Inc. for an extract from *The Franco-Prussian War* by Michael Howard, 1961.
Every effort has been made to trace all copyright holders, but if any have been inadvertently overlooked the Publishers will be pleased to make the necessary arrangements at the first opportunity.

Orders: please contact Bookpoint Ltd, 130 Milton Park, Abingdon, Oxon OX14 4SB. Telephone: (44) 01235 827720. Fax: (44) 01235 400454. Lines are open 9.00–5.00, Monday to Saturday, with a 24-hour message answering service. Visit our website at www.hoddereducation.co.uk

© Alan Farmer and Andrina Stiles 2007
First published in 2007 by
Hodder Education, An Hachette UK Company
338 Euston Road, London NW1 3BH

Impression number   5 4
Year   2011 2010 2009

Cover photo AKG-images
Illustrations by Gray Publishing
Typeset in Baskerville and produced by Gray Publishing, Tunbridge Wells
Printed in Malta

A catalogue record for this title is available from the British Library

ISBN: 978 0340 929 292

Contents

Dedication

Keith Randell (1943–2002)

The *Access to History* series was conceived and developed by Keith, who created a series to 'cater for students as they are, not as we might wish them to be'. He leaves a living legacy of a series that for over 20 years has provided a trusted, stimulating and well-loved accompaniment to post-16 study. Our aim with these new editions is to continue to offer students the best possible support for their studies.

1

Germany 1815–48

POINTS TO CONSIDER

Before 1871 Germany did not exist as a country in the sense of being a unified political state. However, in 1815 there were tens of thousands of people, especially among the young, the educated, and the middle and upper classes, who longed passionately for a unified Germany. The numbers of these German nationalists grew greatly in the years after 1815. The years 1815–48 are often called the *Vormärz* or pre-March (a prelude to the March revolution in Berlin in 1848). Associated with the Austrian statesman Metternich, the *Vormärz* is usually seen as a period of reaction and repression. Is this fair? To what extent did the period see the development of a nationalist and liberal opposition? Was there any real sense of German unity by 1848? This first chapter tries to answer these questions by examining:

- The situation in Germany by 1815
- Reform and repression 1815–40
- Economic developments 1815–48
- Germany 1840–8

Key dates

1813	Battle of Leipzig
1814–15	The Vienna Peace Settlement
1815	German Confederation established
1817	Wartburg festival
1818	Constitutions granted in Baden and Bavaria
1819	Carlsbad Decrees
1832	Nationalist festival at Hambach
	The Six Articles
1834	*Zollverein* came into operation
1840	Frederick William IV became King of Prussia
1847	Meeting of the Prussian United *Diet* in Berlin

Key question
Was 'Germany' a meaningful concept in 1815?

1 | The Situation in Germany by 1815

The term 'Germany' had no real political significance before the nineteenth century. There was no single German state. By 1800, some 23 million Germans were divided into 314 states, varying in size from the 115,533 square miles of the Habsburg monarchy to the 33 square miles of Schwartzburg-Sonderhausen. These states were loosely united under the nominal rule of the Holy Roman Emperor, who was also Emperor of Austria.

To make the situation more complicated, Germany lacked clear natural frontiers, especially in the east and south. It was not even possible to define Germany's extent on ethnic grounds. The Holy Roman Empire included land peopled by French, Dutch, Danish, Polish and Czech speakers and excluded sizeable territories with a predominantly German population.

Apart from Austria, only one state within the **Holy Roman Empire** had any real power or importance in domestic and international affairs, and that was Prussia. When Austria and Prussia were defeated by Napoleon Bonaparte in 1805–6, the Empire collapsed.

Napoleon's impact on Germany

In 1806 Napoleon re-organised the old hotchpotch of German states:

- France annexed the territory on the left bank of the Rhine.
- Elsewhere many small states were amalgamated: the total number was reduced to 39.
- Bavaria, Saxony, Baden and 14 other states were formed into the Confederation of the Rhine. This was under direct French control. The French legal system replaced the different laws and judicial procedures of the separate states.

The Napoleonic conquests transformed the German political landscape in other ways. French ideas of liberty and equality created a new context for German politics. There was increased middle-class involvement in government and in administration. Many Germans were released from **feudal restrictions**.

Prussia 1806–13

After the devastating defeat by Napoleon in 1806, Prussia was determined to recover her position as a leading German state. The Prussian government made great efforts to reform Prussian institutions:

- The army was re-organised.
- The government was overhauled to provide a more efficient central authority.
- A new system of education was introduced.

The War of Liberation

Popular anti-French opinion encouraged the Prussian King Frederick William III to overcome his natural indecisiveness and in January 1813 he made an alliance with Russia against France. Russian and Prussian armies drove Napoleon's forces back towards France. In June, Austria also declared war on France and in October, Napoleon was defeated at the Battle of Leipzig.

Key terms

Holy Roman Empire
Formed in the ninth century, the Empire had little power or meaning by 1800. The French philosopher Voltaire said it was not holy, Roman or an empire.

Feudal restrictions
The feudal system was a system of social organisation prevalent in much of Europe in the Middle Ages. Powerful landowning lords limited the freedom of the people who worked on their estates.

Key date

Battle of Leipzig: 1813

Key terms

Nationalism
The belief in – and support for – a national identity.

Habsburg
The ruling family of the Austrian Empire.

Within a few months the allied armies invaded France and forced Napoleon to abdicate.

This so-called War of Liberation has often been seen as the first collective action of the German nation. However, later nationalist myths about it bore little relation to reality. Although the unacceptable behaviour of French occupying troops had helped to fuel **nationalism**, German resistance to France never became a mass national uprising. South Germans tended to look to Austria for political leadership, North Germans tended to look to Prussia. It was clear that the future of Germany would be decided, not by German patriots but by the particular interests of Prussia and Austria.

Key question
How did the Vienna Peace Settlement affect Germany?

The Vienna Settlement

In 1814–15 German unification was not a practical proposition. Too many deep-seated divisions stood in the way of national unity. Perhaps the most important was the rivalry between Austria and Prussia. These two states were obvious rival candidates for the control of any united Germany. However, at this stage, they were content to exist side by side in what Austrian Foreign Minister Metternich called 'peaceful dualism'. Both were among the Great Powers who drew up the peace treaty at the Congress of Vienna in 1815. Not surprisingly, both benefited substantially from the Vienna settlement.

Key dates

The Vienna Peace Settlement: 1814–15

German Confederation established: 1815

Austrian gains

Most of Austria's territorial gains came in Italy, not Germany. Austria secured Lombardy and Venetia in northern Italy, while **Habsburg** rulers were restored to the central Italian duchies of Parma, Modena and Tuscany.

Prussian gains

Prussia gained considerable areas of territory, including part of Saxony, the Rhineland, Westphalia and Pomerania (see Map 1.1 on page 4). Prussia's population had been more than doubled to ten million. The sudden increase in size brought problems, particularly with the Rhineland. The Catholic Rhinelanders resented being annexed to Protestant Prussia from which they were separated by more than 80 kilometres and with which they had little in common. The industrialised Rhineland with its numerous towns contrasted sharply with rural Prussia. It had come under French influence while part of Napoleon's Confederation of the Rhine, and many Rhinelanders regarded the Prussians as an alien culture from the east.

Key question
How important was the German Confederation?

The German Confederation

The most important influence on the future of the German states after 1815 was that of Prince Metternich, Austrian chief minister until 1848. Metternich's aim was the maintenance of Austria's traditional authority over the German states. He was not concerned with German political unity, and his

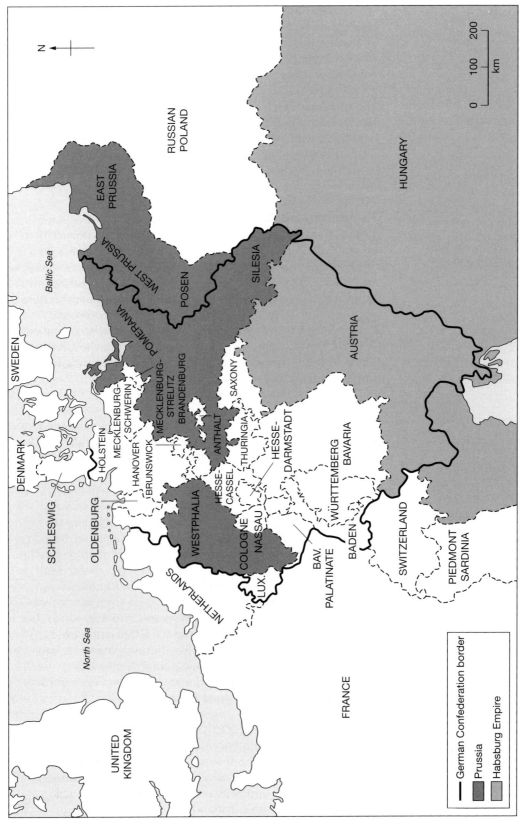

Map 1.1: Germany in 1815.

negotiations at Vienna ensured that Germany would become a loose confederation of states under Austrian control.

In June 1815 the German Confederation, comprising 39 states, was established with the aim of 'maintaining the external and internal security and the independence and integrity of the individual states'. Its declared aim was therefore the maintenance of the **status quo** in individual states through a system of mutual assistance in times of danger, such as internal rebellion or external aggression. It was not concerned with promoting a united Germany. In fact its aim was exactly the opposite, for none of the rulers of the separate states wished to see their independence limited by the establishment of a strong central German government.

Thus, no objection was raised when the boundaries of the Confederation were modelled on those of the old Holy Roman Empire rather than on ones that would encourage the development of a nation state of Germany. So areas peopled by Poles, Czechs, Danes and French were included and provinces with largely German-speaking populations were excluded. States such as Luxemburg, Hanover and Holstein, which were ruled by foreign monarchs (the Dutch King ruled Luxemburg, the British King Hanover and the Danish King Holstein), were within the Confederation while parts of German-speaking Austria and Prussia were not.

The *Diet*

The Confederation had only one **executive** body, the *Diet*, which met at Frankfurt. This was a permanent conference of representatives, who were not elected but were sent by their governments with instructions how to act. It was presided over by the Austrian representative. Given that the agreement of every state government was required before any measure could be passed, little was ever achieved. Representatives were more concerned with safeguarding the interests of their own states than working for the Confederation as a whole.

The weakness of the German Confederation

Each state had its own independent ruler, its own government and its own army. The Confederation appointed ambassadors and could make foreign treaties on behalf of its members. Otherwise it had very little direct control over the 39 individual states, apart from being able to prevent them making foreign alliances which might threaten the security of the Confederation, or concluding separate peace agreements in the event of the Confederation being involved in war. The Constitution of the Confederation, the Federal Act, had empowered the *Diet* to organise a federal army and to develop commercial and economic co-operation between the states, but local jealousies and fiercely guarded independence meant that nothing of importance was done to unify the Confederation militarily or economically. The defence of the Confederation depended upon the continued co-operation of Austria and Prussia.

The Confederation thus disappointed those Germans who hoped for greater national unity. It has also been criticised by historians who see it as being essentially the Holy Roman Empire mark II – an organisation which had no place in the age of emergent nation states. However, the Confederation at least provided a framework within which German states co-existed, albeit uneasily.

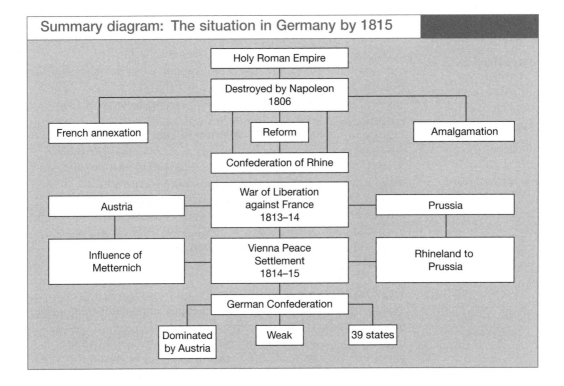

Summary diagram: The situation in Germany by 1815

- Holy Roman Empire
- Destroyed by Napoleon 1806
- French annexation
- Reform
- Amalgamation
- Confederation of Rhine
- Austria
- War of Liberation against France 1813–14
- Prussia
- Influence of Metternich
- Vienna Peace Settlement 1814–15
- Rhineland to Prussia
- German Confederation
- Dominated by Austria
- Weak
- 39 states

2 | Reform and Repression 1815–40

Absolute rule was restored in most German states in 1815. All but four were **dynastic** states – monarchies, **duchies** and **principalities**. However, one of the Articles of the Federal Act laid down that the ruler of each state should sooner or later give his subjects a 'Constitution of Regional Estates', that is, some kind of parliament. The response varied:

- Some rulers totally ignored the Article.
- Most north German states allowed the 'estates' to meet. These 'estates' were traditional representative bodies, not always elected, and usually composed largely of nobles.
- In southern and central Germany there was more compliance with the Federal Act. Between 1818 and 1820 Bavaria, Baden, Württemberg and Hesse-Darmstadt introduced constitutions that created elected assemblies. These assemblies had the

power to make laws and control taxation. However, even in these states the assemblies had limited influence. The monarchs continued to appoint their own ministers and retain real power.

Developments in Austria and Prussia

Little was done to encourage democratic reform in Austria. The Austrian kings Francis I (1804–35) and his weak-minded successor Ferdinand I (1835–49) wished to maintain their absolute power. The old provincial *Diets* were eventually revived, but only as a means of preserving the existing social order. They were dominated by the local aristocracy.

In Prussia, Frederick William III (1797–1840) showed little interest in liberal reform. Prussia was a patchwork of disparate territories, divided culturally, economically and in religious terms, particularly between east and west. The country was divided into provinces, each with a president, who was appointed by the central government in Berlin. Each province enjoyed a high degree of independence and each maintained its own distinct identity. Although Frederick William III did agree to set up provincial estates with limited advisory powers in 1823, these were controlled by large landowners. Essentially Prussia remained a state without a **constitution** until 1848.

Monarchical rule

The majority of German rulers, following the lead of Austria and Prussia, clung obstinately to their absolute power. Noble families continued to wield huge influence. However, many states emerged from the years of war with better organised and stronger **bureaucracies**. This was the result of French occupation, imitation of French methods, or simply financial necessity. The bureaucracies were active in a host of areas – economic, financial, legal and educational. They ensured, for example, that educational provision in Germany was the best in Europe.

Student movements

Student societies with a strong political flavour had grown up in the universities in 1813 after the battle of Leipzig that had driven the French out of the German states. The defeat of Napoleon was a great encouragement to German nationalism. In the years after 1815, thousands of young middle- and upper-class Germans, hoping to give practical form to their romantic sense of national identity, joined societies campaigning for a united Germany.

In 1817, nationalist students converted the Wartburg Festival from a celebration of the tercentenary of **Martin Luther's stand against the Pope** and the fourth anniversary of the victory of Leipzig into a demonstration against the princes. Given that fewer than 500 students attended the Festival, its importance has often been exaggerated.

Key terms

Constitution
A set of rules by which a state is governed.

Bureaucracies
Systems of administration.

Martin Luther's stand against the Pope
In 1517 German religious leader Martin Luther protested against a number of practices within the Catholic Church. His move led to a bitter religious divide. Luther's followers became known as Protestants.

Key question
To what extent did nationalist and liberal ideas develop in the period 1815–40?

Key date
Wartburg festival: 1817

This print published in 1817 shows a procession of students on their way to the Wartburg Festival.

The Carlsbad Decrees

Metternich certainly exaggerated the importance of the student movements, especially when in 1819 a member of an extreme student society murdered Kotzebue, a secret agent of the Russian Tsar. This murder prompted Metternich to take action. He consulted the King of Prussia and then summoned representatives of the German states to meet him at Carlsbad. Their decisions were ratified by the *Diet* as the Carlsbad Decrees. These Decrees:

- provided inspectors for universities
- ensured that student societies were disbanded
- introduced press censorship
- set up a commission to investigate 'revolutionary' movements.

As a result of the Decrees, a number of professors were dismissed from their posts and a few radical leaders were imprisoned. It seemed that **reactionary** forces had triumphed.

Carlsbad Decrees: 1819

Key date

Reactionary
Opposing political or social change and wanting to revert to past conditions.

Key term

Liberal reform

The liberal ideas Metternich so distrusted were concerned with constitutional reform and the replacing of absolute government by a parliamentary system. Liberals also wanted:

- freedom of speech
- freedom of the press
- freedom of worship
- freedom to form political associations and hold political meetings.

Key term

Franchise
The right to vote.

However, their ideas on parliamentary representation were restricted to giving the vote to men of property. Few supported a universal **franchise**. Liberals were almost exclusively well-educated, well-to-do members of the middle class concerned with their own economic and political interests and not with radical changes in the structure of society. Most were opposed to violence and hoped to achieve their aims by intellectual argument and peaceful persuasion. Too often though, talk became a substitute for action.

German nationalism

The seeds of German nationalism had been sown by the philosopher Johann Herder in the eighteenth century. He believed that all people or cultures had their own special and unique spirit, which made them different from neighbouring peoples. These cultures, Herder argued, should be cherished and developed as the basis for a national identity.

Some nationalists, like the writer Johann Goethe, believed that there was no need for the formation of a nation state. Instead, Germany should essentially be a cultural community, based on the model of ancient Greece.

Others, like George Hegel, a professor in the University of Berlin, claimed that man only achieved his full potential as a human being by service to the state. As an individual he was nothing; as part of a national community he was everything.

By the early nineteenth century, most German nationalists wanted an independent German state with fixed geographical boundaries and its own government. One problem was there were no clearly defined frontiers. Nor was there religious unity; the south and west were mainly Catholic and the north Lutheran Protestant. However, there was a common language and a shared cultural tradition based on a literary and artistic heritage. In addition there was felt to be an ethnic bond uniting all true Germans, and this was to become more important over the years.

How strong were German nationalism and liberalism?

It is difficult to know how far liberal and nationalist ideas filtered down from the educated minority to the rest of the population. For many ordinary Germans, nationalism arose simply as a resentment of French rule. Once French occupation had ended, nationalist sentiment declined. The middle classes, many of whom believed that German culture – literature, music, art, and philosophy – was pre-eminent in Europe, tended to have more positive views about nationalism. There were a remarkable number of national associations and festivals. German artists painted canvases of Germany's heroic past. German architects tried to build in a German style (although there was some uncertainty about what that style should be). Nevertheless, only a small minority envisaged a strong united German nation that would dominate Europe.

The *Vormärz* years were certainly a time of political excitement. However, much of it was of an intellectual and theoretical kind. Lectures, books and pamphlets, which put forward the new ideas, reached only a limited audience, rarely filtering down from the educated minority to the rest of the population.

In some cases, however, the message was carried to the workers in the cities by well-meaning liberals who set up study groups. Moreover, groups were sometimes formed by workers themselves. Some groups had several hundred members and discussed the possibility of revolution. Their politics often became democratic rather than liberal, centred on the **sovereignty** of the people rather than on the sovereignty of parliament, on a republic rather than a monarchy, and on violence rather than on peaceful means to obtain their ends. But however enthusiastic these groups were, they involved only a small proportion of workers in the cities and the workers on the land hardly at all.

Metternich

Metternich believed that the maintenance of international peace was directly linked with the prevention of revolution in individual states. Internal and international affairs were inseparable. What happened inside one state was of concern to other states, and entitled them to intervene if they considered it necessary. The social order had to be defended against the forces of destruction. For Metternich these forces were liberalism and nationalism. If these – in his view – revolutionary ideas spread, they could lead to the overthrow of absolute monarchy and the end of the **multinational Austrian Empire**. He, therefore, set his face against any constitutional change, however modest.

The Congress of Troppau

Metternich supported the idea of European Congresses – meetings of the Great Powers to discuss and settle international disagreements and maintain peace. At the Congress of Troppau in 1820 discussion centred on revolutions which had broken out in Spain, Portugal, Piedmont and Naples. Tsar Alexander I of Russia, in sympathy with Metternich's reactionary beliefs, put forward a proposal that Russia, Austria and Prussia should act jointly, using force if necessary, to restore any government which had been overthrown by force. The proposal was accepted and in the Protocol of Troppau, Russia, Austria and Prussia announced that they 'would never recognise the rights of a people to restrict the powers of their King'. This ran directly contrary to the

Key question
How successful were Metternich's repressive policies?

Vormärz
The period from 1815 to 1848.

Sovereignty
Supreme power.

Multinational Austrian Empire
The Austrian Empire contained people of many different nationalities. Although a relatively small minority, the Germans were the dominant ethnic group within the Empire.

Key terms

Profile: Clemens von Metternich 1773–1859

1773	– Born into high German nobility in the Rhineland
1794	– Family moved to Vienna to escape a French invasion of the Rhineland
1809	– Became Foreign Minister of Austria
1814–15	– Played a key role at the Vienna Peace Settlement
1821	– Became Austrian Chancellor
1848	– Forced to resign and flee to England
1859	– Died

Metternich was a complex personality. Vain, arrogant and pompous, he was also extremely able. In 1819 he said:

> There is a wide sweep about my mind. I am always above and beyond the preoccupations of most public men; I cover a ground much vaster than they can see or wish to see. I cannot keep myself from saying about twenty times a day: 'O Lord! how right I am and how wrong they are.'

Although confident in his own abilities and ideals, he was pessimistic about the future:

> My life has coincided with a most abominable time ... I have come into the world too soon or too late. I know that in these years I can accomplish nothing ... I am spending my life underpinning buildings which are mouldering into decay.

He was totally opposed to democracy. He wrote:

> It is true that I do not like democracies. Democracy is in every case a principle of dissolution, of decomposition. It tends to separate men, it loosens society. I am opposed to this because I am by nature and by habit constructive. That is why monarchy is the only government that suits my way of thinking ... Monarchy alone tends to bring men together, to unite them in compact, efficient masses, and to make them capable by their combined efforts of the highest degree of culture and civilisation.

Metternich believed that popular challenges to legitimate authority would result in chaos, bloodshed and an end to civilisation. His single-mindedness prompted contemporaries to speak of a 'Metternich System' and historians have subsequently found this a useful concept to help to analyse his actions. Some think his 'System' was based on a complex philosophy. Others, like A.J.P. Taylor, have doubted whether there was a 'System', believing that Metternich was simply a traditional conservative with no profound philosophical beliefs. His main aims were simply to maintain the Austrian Empire and maintain himself in office.

ambitions of liberals and nationalists everywhere, and was particularly disappointing to those in the German states. Prussia as well as Austria was firmly ranged on the side of reaction.

Repression in the 1820s

As well as the weapons of diplomacy and threats of force, Metternich used those of the police state to maintain the *status quo*. A special office was set up in Vienna to open, copy and then reseal foreign correspondence passing through Austria. This gave him an enormous amount of secret information and it was backed up by reports from his network of spies throughout Europe and by the work of his secret police. His efforts to turn the Confederation into a police state were only partially successful. Repression and press censorship varied in severity from state to state. Nevertheless, Metternich was generally successful in keeping Germany (and indeed Europe) quiet throughout the 1820s.

Liberal reform in the 1830s

In the 1830s the picture changed. The **July Revolution in Paris** of 1830 sparked off demonstrations and riots in several south German states. The demands were for a constitution as laid down in the Federal Act of 1815; or, if a constitution already existed, for its liberalisation.

- In Brunswick the Duke was driven out and his successor was forced to grant a more liberal constitution.
- In Saxony and Hesse-Cassel more liberal constitutions were obtained.
- In Bavaria, Baden and Württemberg liberal opposition parties gained parliamentary seats and greater freedom of the press allowed criticisms of the government.
- In Hanover the King granted a constitution in 1832.

The growth of German nationalism in the 1830s

In the early 1830s, a number of republican groups were busy with plans for the unification of Germany. In 1832 some 25,000 nationalists met at the Hambach Festival in Bavaria to drink, talk and plan revolution. The tricolour flag, symbol of revolution, was hoisted and toasts drunk to the notion that power should lay with the people.

Metternich, not surprisingly, was thrown into a panic. In 1832, with Prussian support, he persuaded the *Diet* to pass the Six Articles. These increased the *Diet*'s control over the internal affairs of individual states, and, in particular, its control of the universities and the press. The effect was to make the *Diet* hated by nationalists and, in 1833, an armed student rising tried to take it over. The rising was quickly defeated and the *Diet* set up a special commission to round up young student agitators, many of whom were forming themselves into a 'Young Germany' movement dedicated to establishing a united Germany.

Key question
To what extent did nationalist and liberal ideas develop in the 1830s?

July Revolution in Paris
In 1830 the reactionary King Charles X of France was overthrown and replaced by the more liberal Louis Philippe.

Key term

Nationalist festival at Hambach: 1832

The Six Articles: 1832

Key dates

Faced with such developments, Metternich again summoned representatives from the Confederation to meet him in Vienna in 1834 to discuss the need for yet sterner action against subversive elements. Press censorship was intensified and new controls were placed on universities.

Liberals and nationalists were powerless against Metternich's domination. The *Diet*, little more than an Austrian tool, would do nothing to aid the liberal or nationalist causes. As long as Prussia remained Austria's ally and equally reactionary, there was little hope of a change in the situation.

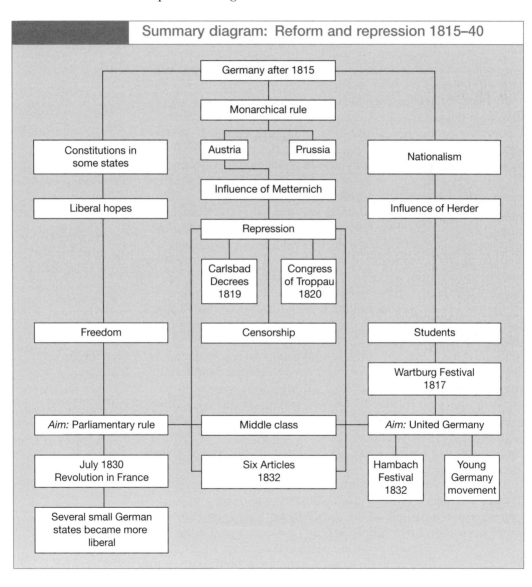

Summary diagram: Reform and repression 1815–40

3 | Economic Developments 1815–48

Few liberal-nationalists in the period 1815–48 would have foreseen that political unification of Germany would eventually be brought about by Prussia, one of the most reactionary of the German states. Nevertheless, the basis for the unification of Germany had already been laid by Prussia before 1840, and that basis, which was not political but economic, was the *Zollverein* (see page 15).

The Prussian Customs Union

After 1815, the 39 German states managed their own economies. Innumerable customs barriers and internal **tariffs** restricted trade. Even within a single state there were large numbers of tolls. Variations in currency values within the Confederation were an added problem.

In 1818, Rhineland manufacturers complained to the King of Prussia about the massive burden on home industry, and about competition from unrestricted foreign imports, on which no duty was charged. As a result, in the same year, the Prussian Tariff Reform Law brought into being the Prussian Customs Union. The law did away with the web of internal customs duties and replaced them with a tariff to be charged at the Prussian frontier.

However, the customs union was not quite what the Rhineland industrialists sought: they had hoped for a high protective tariff, particularly against British goods. Instead, the tariff was low: nothing at all on raw materials, an average of only 10 per cent on manufactured goods and 20 per cent on luxury goods such as sugar or tea. High tariffs would have encouraged smuggling, which was already widespread. Moreover, they would have led to a tariff war: other countries would have responded by putting high duties on Prussian exports.

Later, Prussia did introduce customs duties on raw materials, especially iron and cotton yarn, as it tried to protect home industry from foreign competition. Nevertheless, it was also working to extend **free trade**, first within Prussia and then within other states in the Confederation. The aim was to get rid of as many internal trade barriers as possible so goods could move more freely. This meant wider markets for home-produced goods at cheaper prices.

Some smaller north and central German states, impressed by Prussia's economic success or forced by economic pressure, agreed to join a customs union with Prussia. They even allowed Prussian customs officers into their territories to operate the system. In 1828 Prussia persuaded Hesse-Darmstadt to join the Prussian Customs Union, thus establishing a foothold south of the river Main.

However, some northern states, like Hanover and Hesse-Cassel, which stood between east Prussia and the western Prussian provinces, stubbornly resisted all Prussia's efforts to win them over.

Key question
To what extent did economic developments encourage German unity?

Key terms

Zollverein
The Prussian Customs Union.

Tariffs
Import duties, intended to raise money or protect domestic industry and agriculture from foreign competition.

Free trade
Unrestricted trade without protective import duties.

Other customs unions

By 1830 there were two other important customs unions. One was between Bavaria and Württemberg: the other, known as the Middle German Commercial Union, was made up of Hanover, Brunswick, Saxony and several smaller states. This union was not so much concerned with encouraging its own trade as spoiling that of Prussia.

Prussia was geographically well placed to control north–south routes through north Germany and to generate a large income out of duties charged on foreign goods carried along these routes. The Middle Union worked to protect and keep open the existing roads from the North Sea ports to the central German cities of Frankfurt and Leipzig and to build a series of new roads which would go round the states of the Prussian Customs Union. In this scheme they were thwarted by the Prussian finance minister, who:

- encouraged the building of roads joining Prussia directly with Bavaria, Württemberg and Frankfurt
- extended Prussian trade along the Rhine through a customs agreement with the Dutch.

The *Zollverein*

Key question
What was the importance of the *Zollverein*?

Key date
Zollverein came into operation: 1834

Key term
Hanseatic towns
A league of German commercial cities on the Baltic Sea coast.

In 1830 Hesse-Cassel, one of the smaller but vitally important states of the Middle Union, ran into financial difficulties and revolutionary upheavals. The following year it joined the Prussian Customs Union – to the horror of its Middle Union partners. The Middle Union, which was already in trouble, collapsed soon afterwards, while the Prussian Customs Union went from strength to strength.

In 1834 Bavaria and Württemberg joined the Prussians. This new enlarged Customs Union, the *Zollverein*, now covered 18 states with 23 million people. In 1836, when Baden and Frankfurt joined, it included 25 states with a population of 26 million. By 1844 only Hanover, Oldenburg, Mecklenburg, the **Hanseatic towns** and Austria were not members. The organisation and supervision of the *Zollverein* was carried out by a specially appointed body, the *Zollverein* Congress. All *Zollverein* member states had a common system of tariffs and abolished all internal customs barriers.

In the next few years a start was made on unifying both the currency and the system of weights and measures in the states of the *Zollverein*. The railways were greatly extended to make a quick and efficient means of communication between *Zollverein* members.

There were some difficulties:

- The *Zollverein* administration did not always work smoothly.
- As any member state could veto a proposal at the *Zollverein* Congress, decisions were often held up or not made at all.

Nevertheless, the *Zollverein* experiment was generally successful, certainly from Prussia's point of view. The member states worked together and Prussia achieved a position of economic leadership within the Confederation.

Prussia's aims

Successive Prussian finance ministers realised that doing away with internal customs duties, first within Prussia, and then between Prussia and neighbouring states, would increase trade and bring prosperity. However, as early as 1830, even before the *Zollverein* was formed, Prussian Finance Minister Frederick Motz pointed out to his King that such a free trade organisation would not only bring prosperity to Prussia but also isolate Austria. This isolation would eventually weaken Austria's political influence within the Confederation.

It does seem that Prussia deliberately used the *Zollverein* to achieve dominance in Germany. Prussian ministers realised that those states which found financial advantage in an economic union under Prussian leadership might well take a favourable view of similar arrangements in a political union. Moreover, the *Zollverein* was itself a force for unity and therefore a focal point for nationalist sentiments. Accordingly, Prussia, despite her reactionary political sympathies, came to be regarded by many northern states as the natural leader of a united Germany.

Austrian isolation

Austria had refused to join the *Zollverein* because she disagreed with the policy of free trade. Austria's policy was **protectionist**. It already had large markets within the **Austrian Empire** for home-produced goods, and therefore wanted high import duties to protect its industries and markets from cheap foreign imports. Joining the *Zollverein* would have meant reducing import duties to the same level as the other states, and this it would not consider.

Austria gave Prussia a great opportunity when it refused to join. Prussia took this opportunity, established a position of leadership, and made sure that Austria would stay outside. By 1848, while Austria still retained political control of the Confederation, Prussia had the economic leadership.

Key question
What was Prussia's aim in setting up the *Zollverein*?

Key question
Why did Austria stay outside the *Zollverein*?

Key terms

Protectionist
Favouring the protection of trade by having duties on imports.

Austrian Empire
The Austrian Empire included much of what is today Austria, Hungary, Poland, the Czech Republic, Slovakia, Croatia and northern Italy.

Summary diagram: Economic developments 1815–48

```
                        ┌─────────────────────┐
                        │  Problem of tariffs  │
                        └─────────────────────┘
                                  │
                        ┌─────────────────────┐
                        │ Prussian Customs Union│
                        │        1818          │
                        └─────────────────────┘
              ┌───────────────┘         └───────────────┐
   ┌──────────────────┐                        ┌──────────────────┐
   │ Links with other │                        │  Proliferation of │
   │  German states   │                        │ other custom unions│
   └──────────────────┘                        └──────────────────┘
              │                                          │
   ┌──────────────────┐                        ┌──────────────────┐
   │ Prussia's strong │                        │   Hesse-Cassel    │
   │   geographical   │                        │    problems       │
   │    position      │                        │                   │
   └──────────────────┘                        └──────────────────┘
              └──────────────┐        ┌─────────────┘
                        ┌─────────────────────┐
                        │     Zollverein      │
                        │        1834         │
                        └─────────────────────┘
      ┌────────────┬───────────┤        ├──────────┬────────────┐
 ┌──────────┐      │      ┌──────────┐   │    ┌──────────────────┐
 │ Prussian │      │      │ Success  │   │    │  Why did Austria │
 │   aims   │      │      └──────────┘   │    │     not join?    │
 └──────────┘      │                     │    └──────────────────┘
 ┌──────────┐ ┌──────────┐ ┌──────────────────┐  ┌──────────────┐
 │ Economic │ │ Political│ │ Growing economic │  │ Protectionism│
 └──────────┘ └──────────┘ │      unity       │  └──────────────┘
                           └──────────────────┘
                        ┌─────────────────────┐
                        │   Austria isolated   │
                        └─────────────────────┘
```

Key question
How strong was
German nationalism
by 1848?

Key term

Deutschland über
Alles
This means
'Germany above the
others'. It
eventually became
Germany's national
anthem, the words
being set to a
popular melody by
the eighteenth-
century composer
Joseph Haydn.

4 | Germany 1840–8

The growth of nationalism

Despite the problems, the emotional appeal of nationalism was
experienced by increasing numbers of Germans. It was inflamed
by poetry, music, history and philosophy. It was also fuelled by
several situations in which foreign governments (especially
France) appeared to threaten Germany as a whole. This made
many Germans, who were normally content to think of
themselves as Bavarians, Hessians or members of other states,
discontented that Germany could not speak with a single, strong
voice at times of crisis.

The 1840 crisis

Nationalist feelings were particularly widespread in 1840 when it
seemed likely that France would invade the German states along
the Rhine in an attempt to force the other major powers to bow
to its wishes over a crisis in the Near East. The German press
threw its weight behind the nationalist upsurge and there was a
flurry of songs and poems such as ***Deutschland über Alles***. France
backed down, but not before much nationalistic feeling had been

generated throughout Germany in the face of a threat from the 'old enemy'.

Schleswig and Holstein

It is easy to understand why a threat from France should evoke such a response. After all, only 25 years had elapsed since the defeat of Napoleon. Less immediately understandable is the reaction to a threat from Denmark, which was relatively small, weak and internationally insignificant. Yet in 1846 Denmark did as much to create support for the idea of German unification as had France in 1840.

Immediately to the south of Denmark proper lay the duchies of Schleswig and Holstein (see Map 1.1, page 4). They were ruled by the King of Denmark.

- Schleswig, half German and half Danish-speaking, was not a member of the German Confederation.
- Holstein, by contrast, had an overwhelmingly German-speaking population and was one of the member states of the Confederation.

When it seemed that the King of Denmark was about to incorporate the duchies into his kingdom, the outcry throughout Germany was enormous. What to most Europeans, including the King of Denmark, seemed merely legal technicality was viewed by Germans as a violation of the Fatherland to be resisted by force if need be. Bavarian, Prussian and Austrian leaders all spoke against the Danish action. This strength of feeling was enough to persuade the Danish king to abandon his plans.

Railway development

Another factor of great significance in the development of nationalism was the coming of the railway. One German economist described the growing railway network as 'the firm girdle around the loins of Germany binding her limbs together into a forceful and powerful body'. The railways made Germans more mobile and contributed to the breakdown of local and regional barriers.

The growth of liberalism

The 1840s were to bring new and hopeful developments for liberals. In the south-western states the liberals increased their popular support.

> **Key question**
> How strong were German liberal movements by 1848?

- In 1846 the liberals in Baden managed to obtain a relaxation of press censorship, and reforms of the police and of the judicial system.
- In Hesse-Darmstadt there were strong liberal parliamentary campaigns for changes in electoral rules and for a free press.
- In Bavaria the liberals were helped by an unexpected change of policy on the part of the half-mad King, Ludwig I. His passion for a dancer led him to propose that she should be given a title

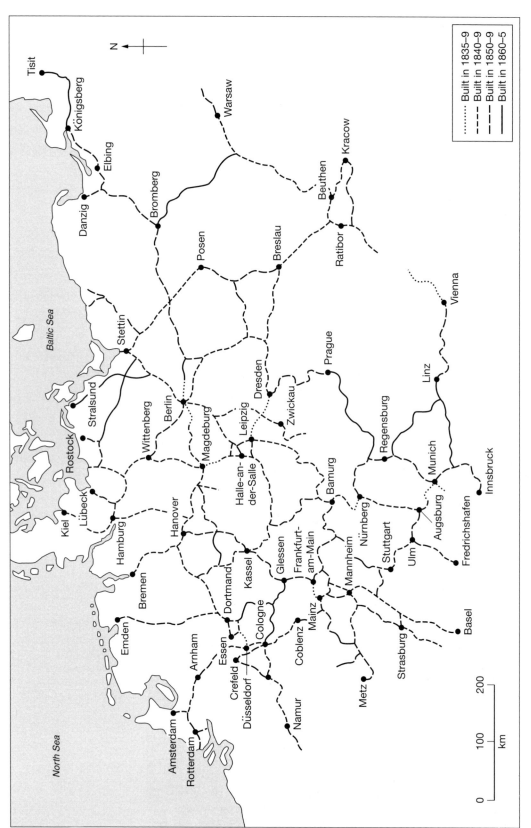

Map 1.2: German railways 1835–65.

and land and be introduced to court. When his advisers criticised him, he replaced his reactionary ministers with liberal ones.

Developments in Prussia

Developments in Prussia also seemed promising. King Frederick William III, who had ruled as an absolute monarch for over 40 years, died in 1840. Although he had agreed to the establishment of provincial *Diets* in 1823, he had avoided granting a constitution. Throughout his reign he had close ties with Austria.

Frederick William III was succeeded by his son Frederick William IV – an intelligent, cultured, but very unstable man whose policies were to fluctuate widely throughout his reign. Sometimes he behaved as a reactionary absolutist, sometimes as a **constitutional monarch**. He started by acting as many liberals wished:

- He released many political prisoners.
- He abolished censorship.
- In 1842 he arranged for the Prussian provincial *Diets* to elect representatives to meet as an advisory body on a temporary basis in Berlin.
- He extended the powers of the provincial *Diets* and allowed them to publish reports of their debates.

Frederick William IV crowned King of Prussia: 1840

Meeting of the Prussian United *Diet* in Berlin: 1847

Key dates

Constitutional monarch
A king or queen whose powers are limited by a constitution and who usually rules in co-operation with an elected parliament.

Key term

King Frederick William IV 1795–1861.

Junkers
The conservative landed aristocracy of Prussia.

Standing army
A state's main military force. The army usually supported the government against revolutionary activity.

National guard
A national guard had first appeared in France during the French Revolution. It was supposed to be a force of the people and thus less under the control of the monarch.

Encouraged by this, liberals in the Rhineland agitated for a constitution and the calling of a single *Diet* for all Prussian territories. The *Junkers*, watched the activities of the King with anxiety and even considered a *coup* to replace him with his brother, William.

Frederick William, taking fright at finding himself under political attack from both left and right, re-imposed press censorship in 1843. However, in 1847 he called a meeting of the United *Diet* in Berlin to vote on a loan for building a railway to link East Prussia and Berlin. The 600 delegates were all men of substance: more than half of them were aristocrats. They were prepared to support the railway, but insisted on a guarantee that the United *Diet* should meet on a regular basis. Frederick William promptly sent the United *Diet* packing. The King's action strengthened the determination of Prussian liberals to push for constitutional change.

German newspapers

In the 1840s the pace of political debate picked up and public opinion grew bolder. More books were published. Newspapers and political journals flourished. The fact that Germans were the most literate people in Europe helped. Popular journals played a crucial role in arousing interest in issues such as Schleswig-Holstein in 1846. In 1847 liberal and nationalist sentiments found expression in the foundation at Heidelberg of a newspaper with the prophetic title of *Die Deutsche Zeitung* ('The German Newspaper').

The Hippenhelm meeting

In 1847, liberal representatives of the south-western states met at Hippenhelm. They demanded an elected national *Diet* and detailed their complaints which were published in *Die Deutsche Zeitung*:

> The *Diet* has so far not fulfilled the tasks set it by the Act of the Confederation in the fields of representation by estates, free trade, communications, navigation, freedom of the press, etc.; the federal defence regulation provides neither for the arming of the population nor for a uniformly organised federal force. On the contrary the press is harassed by censorship; the discussions of the *Diet* are enveloped in secrecy.

As well as supporting constitutional change, the Hippenhelm delegates proposed:

- the liberation of the press
- open judicial proceedings with juries
- the end of feudal restrictions
- reduction of the cost of the **standing army** and the creation of a **national guard**
- reform of the system of taxation.

Conclusion

The *Zollverein*'s example of economic co-operation between the German states encouraged the liberals and nationalists. It made their dreams of a politically united Germany seem more attainable. By the late 1840s there was a growing call for the setting up of a nation state. The greatest support for nationalism and liberalism came from the middle classes. Most liberal-nationalists envisaged a **federation** of states under a constitutional monarch. Suspicious of full democracy, they wanted to limit the vote to the prosperous and well educated. Radicals, by contrast, favoured universal manhood suffrage and pressed for a German republic.

However, it is wrong to over-estimate the degree of political consciousness attained by Germans on the eve of the 1848 revolutions. Even among the middle classes only a minority were liberal-minded and even fewer were politically active. Most liberals were concerned with developments in their own states, not in the situation across Germany as a whole. Small in number and far from unified, they were also isolated from the mass of the people.

In truth, nationalists, liberals and radicals had not achieved much by 1848. As long as Metternich remained in power and Prussia remained Austria's ally, there seemed little chance of changing the situation. German nationalism as a mass phenomenon tended to be reactive, erupting in response to perceived threats and then subsiding again. Although nationalist organisations grew at an impressive rate in the mid-1840s, loyalty to individual states and dynasties remained strong. There was still a major division between the Catholic south and the Protestant north. There were also cultural differences between the more industrialised and liberal west and the agrarian, autocratic east.

Key question
How strong was German liberalism and nationalism by 1848?

Federation
A group of states joined together in some form of union.

Key term

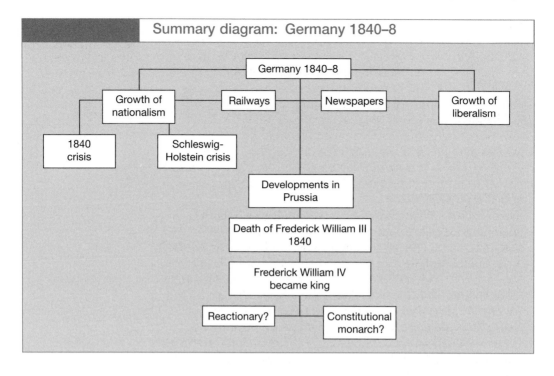

Summary diagram: Germany 1840–8

- Germany 1840–8
  - Growth of nationalism
    - 1840 crisis
    - Schleswig-Holstein crisis
  - Railways
  - Newspapers
  - Growth of liberalism
  - Developments in Prussia
    - Death of Frederick William III 1840
    - Frederick William IV became king
      - Reactionary?
      - Constitutional monarch?

2 Germany in Revolution 1848–9

POINTS TO CONSIDER

In 1848 France, the German Confederation, Habsburg lands including Austria and Hungary, and Italy experienced revolution. One striking feature of the 1848 revolutions, both in Germany and elsewhere, was the rapidity of the success they enjoyed. Another was the fact that all – equally rapidly – failed. The revolutions are complex affairs. Some historians claim that general – European-wide – factors explain the cause, course and failure of the revolutions. Others stress that revolutionaries in different areas had very different grievances and demands. Even within specific countries, there was often little cohesion among the revolutionaries and what there was soon collapsed. This chapter will consider the German revolutions through the following sections:

- The causes of the German revolutions
- The course of the revolutions
- The Frankfurt Parliament
- The revolution in Prussia
- The failure of the German revolutions

Key dates

1848	March 5	Declaration of Heidelberg
	March 13	Metternich fell from power
	Mid-March	Riots in Berlin
	Late March	King Frederick William made concessions to liberals
	March 31	Meeting of the *Vorparlament*
	May	Meeting of Frankfurt Parliament
	November	Frederick William re-established control in Berlin
	December	New Prussian constitution
1849	March	Frankfurt Parliament agreed on a constitution
	April	Frederick William rejected the offer of the German crown
	June	Frankfurt Parliament dispersed

1 | The Causes of the German Revolutions

Key question
To what extent was there a general European revolutionary movement in 1848?

In Europe, 1848 was a year to remember, a year of dramatic, violent events, of hope and of failure. It was the year of death as a cholera epidemic swept across Europe, causing such loss of life that for a while society in many areas was totally disorganised. It was the year that Karl Marx's *The Communist Manifesto* was published. This did not have the drama of the cholera epidemic and attracted little attention at the time, but in 20 years its message had spread across Europe and beyond to become, a century later, the basis of the political system of half the world. In the spring of 1848, revolutionaries, to the delight of Marx, seemed to carry all before them across Europe.

Why did revolutions in France, Germany, Prussia, Austria, Hungary and Italy all happen in the same year? Historians used to think that the French troubles, beginning in Paris in February 1848, triggered off copycat revolutions in other countries. Now, a generally accepted view is that the revolutions took place at about the same time because conditions across Europe were very similar. These conditions – economic, social and political – are seen as giving rise to revolutions. The sections that follow focus on Germany. However, much – indeed most – of what is said applies to many parts of Europe.

Economic and social problems

Key question
What were the main economic and social problems in Germany in the late 1840s?

Most historians agree that the German revolutions resulted, at least in part, from a social and economic crisis. However, the precise nature of this crisis and its effects on different classes have generated much debate.

Increasing population
Since the middle of the eighteenth century, Germany's population had grown dramatically, doubling in the century up to 1848. (The rise was probably due more to a declining death rate than to an increasing birth rate.) The result was that some areas found it difficult to sustain their populations. Thus, people left the land and drifted to the towns in search of work or went to other parts of the world, hoping to better themselves. Of the 250,000 who left Germany in the 1840s, most went to the USA.

Problems in the countryside
Those people who remained in the countryside found life hard. In eastern Prussia much of the land belonged to the *Junkers* and was worked by landless peasants. Even in the parts of Germany where the peasants had become **tenant farmers** rents were high and it was difficult to make a living.

Problems in the towns
In most towns there were insufficient jobs and housing to cope with the influx of migrants from the countryside. Living and working conditions were often atrocious. Even in good times workers were poorly clothed and fed. From the mid-1840s there

Key terms

The Communist Manifesto
This book, written by Karl Marx, supported the idea of class revolution. It encouraged workers everywhere to unite.

Tenant farmers
Farmers who rented their land from a landowner.

was unemployment in many industries. One observer reported that unemployed factory workers were living in dirty, damp and overcrowded accommodation, often 20 people to a room, six or seven to a bed.

When work was available, working conditions were grim. The machines, especially in the textile factories, were not designed with the workers in mind. Men, women and children worked for 13 or more hours a day, often in awkward positions, crouched over the machines.

Inadequate sanitation encouraged diseases like typhoid and cholera. Many newcomers, unable to find work, depended on charity or turned to crime. Strikes and riots among the urban working class multiplied in the 1830s and 1840s. Towns had concentrations of discontented people who were far more likely to act together than their rural counterparts. It is worth noting that the 1848 revolutions in Germany were overwhelmingly urban.

Across Germany industry was growing in the early nineteenth century. Skilled workers felt threatened by the advance of mechanisation that forced down the costs of production and made hand-produced goods relatively expensive.

The economic crisis: 1846–7

In 1846 and 1847 the corn harvests were disastrous and the situation was made worse by a serious outbreak of **potato blight**. Potatoes were the main item of diet for most German peasants, and failure of the crop meant starvation. There was distress and unrest, and food riots broke out. There had been poor harvests before, but the increased population made the position worse.

In the industrial towns there was a sharp rise in food prices. Cereal prices increased by nearly 50 per cent in 1847. In Berlin, the 'potato revolution' occurred. Barricades were erected, shops looted and the Crown Prince's palace stormed before soldiers restored order.

Across Germany, the rise in food prices led to a reduction in consumer spending on items other than foodstuffs. Consequently, craft and industrial production suffered a steep fall in demand, to which employers responded by laying off workers. There was thus a rapid increase in unemployment, particularly in the textile industry. Even those in work found their wages cut. The standard of living of most workers fell alarmingly as higher food prices coincided with lower wages.

Growing unrest

In both town and country, there was growing unrest. Dissatisfied with the existing state of affairs, workers and peasants demanded a better life for themselves and their families. Most of the demands were concerned with practical matters – higher wages, better housing, a shorter working day – not politics and political theories.

There were some exceptions. In towns such as Cologne and Bonn, skilled craftsmen had their own trade organisations, and kept themselves apart from the unskilled factory workers, whom

Potato blight
A destructive disease of the potato caused by a parasitic fungus.

Key term

they despised and feared. During 1848 the leaders of the skilled workers staged demonstrations and elected representative assemblies to discuss their grievances.

Class consciousness

Key question
To what extent was class consciousness developing in Germany?

Historians remain divided about whether 'class consciousness' was developing among industrial workers. This was a key issue for **Marxist historians** who believed that historical change grew out of conflicts between classes. Karl Marx, a German revolutionary, argued that as industrialisation developed, so each class evolved its own consciousness. He believed that the **proletariat** was inevitably opposed to the **bourgeoisie**. Marx and Marxist historians since argued that the 1848 revolutions were caused by the effect of industrialisation on the working class. Certainly, in Germany it was often workers who fought and died in the streets behind the barricades. However, it was not only the workers who made the German revolutions. Others played an important part, particularly the liberal middle classes.

Political problems

Key question
What were the main political problems in Germany?

The economic crisis helped to shake the prestige and self-confidence of many existing regimes. Most lacked the financial and bureaucratic resources – and also possibly the will – to intervene effectively to alleviate the social distress and reverse the economic collapse. The calibre of rulers was not high and many monarchs and their ministers attracted a great deal of personal unpopularity, particularly from the growing number of educated middle class – lawyers, doctors, journalists, teachers and civil servants.

Key terms

Marxist historians
Historians who accept the ideas of Karl Marx and believe that history is essentially about class conflict.

Proletariat
The exploited industrial workers who (Marx claimed) would triumph in the last great class struggle.

Bourgeoisie
The upper and middle classes who owned the capital and the means of production (factories, mills, mines, etc.), who (Marx claimed) exploited the workers.

In 1848 power lay where it always had – with the nobility who owned the land, filled senior government jobs and officered the army. They guarded their privileges jealously against any infiltration by the middle classes. Middle-class Germans were critical of systems which largely excluded them from participation in the political process, and in which they were restrained from free expression of their grievances by the censor and the secret police. Many of the dissatisfied middle classes wanted the establishment of some form of parliamentary system and the guarantee of basic civil rights.

Middle-class Germans also wanted to see the establishment of a united Germany, which they claimed would ensure national prosperity. By 1847 patriotism was running high, and the feelings of many Germans were expressed in a memorandum written by Prince Hohenlohe:

> In the history of every nation there is an epoch in which it comes to full self-consciousness and claims liberty to determine its own destiny. … We Germans have reached this stage. … No one will deny that it is hard on an energetic thinking man to be unable to say abroad 'I am a German' – not to be able to pride himself that the German flag is flying from his vessel, to have no German consul in case of emergency, but have to explain 'I am a Hessian, a Darmstadter, a Buckeburger'.

Baden

The impetus for a German national revolution came from the small state of Baden in south-west Germany. In 1846 the Grand Duke of Baden had been forced to accept a liberal constitution. In consequence, the Baden representative assembly was elected on a wider franchise than in any other German state. Not surprisingly, the people of Baden were more politically conscious than most Germans.

Throughout the 1840s liberal politicians in Baden had supported a united Germany. Now they put their views forcefully to an assembly of liberals from all the south-west German states (see page 21). This assembly, which met in October 1847, agreed on the urgent need for a German People's Parliament.

While this meeting was going on, radical politicians (mainly from Baden) were holding their own meetings in south-west Germany. The radicals wanted fairer taxation, education for all, a people's army, better relations between employees and workers, and most importantly, the establishment of a united German Republic.

The situation in early 1848

In 1848 few Germans expected revolution. There was still widespread loyalty to the established dynasties. Moreover, the economic situation was beginning to improve slightly. Nevertheless, economic distress in the major cities, which continued over the winter of 1847–8, helped to foment revolution. The urban and rural poor, however, did not have a clear set of aims and were often untouched by the radical, liberal and nationalist ideologies of the middle classes.

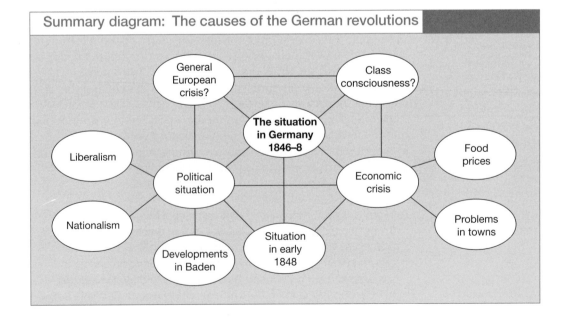

Summary diagram: The causes of the German revolutions

Key question
What sparked the revolutions in Germany?

Key date

Metternich fell from power: 13 March 1848

2 | The Course of the Revolutions

On 24 February 1848 King Louis Philippe was overthrown and a republic was established in France. French revolutionaries' proclamation of the idea of the sovereignty of the people called into question all established authority.

News of events in France helped to spark revolution in Austria. On 13 March there were mass demonstrations in Vienna. The situation quickly got out of hand, especially in working-class areas where there was widespread looting. Metternich fled and the army, whose loyalty was suspect, was withdrawn from the capital. The city was left in control of radical students and their working-class supporters.

Metternich's fall had a profound effect on most Germans and added fuel to the revolutionary conflagration. In some places, peasants attacked their landlords, stormed castles and destroyed feudal records. Elsewhere artisans used the opportunity of the breakdown of law and order to destroy new machines that they saw as a threat to their livelihood. In Baden radical republicans tried to lead a peasant and worker rising. This attracted little support and was quickly suppressed by the liberal government. Meetings, demonstrations and petitions, not armed risings, were the chief weapons of the middle-class revolutionaries who hoped to work with, not destroy, the princes.

Most German rulers lost their nerve, giving in easily, if temporarily, to demands for more representative government. Almost everywhere, elections were held, liberal ministries appointed, constitutional changes set in train and the remnants of the old feudal order abolished. There was relatively little violence. Only in Austria and Prussia were there serious confrontations between the people and the military.

For a time, the revolutionary fire seemed irresistible because no one was fighting it. Although the eccentric Bavarian King Ludwig was forced to abdicate, in most states the old rulers survived and watched developments. Moreover, it was soon obvious that the urban liberals had little sympathy with the peasant revolts in the countryside. In some instances new liberal governments, appalled by the destruction of private property, sent in troops to restrain the peasantry.

The situation in Austria and Prussia

In May 1848 Austrian Emperor Ferdinand agreed to summon a constituent assembly, elected by universal suffrage, to draw up a new constitution. The government, which moved to Innsbruck, was reformed to include a few liberals. Faced with serious revolts in Italy, Hungary and Bohemia, Austria was too engrossed in its own affairs in the spring and summer of 1848 to exert its customary influence on Germany. Events in Berlin in March 1848 (see pages 40–1) prevented Prussian King Frederick William from taking action against the revolutionaries.

The Declaration of Heidelberg

In March 1848, at a meeting in Heidelberg, 51 representatives from six states (Prussia, Bavaria, Württemberg, Baden, Nassau and Frankfurt), discussed changes to Germany's political institutions. They did so before revolutions had made an impact on the individual German states. On 5 March their decisions were published in the Declaration of Heidelberg:

> The meeting of a national representation elected in all the German lands according to the number of the people must not be postponed, both for the removal of imminent internal and external dangers, and for the development of the strength and flowering of German national life!

Key date

Declaration of Heidelberg: 5 March 1848

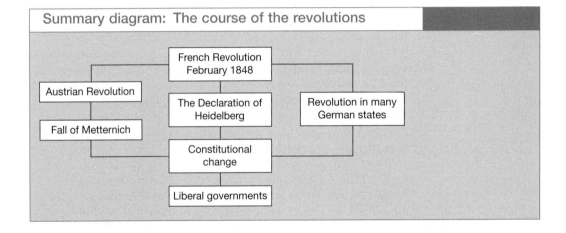

Summary diagram: The course of the revolutions

- French Revolution February 1848
- Austrian Revolution
- Fall of Metternich
- The Declaration of Heidelberg
- Revolution in many German states
- Constitutional change
- Liberal governments

3 | The Frankfurt Parliament

The *Vorparlament*

Following the Declaration of Heidelberg, invitations for a proposed 'assembly of German men' were quickly issued. This move, which looked directly to the German people for support, was unexpectedly successful. On 31 March, 574 representatives, from almost all the states of the Confederation, squeezed themselves into the pews of the *Pauluskirche* (St Paul's Church) in Frankfurt. This assembly is known as the **Vorparlament**. After 5 days of debate, the *Vorparlament* members reached an agreement on how to elect a national Parliament that would draw up a constitution for a united Germany. It was decided that the Parliament:

- would meet in Frankfurt
- should consist of one representative for every 50,000 inhabitants
- should be elected by citizens, who were of age and 'economically independent'.

Key question
How and why was the Frankfurt Parliament created?

Key date

Meeting of the *Vorparlament*: 31 March 1848

Key term

Vorparlament
This is usually translated as 'pre-parliament', but it is better thought of as 'preparatory parliament', which was preparing the way for the real parliament.

It was left to individual states to decide who was an independent citizen. Most states decided on a residence qualification, some on ownership of property. Although the *Vorparlament* did not actually say so, it was assumed that only men could vote, so women (who had played an active role in demonstrations) were excluded from the franchise, along with servants, farm labourers and anyone receiving poor relief. This last category alone excluded large numbers: in Cologne, for example, nearly a third of the population was on poor relief.

The election of the Frankfurt Parliament

The elections, arranged at short notice and in all 39 states, were carried out peacefully and successfully. Probably 75–90 per cent of men, depending on the state, were able to vote. However, in most of the states the elections were indirect. The voters elected 'electors', who then chose representatives. The Parliament, which met in Frankfurt in May 1848, did not represent the population as a whole. Most of those elected were prominent figures in the local community. Of the 596 members, the vast majority were middle class. There were large numbers of teachers, professors, lawyers and government officials. It was probably the best-educated German Parliament ever – over 80 per cent of the members held university degrees. There were a few landowners, four craftsmen and one peasant.

Key date

Meeting of Frankfurt Parliament: May 1848

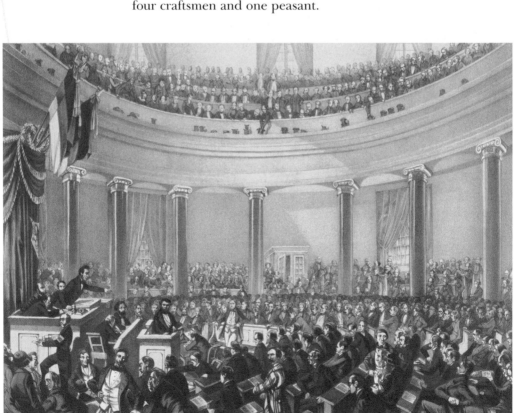

The Frankfurt Parliament. How far does the illustration, painted in 1848, suggest that the Parliament was a significant body?

The Parliament was essentially moderate and liberal. It intended to establish a united Germany under a constitutional monarch who would rule through an elected Parliament. Only a small minority of its members were radical, revolutionary or republican. Reactionary conservatives were similarly scarcely represented.

The work of the Frankfurt Parliament

It had been a great achievement to have had the Frankfurt Parliament elected, convened and ready to begin work in little over a month. For the moment, the Parliament filled a power vacuum that had been created by the revolutions:

Key question
What were the main concerns of the Frankfurt Parliament?

- Austria was absorbed in suppressing uprisings throughout its multinational empire.
- Prussia was in a state of disarray after events in March 1848 (see pages 40–1).
- The Frankfurt Parliament started with the advantage that the old *Diet* of the Confederation, with representatives appointed by new liberal governments, had agreed to its own demise and nominated the Parliament as its legal successor.

The key issue was whether the Parliament would be able to draw up a national constitution which would be accepted by all Germans. As well as drawing up a constitution, it hoped to agree a series of 'Basic Rights and Demands', such as:

- freedom of the press
- fair taxation
- equality of political rights without regard to religion
- German citizenship for all.

The Parliament began by considering the relationship between itself and the individual states. The Confederation had been an association in which the states had a very large degree of independence from federal control. The Frankfurt Parliament's intention was that the new Germany should have much stronger central government, with correspondingly greater control over the actions of the states. It quickly decided that any national constitution it framed would be sovereign, and that while state parliaments would be free to make state laws, these would only be valid if they did not conflict with that constitution. So by the end of May the Frankfurt Parliament had declared its authority over the states, their parliaments and princes. Now it remained to draw up a constitution and to organise a government.

Most members of the Parliament accepted that the logical approach would be to agree a constitution and then to set up a government according to its terms. But it was another matter to find a majority of members who favoured any one procedure for carrying out these tasks, or who agreed on the type of constitution that should be established. Without the discipline imposed by well-organised political parties and without the leadership provided by outstanding individuals, the Frankfurt Parliament became a 'talking shop' in which it was difficult to reach agreement on anything.

The Provisional Central Power

Once it became clear that it would not be possible to reach rapid agreement on a constitution, steps were taken to establish a provisional government to rule in the meantime. But, so little was agreed about the specific ways in which its powers were to be carried out that the 'Provisional Central Power', established at the end of June, was largely ineffectual. It provided for an Imperial Regent of the Empire, to be elected by the Parliament. He was to govern through ministers, appointed by him and responsible to Parliament, until such time as a decision about the constitution could be reached. An elderly Austrian Archduke, John, was elected as Regent. He was an unusual Archduke, married to the daughter of a village postmaster, and with known liberal and nationalist sympathies. He duly appointed a number of ministers but, as they did not have any staff or offices or money, and their duties were not clearly defined, they could do little.

The Fifty Articles

As the summer went on, it seemed less and less likely that the Frankfurt Parliament would be able to create a viable united Germany. Nevertheless, the Parliament did not give up and continued its interminable debate over the constitution.

In December, the Fifty Articles of the fundamental rights of the German citizens were approved and became law. For the Parliament to have reached this degree of agreement was an unexpected achievement. The Articles included:

- equality before the law
- freedom of worship
- freedom of the press
- freedom from arrest without warrant
- an end to discrimination because of class.

The problem of 'Germany'

Apart from the constitution, other problems beset the Parliament. One concerned the territorial extent of 'Germany'. The existing boundaries of the Confederation did not conform to any logical definition of 'Germany'. Parts of Prussia and the Austrian Empire were included while others were not. Those parts that were within the Confederation contained many Czechs and Poles while some of the excluded provinces had an overwhelmingly German-speaking population.

The Austrian Empire, which comprised a host of different nationalities and in which Germans were a minority, was a major problem. Should all the Austrian Empire be admitted into the new Germany? Should only the German part of it be admitted? Should none of it be admitted?

Key question
Why was the Frankfurt Parliament unable to agree on the concept of Germany?

The Parliament was divided between the members who wanted a *Grossdeutschland* (Greater Germany), which would include the pre-dominantly German-speaking provinces of the Austrian Empire, and those who favoured a *Kleindeutschland* (Little Germany), which would exclude Austria but include the whole of Prussia. The *Grossdeutschland* plan would maintain the leadership of Germany by Catholic Austria, while the *Kleindeutschland* plan would leave Protestant Prussia as the dominant German state. The Parliament was unable to decide between the two proposals and debate dragged on inconclusively.

It had been an article of faith among most European liberals that all people would live in peace and harmony once they had thrown off the yoke of oppression. The events of 1848–9 were to destroy these naïve illusions. Relations between the peoples of central Europe deteriorated as national conflicts broke out between Magyars, Czechs, Croats, Poles, Italians and Germans.

In general, the Frankfurt Parliament had little sympathy for non-Germans within Germany. Not wishing to see a diminution of German power, it opposed the claims of Poles, Czechs and Danes for territory seen as part of Germany, namely Posen, Bohemia and Schleswig-Holstein. The Parliament applauded many of the actions of Austria in re-establishing control in Prague and northern Italy.

Key terms

Grossdeutschland
A greater Germany that would include the German-speaking provinces of the Austrian Empire.

Kleindeutschland
A little Germany that would exclude Austria.

The weakness of the Frankfurt Parliament

From the start the Frankfurt Parliament lacked real muscle. Unable to collect taxation, it had no financial power. Nor did it have an army. The only army in any way capable of acting as a national army in 1848 was the Prussian one. A Prussian general was appointed as Minister of War, but he agreed to accept the post only on condition that he would not be expected to act in any way contrary to the wishes of the King of Prussia. As Minister of War he did try to persuade the rulers of Bavaria and Austria, the only other states that had armies of any significance, to join with Prussia if 'exceptional circumstances' should make it necessary to field a national German army, but he failed. Without an army loyal to it, the authority of the Frankfurt Parliament remained theory rather than fact.

Key question
What problems did the Frankfurt Parliament face?

Lack of popular support

The Parliament was not in tune with the views of a large segment of the working class. German artisans established their own assemblies in 1848, the two most important being those meeting in Hamburg and Frankfurt. The Industrial Code put forward by the Artisan Congress in Frankfurt, as well as regulating hours of work and rates of pay, proposed to retain the restrictive practices of the old guild system. The Frankfurt Parliament delegates were mainly liberal. Regarding political freedom and economic freedom as inseparable principles, they rejected the Industrial Code out of hand. Many workers thus lost faith in the Frankfurt Parliament.

Divisions within the Frankfurt Parliament

The Frankfurt Parliament was seriously divided. The radical minority, who wanted to do away with the princes and replace them with a republic, found themselves in conflict with the majority of liberal members who wanted a moderate settlement which would safeguard both the rights of individual states and of the central government, and with a minimum of social change. There was also a small conservative group who wanted to preserve the rights of individual states and ensure that neither the Frankfurt Parliament nor the central government would exercise too much control.

These groups were simply loose associations within which there were many shades of opinion. In addition to the three main groups there were a large number of independent, politically uncommitted members. For much of the time it proved impossible to resolve the differences between the members sufficiently to reach any decision.

Other problems

The Parliament was handicapped by its unwise choice of leader, Heinrich Gagern. He was a distinguished liberal politician, sincere and well meaning, but without the force of character needed to dominate the assembly.

Events in Schleswig-Holstein showed the Parliament's weakness. Denmark's decision to absorb the two provinces brought a noisy protest from Frankfurt. Lacking an army of its own, it had to look to Prussia to defend German interests. Prussia did occupy the two duchies in April–May 1848 but King Frederick William, aware of Russian and British opposition and doubting the wisdom of war with Denmark, agreed, in August, to the armistice of Malmo. The Frankfurt deputies regarded the Prussian withdrawal from Schleswig-Holstein as a betrayal of the German national cause but could do nothing about it.

Key question
Why did the radicals pose a threat to the Frankfurt Parliament?

The radical challenge

Radicals, both within and outside the Frankfurt Parliament, continued to demand widespread political and social reform. Some 200 delegates, representing radical associations from across Germany, met in Frankfurt in mid-June. They agreed to form a national democratic and republican movement, based in Berlin. They gained considerable support from urban workers. The acceptance of the Malmo armistice by the Frankfurt Parliament brought matters to a head.

On 18 September 1848, a radical mob stormed the *Pauluskirche*, which was defended by Austrian, Prussian and Hessian troops. Eighty people were killed, including two conservative deputies. Archduke John placed Frankfurt under martial law. This violence discredited the radicals in the eyes of many Germans. Moderate liberals, horrified by the prospect of further violence, joined forces with the conservatives to combat the radicals. They regarded law and order as more important than freedom and equality.

The radicals refused to give up the struggle. At the second Democratic Congress, held in Berlin in October 1848, they pronounced the Frankfurt Parliament illegitimate and demanded new elections. However, by this time the **counter-revolution** was in full swing. Moreover, the radicals were hopelessly divided into various rival factions.

A German Constitution

In March 1849 a Constitution for a German Empire was finally agreed:

- There were to be two houses, the lower house to be elected by a secret ballot among men over the age of 25 and of 'good reputation', the upper house to be made up of the reigning monarchs and princes of the Confederation.
- The two houses would have control over legislation and finance.
- There was to be an Emperor who had considerable power. However, he would only be able to hold up legislation for a limited time.
- The new Germany was to be a 'little' rather than a 'greater' Germany.

The failure of the Frankfurt Parliament

In March 1849 the Frankfurt Parliament voted, half-heartedly (290 votes in favour, 240 abstentions), to elect Prussian King Frederick William as Emperor of Germany. However, Frederick William refused to accept on the grounds that it was not the Parliament's to offer. He distrusted 'the gentlemen of Frankfurt' who had, he believed, taken it upon themselves to speak for a united Germany without any legal authority. In any case, he was not prepared to be Emperor of Germany if it meant putting himself and Prussia under the control of the Frankfurt Parliament. Moreover, Frederick William was aware that if he accepted the crown, this would have serious foreign policy implications and might even lead to war with Austria.

The rulers of Bavaria, Saxony and Hanover, together with Prussia, rejected the German constitution. In the face of these disappointments, many members of Parliament lost heart and went home. The remnants, about 130 of them, mostly from south German states, made a last attempt to recover the situation. They called for the election of the first new German Parliament, or *Reichstag*. The call fell on deaf ears. The moment was past, the high hopes gone.

The Parliament, driven out of Frankfurt by the city government, now moved to Stuttgart, the capital of the Kingdom of Württemberg. There it was forcibly dispersed by the King's soldiers in June 1849. So ended the Frankfurt experiment.

Key term

Counter-revolution A subsequent revolution (usually by conservative forces) counteracting the effect of a previous one.

Key question Why did the Frankfurt experiment fail?

Key dates

Frankfurt Parliament agreed on a constitution: March 1849

Frederick William rejected the offer of the German crown: April 1849

Frankfurt Parliament
dispersed: June 1849

Why did the Frankfurt Parliament fail?

The Frankfurt Parliament has been harshly treated, particularly by Marxist historians. Marx's friend Engels described it as 'an assembly of old women' and blamed it for not overthrowing the existing power structures. However, it is unfair to condemn the Parliament for failing to do something that it did not want to do. Most of its members had no wish to be violent revolutionaries.

Another charge levelled against the Parliament is that its members were impractical idealists who wasted valuable time (6 months) discussing the fundamental rights of the German people. Unable to agree on a new constitution, it failed to grasp the opportunity of filling the power vacuum in Germany in 1848. In reality, however, there probably never was a real possibility of creating a unified German nation in 1848–9. Had the members of the Frankfurt Parliament acted as decisively as their critics would have them act, they would probably have been dispersed far earlier than they were. Dependent on the willing co-operation of the individual states, the Parliament lacked the power to enforce its decrees.

The attitude of Austria and Prussia was crucial. Constitutional government and national unity could only be achieved on their terms. Austria had no wish to see a more united or democratic Germany: she hoped to dominate Germany by keeping it weak and divided. The best, perhaps only, chance of the Frankfurt liberals lay in working out an agreement with Prussia. The chaos in Austria in 1848 gave Prussia a unique chance to play a dominant role in German affairs. Prussia did not grasp this opportunity. This was a failure not just on the part of King Frederick William, but also on the part of the Prussian liberal ministry (see page 41). Both King and ministry ultimately failed because they were not at all anxious to succeed. Frederick William, like most of his subjects, was unwilling to see Prussia merged in a united Germany at least in the way envisaged by the Frankfurt Parliament.

In fact, the authority of the Frankfurt Parliament was never accepted wholeheartedly by most of the individual states. When the ruling princes feared that they were about to lose many of their powers or even their thrones because of revolutions within their territories, they were prepared to support the Parliament. They feared that by opposing it, they would stir up even more opposition. But once the rulers had re-established their authority, their enthusiasm waned. Attractive as might be the idea of a united Germany in theory, in practice they had no wish to see their powers limited by liberal constitutions and a strong central authority.

When the Austrian Emperor, Franz Joseph, regained control of all his territories in 1849, all hope of the Frankfurt Parliament experiment ended. The Austrian government opposed all revolutionary change. Once effective Austrian opposition was established, no other ruler dared to be seen to be taking the lead in establishing a German Empire.

By 1849 the Frankfurt Parliament, which had once seemed to offer the way forward for national revival, became an irrelevance and embarrassment. Most rulers were pleased to see it go.

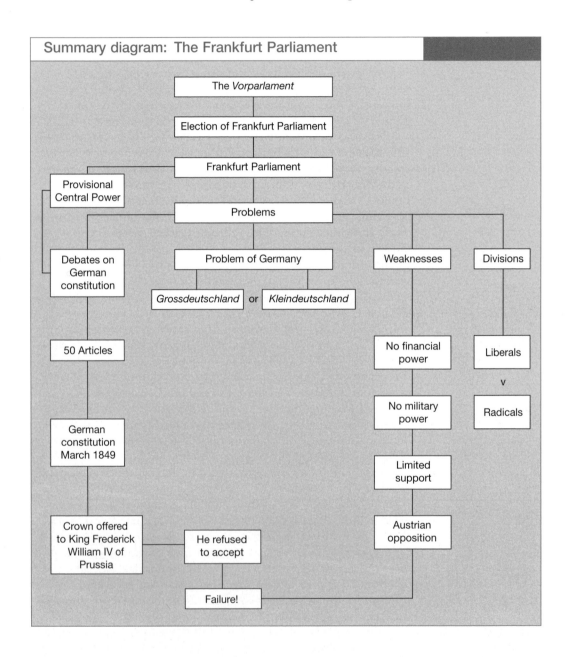

Summary diagram: The Frankfurt Parliament

4 | The Revolution in Prussia

In 1848–9 the hopes of the Frankfurt Parliament lay with Prussia, and King Frederick William IV. Frederick William was a strange and complex character, sensitive, cultured and charming, but moody and unpredictable and so unstable that later in life he was

Key question
Was King Frederick William IV a liberal or a reactionary?

Key term

Divine right of kings
The notion that kings are God's representatives on earth and thus entitled to full obedience from their subjects.

to be declared insane. A fervent believer in the **divine right of kings**, he had a mystical idea of kingship and its privileges and duties:

> I am moved to declare solemnly that no power on earth will ever succeed in prevailing on me to transform the natural relationship between prince and people … into a constitutional one. Never will I permit a written sheet of paper to come between our God in Heaven and this land … to rule us with its paragraphs and supplement the old sacred loyalty.

However, at the beginning of his reign in 1840 it seemed that he might be a reforming monarch (see pages 20–1). But angered by opposition, Frederick William returned to restrictive policies. For most of the 1840s, he was a friend and ally of Metternich and dedicated to maintaining the old order in Europe.

Then, in 1847, he swung back to what at first seemed more liberal ideas and called a meeting of the United *Diet* in Berlin, which included representatives from all the provincial *Diets* (see page 41). Having called the *Diet*, the King made few concessions

This is a contemporary illustration of street fighting in Berlin in 1848. What does it suggest about the threat posed by the Berlin rioters?

to its demands for a written constitution. This uncertain wavering between the conservative autocrat and the liberal monarch was a pattern which Frederick William was to repeat many times during 1848–9.

Revolution in Berlin

On 13 March 1848 a demonstration by workers, mostly self-employed craftsmen, took place in the palace square in Berlin. The demonstrators threw stones at the troops and the troops replied by opening fire. Deputations of leading citizens called on the King and asked him to make political concessions. Fighting continued in a confused way during the next 2 days. The original demonstrations, begun as a protest about pay and working conditions, quickly turned into a general, if vague, demand for 'the maintenance of the rights irrefutably belonging to the people of the state'.

On 16 March, news of revolution in Vienna and the dismissal of Metternich reached Berlin, and popular excitement rose even further. Frederick William accepted the idea of a new German constitution and agreed to recall the United *Diet* and to end censorship.

On 18 March a large crowd collected outside the royal palace. The King appeared on the balcony and was loudly cheered. He then ordered the troops to clear the crowds, and shots were fired either in panic or by accident after some jostling had taken place. Students and workers immediately set up barricades and serious fighting erupted. At least 300 rioters were killed as troops won control of the city.

The King, who all his life hated bloodshed and, most untypical for a Prussian leader, disliked the army and all military matters, decided to make a personal appeal for calm. He wrote a letter 'To my dear Berliners' at 3am. Copies were quickly printed and were put up on trees in the city centre early on the morning of 19 March. It promised that the troops would be withdrawn if the street barricades were demolished.

Troops were indeed withdrawn, largely due to a misunderstanding, so that the King was left in his palace guarded only by Berlin citizens who formed a **Civic Guard**. On 19 March he had little option but to appear on the balcony and salute the bodies of the dead rioters. Berliners hoped that Frederick William might become a constitutional monarch and that he might also support the German national revolution. On 21 March he appeared in the streets of Berlin with the German colours, black, red and gold, round his arm. He was greeted with tumultuous applause and declared: 'I want liberty: I will have unity in Germany'. In the following days Frederick William granted a series of general reforms, agreeing to the election of an assembly to draw up a new constitution for Prussia, and appointing a liberal ministry.

Key question
Why did Frederick William apparently support the revolution?

Key dates

Riots in Berlin: mid-March 1848

Frederick William made concessions to liberals: late March 1848

Key term

Civic Guard
A military force composed of ordinary people, not professional soldiers.

Frederick William's motives

Did Frederick William submit to the revolution from necessity, join it out of conviction, or, by putting himself at its head, try to take it over? Given his unstable character, he may well have been carried away by the emotion of the occasion and felt, at least for a short time, that he was indeed destined to be a popular monarch.

But the King's apparent liberalism did not last long. As soon as he had escaped from Berlin and rejoined his loyal army at Potsdam, he expressed very different feelings. He spoke of humiliation at the way he had been forced to make concessions to the people and made it clear that he had no wish to be a 'citizen' king. However, he took no immediate revenge on Berlin and allowed decision-making for a time to pass into the hands of the new liberal ministry.

The liberal ministry and the Prussian Parliament

The liberal ministry was hardly revolutionary. Its members were loyal to the crown and determined to oppose social revolution. Riots and demonstrations by workers were quickly brought under control. Meanwhile the ministry, supporting German claims to the Duchies of Schleswig-Holstein, declared war on Denmark (see page 35). It also supervised elections to a Prussian Parliament on the basis of manhood suffrage.

The new Parliament met in May. Although it was dominated by liberals, a third of its members were radicals and there was no agreement about the nature of the new constitution. Its main achievement was to abolish the feudal privileges of the *Junker* class.

Conservative reaction

Determined to defend their interests, Prussian landowners and nobles formed local associations. In August 1848 the League for the Protection of Landed Property met in Berlin. This *'Junker* Parliament', as it was dubbed by the radicals, pledged itself to work for the abolition of the Prussian Parliament and the dismissal of the liberal ministry. The conservatives' main hope was the army. Most army officers were appalled at the triumph of the liberals.

In Potsdam, Frederick William was surrounded by conservative advisers who urged him to win back power. The conservatives – *Junkers*, army officers and government officials – were not total reactionaries. Most hoped to modernise Prussia but insisted that reform should come from the King, not from the people. The tide seemed to be flowing in their favour. By the summer most Prussians seemed to have lost their ardour for revolution and for German unity. The liberal ministry was increasingly isolated.

In August the King resumed control over foreign policy and concluded an **armistice** with the Danes, to the disgust of the Frankfurt Parliament. Riots by workers in Berlin in October ensured that the middle classes drew closer to the traditional

Key question
Why did the Prussian liberals fail?

Key dates
Frederick William re-established control in Berlin: November 1848

New Prussian constitution: December 1848

Key term
Armistice
Ceasefire.

ruling class. Habsburg success in Vienna in October (see page 44) also encouraged the King to put an end to the Prussian Parliament and to dismiss the liberal ministers.

In November 1848 Frederick William appointed his uncle Count Brandenburg to head a new ministry. Almost at once Brandenburg ordered the Prussian Parliament out of Berlin. The Civic Guard was dissolved and thousands of troops moved into Berlin. **Martial law** was proclaimed. All political clubs were closed and all demonstrations forbidden. There was little resistance to the counter-revolution. The army made short work of industrial unrest in the Rhineland and Silesia. The Prussian Parliament, still unable to agree a constitution, was dissolved by royal decree in December. Frederick William now proclaimed a constitution of his own.

Martial law
The exercise of military power by a government in time of emergency with the temporary suspension of ordinary administration and policing.

Key term

The Prussian constitution

The Prussian constitution of late 1848 was a strange mixture of liberalism and absolutism:

Key question
How democratic was the Prussian constitution?

- It guaranteed the Prussians freedom of religion, of assembly and of association, and provided for an independent judiciary.
- There was to be a representative assembly, with two houses. The upper house would be elected by property owners, and the lower one by manhood suffrage.
- Voters were divided into three classes, according to the amount of taxes they paid. This ensured that the rich had far more electoral power than the poor.
- In an emergency, the King could suspend civil rights and collect taxes without reference to Parliament.
- Ministers were to be appointed and dismissed by the King, and were to be responsible only to him and not to Parliament.
- The King could alter the written constitution at anytime it suited him to do so.
- The King retained control of the army.

The constitution thus confirmed the King's divine right to rule whilst limiting his freedom to act. A genuine parliament, albeit subservient to the crown, had been created – from above. While Frederick William would not accept that his subjects could limit his power, he was prepared to limit his own powers.

The new proposals were well received in Prussia, and ministers made no secret of the fact that they hoped it would be a better model for a united Germany than the Frankfurt Parliament. They had ambitions to make Prussia the leading state in Germany, and Frederick William the leading monarch.

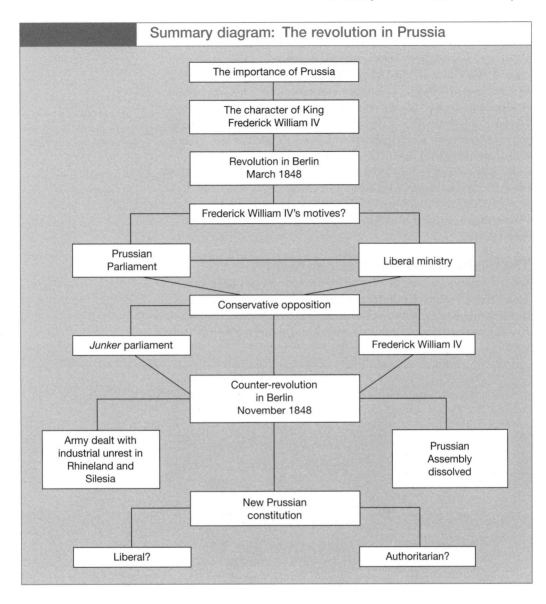

Summary diagram: The revolution in Prussia

The importance of Prussia

The character of King
Frederick William IV

Revolution in Berlin
March 1848

Frederick William IV's motives?

Prussian
Parliament

Liberal ministry

Conservative opposition

Junker parliament

Frederick William IV

Counter-revolution
in Berlin
November 1848

Army dealt with
industrial unrest in
Rhineland and
Silesia

Prussian
Assembly
dissolved

New Prussian
constitution

Liberal?

Authoritarian?

Key question
Why did the
revolutions fail?

5 | The Failure of the German Revolutions

The failure of the Frankfurt Parliament (see pages 36–8) was not
quite the end of the 1848–9 revolutions. A wave of disorder swept
through Germany in the spring and summer of 1849. Popular
uprisings in Saxony, Baden, Bavaria and some Rhineland towns
were put down by Prussian troops. Constitutional changes
obtained from rulers in Saxony, Hanover and several smaller
states were revoked, and liberals all over Germany were arrested
and imprisoned. Some were executed.

By mid-1849, it was clear that the German revolutions had
failed. In Prussia the liberals were defeated. Police powers were
increased and local government powers reduced. The 'three-class
suffrage' for the Prussian lower house ensured that there was no
real democracy.

The counter-revolution went further in Austria than in any of the other German states. In October 1848, 2000 people died in Vienna as government forces regained control of the Austrian capital from radicals. In December, 18-year-old Franz Joseph became the new Austrian Emperor. By mid-1849 his forces had regained control of all the Austrian Empire including Hungary. Dissolving the Austrian Constituent Assembly, he subjected all parts of the Empire to rigid control from Vienna. Martial law was enforced in regions deemed to be infected with liberalism.

By 1850 it seemed as if the events of the previous 2 years had never been; nothing had changed in most of the states. In 1851, as though to complete the restoration of the old order, Metternich returned from exile to Vienna to live as a revered 'elder statesman'.

The failure of revolution across Europe

By 1849 the hopes of the revolutionaries, so high in the spring of 1848, had died. By 1849 the forces of reaction were once again in the ascendant. The three dynastic empires of Austria, Prussia and Russia continued to dominate central and eastern Europe. Most

This German cartoon, entitled 'Panorama of Europe', appeared in August 1849. Explain the significance of the large figure with a broom in the centre of the cartoon.

of the reasons for the failure of the German revolutions relate specifically to the situation in Germany. But the fact that revolutions failed across Europe in 1848–9 had a major impact on Germany.

Limited revolution

In Germany active revolution was comparatively rare. In Prussia it was restricted to riots in Berlin and unrest in the Rhineland and Silesia. In the small states of the south-west, poverty-stricken peasants attacked their landlords, castles were stormed and property was destroyed. In Baden a people's republic existed briefly. but had little support and was quickly suppressed by the liberal government. Most revolutionary activity in Germany did not involve armed uprisings. Meetings, peaceful demonstrations and petitions were the chief weapons of the revolution.

In 1848 most German rulers gave in easily, if temporarily, to demands for more democratic governments, fearing that otherwise they might be overthrown. But almost everywhere, the old rulers retained control of their armed forces and waited for an opportunity to regain power. Growing disunity among the revolutionaries gave them that opportunity.

Revolutionary divisions

There were wide differences in the political aims of liberals and radicals. While the former wanted constitutional government in all states and a united Empire with a national Parliament, the latter worked for complete social and political change within a republican framework. Nor were the nationalists united. There was no agreement on the form the new Germany should take – a unified state or a federation, a monarchy or republic, *Grossdeutschland* or *Kleindeutschland*?

Moreover, different social groups in Germany had very different interests. While popular movements were at the root of the revolutions, it was the propertied classes who seized power. Once middle-class liberals secured the election of their own assemblies, most were as afraid of social revolution as the conservatives.

Working-class movements and the organisation of the radical left were not sufficiently well developed to force social change in their favour. Most workers had a purely practical revolutionary aim: the improvement of their working and living conditions. Unlike their 'intellectual', usually self-appointed, leaders, they were not concerned with – or even aware of – political ideologies that supposedly promoted their cause. Nor were they united. Master craftsmen and the mass of unskilled workers had little in common.

Karl Marx played only a minor role in the revolutions. Hastening back to Germany, like hundreds of other revolutionary exiles in 1848, he was disappointed by the apathy shown by the working class and correctly observed that the revolutions had staff officers and non-commissioned officers, but no rank and file.

Rural apathy

Germany was still essentially agrarian in 1848. The 1847 and
1848 harvests were reasonably good. Consequently, the rural
populations were not in a desperate economic situation in
1848–9. This may explain the unenthusiastic support for
revolutionary movements among peasants and their role in
suppressing revolution by serving as loyal military conscripts.
Across Germany, the peasantry, the vast majority of the
population, lost interest in the revolution once the last remnants
of feudalism had been removed. Indeed, many peasants felt
hostility towards, rather than affinity with, the urban
revolutionaries. The failure of the peasantry to support the
revolutions was of crucial importance.

Loss of support

Popular enthusiasms are often short lived and within a few months
much of the active support for national unity and a national
parliament had disappeared. This loss of support was encouraged
by the slow progress being made by the Frankfurt Parliament. But,
in general, national consciousness failed to develop among the
mass of Germans. Local loyalties remained strong and proved an
important obstacle in the way of national unity.

Conservative strength

In the end the revolutions failed because the enemy was stronger,
better organised and above all possessed military power. The
story might have been very different in Berlin, for example, if
there had not been a well-trained army available – and loyal – to
the King. Given their military advantages, their determination
and often their ruthlessness, the Princes were clear favourites to
win in the end. Constitutional government and national unity
could be achieved only on their terms, not through the well-
intentioned but ineffectual efforts of a liberal parliament, or by
the unco-ordinated actions of popular revolt. Once order was
restored in the Austrian Empire and Austrian policy was still
based on dominating Germany by keeping her weak and divided,
there was no possibility of any moves towards a more united
Germany being allowed to take place. Germany would only be
unified once the military might and moral authority of the
Austrian Empire had been overcome.

Were the revolutions a complete failure?

The 1848–9 revolutions were a severe setback for liberalism, but not a total failure. At least the remnants of feudalism had been swept away. Parliamentary government of a sort had been introduced in Prussia. After 1848 virtually all the monarchical regimes in Germany accepted the need to modernise. Conservatives also accepted the need to show an interest in the social problems of the lower classes if they were to ensure mass support for their policies and/or regimes. Moreover, the 1848–9 revolutions had helped to stir national consciousness across Germany.

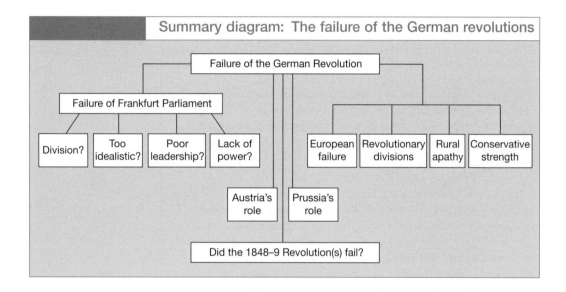

Summary diagram: The failure of the German revolutions

Study Guide: AS Question

In the style of Edexcel

How accurate is it to say that King Frederick William IV of Prussia was responsible for the failure of the Frankfurt Parliament?   (30 marks)

Exam tips

The cross-references are intended to take you straight to the material that will help you to answer the question.

The Frankfurt Parliament was the creation of the 1848 revolution in Germany. Frederick William IV of Prussia, and a host of other princes, had conceded constitutions and the *Vorparlament* led to the Frankfurt Parliament. The aim was a united, constitutional Germany. In 1848 there was great optimism that the aim would be achieved. So what went wrong? Below you will find nine bullet points, all of which help to explain why the Parliament failed. Plan your answer, deciding which ones to emphasise and how to group them effectively. You should devote about a third of your answer to the role of King Frederick William, but you could, of course, include points about Prussian interests also under the heading of his motives and actions.

- The Frankfurt Parliament was the product of a middle-class franchise that omitted the masses (page 31). Thus, the Parliament failed to attract mass support.
- The Parliament was divided. Most representatives wanted a constitutional monarchy incorporating liberal ideals of limited democracy (page 32). This alienated radicals (who wanted to go much further) and outraged conservatives (page 35).
- There was uncertainty about the geographical extent of 'Germany' and no resolution of the *Kleindeutschland–Grossdeutschland* debate (page 34).
- Discussions in the Parliament were ill-organised. There was plenty of talk but little action (see page 33).
- Most states were suspicious of a new German authority. Most (especially Prussia and Austria) were determined to preserve their sovereignty (page 37).
- The Parliament did not have an administration or an army to carry out its decisions (page 34).
- Frederick William of Prussia refused to receive the German crown 'from the gutter' (page 36). There was no other obvious German Kaiser.
- The focus should be on Frankfurt's failure, but the defeat of revolution across Germany is relevant (pages 43–4).
- Once German princes were back in control, the Parliament stood little chance (page 37).

Your conclusion should pull together the main points of your argument. Do not be afraid to say what you think was the main reason for the Frankfurt Parliament's failure. What is your decision? How important was Frederick William IV's role?

3 Prussia and Austria 1849–66

POINTS TO CONSIDER

After the failure of the 1848–9 revolutions, it seemed that Austrian power had revived. Austrian policy was still based on dominating Germany by keeping it weak and divided. Thus, Germany would only be unified once Austrian strength had been broken. The only country that could do that was Prussia. In the 1850s Prussia was regarded as the least important of the major powers. But appearances were deceptive. In 1862 Otto von Bismarck was appointed Minister President of Prussia. Four years later Prussia smashed Austria in the Seven Weeks' War and established the North German Confederation. How much of Prussia's success was due to Bismarck? How much was due to other factors? The chapter will consider these (and other) questions by examining:

- The position of Austria after 1848
- The position of Prussia after 1848
- Bismarck: the man and his aims
- Austro-Prussian conflict
- Prussian ascendancy
- Factors helping Bismarck

Key dates

1849		The Erfurt Plan
1850		The Capitulation of Olmutz
1851		German Confederation restored
1861		William I became King of Prussia
1862		Bismarck became Prussia's Chief Minister
1864		Austria and Prussia fought Denmark
1866	June	Start of Seven Weeks' War
	July	Battle of Sadowa
	August	Treaty of Prague
1867		North German Confederation created

1 | The Position of Austria After 1848

The Prussian Union Plan

Despite his refusal to accept the imperial crown offered by the Frankfurt Parliament, Prussian King Frederick William IV was attracted to the idea of a united Germany with himself at its head, providing he had the consent of the Princes. In 1849 General Radowitz, an ardent nationalist and an old friend of Frederick William, came up with the Prussian Union Plan. His proposal for a *Kleindeutschland*, under Prussian leadership, met with Frederick William's approval.

According to the plan, there would be a German Federal ***Reich***, which would exclude Austria. It would have a strong central government, based on the constitution drawn up by the Frankfurt Parliament (see page 36), with the King of Prussia as Emperor. Although Austria would not be a member of the *Reich*, there would be a special relationship, a permanent 'union', between the *Reich* and the Habsburg Empire.

This complicated plan, which tried to provide both *Kleindeutschland* and *Grossdeutschland* solutions, was not acceptable to Austria. Austrian Chief Minister, Schwarzenberg, saw it as a devious scheme to reduce Austrian influence in Germany. He was not, however, immediately able to mount effective opposition to it, as internal Austrian problems, not least a Hungarian uprising, were occupying his attention. This allowed Prussia, whose army was the strongest authority in Germany in 1849, to press on with the plan. A 'Three King's Alliance' between Prussia, Saxony and Hanover was the first step. Then a number of smaller states were persuaded to fall in with the Prussian proposals. Encouraged by his success, Radowitz called a meeting of representatives of all the German states to Erfurt in March 1850 to launch the new *Reich*. Twenty-eight states agreed to the creation of the Prussian-dominated Erfurt Union. But several important states, suspicious of Prussian ambitions and fearful of Austria's reaction, declined to join.

Austrian opposition

Schwarzenberg, having suppressed the Hungarian rising, was able to reassert Austria's position in Germany. He put forward a scheme of his own for a *Grossdeutschland* to be governed jointly by delegates from Austria, Prussia and the larger German states. Attracted by the way in which this proposal seemed to offer them greater political influence, some of the larger states (for example Hanover and Saxony) deserted Prussia and gave their support to Austria.

Schwarzenberg now summoned the *Diet* of the old German Confederation (see page 5), thought to have been dead and buried, to meet in Frankfurt in May 1850. The response was good and he was able to announce that the *Diet* and Confederation were both alive and well. Thus, by the summer of 1850 there were two assemblies claiming to speak for Germany: the Prussian-led Erfurt Parliament and the Austrian-led Frankfurt *Diet*.

Key question
Why did the Prussian Union Plan fail?

Key date

The Erfurt Plan: 1849

Key term

Reich
The German for empire.

Prussia versus the Confederation

A showdown soon occurred. A revolution in Hesse-Cassel, a member state of the Erfurt Union, prompted its ruler to request help from the Frankfurt *Diet*. But the Erfurt Parliament also claimed the right to decide the dispute. Hesse-Cassel was of strategic importance because it separated the main part of Prussia from the Rhineland, and therefore controlled communications between the two. The Prussian army mobilised. Austria replied with an ultimatum that only the troops of the old Confederation had the right to intervene.

Small-scale fighting broke out between Prussian and Confederation troops. Frederick William, who had no wish for war, dismissed Radowitz. Edwin Manteuffel, the new Prussian Minister-President (Prime Minister), was also anxious to avoid an all-out war.

The 'Capitulation of Olmutz'

Key dates

The 'Capitulation of Olmutz': November 1850

German Confederation restored: 1851

A meeting between Manteuffel and Schwarzenberg was arranged at Olmutz and on 29 November 1850 Prussia agreed to abandon the Prussian Union Plan. The two men also agreed to a conference of states being held at Dresden early in 1851 to discuss the future of Germany. Schwarzenberg had won a major diplomatic victory and Prussia had suffered huge humiliation.

However, the revival of Austria was not allowed to go as far as Schwarzenberg hoped. His proposal for an Austrian-dominated 'Middle Europe', incorporating the 70 million people of all the German states and the Habsburg Empire, was not acceptable to the smaller German states, as it would have increased the power of the larger states at their expense. There was strong pressure for a return to the situation pre-1848. Prussia supported this. Given that the Prussian Union Plan was lost, anything from Prussia's point of view was better than accepting the Austrian counter-plan.

In May 1851 the German Confederation of 1815 was formally re-established and an alliance between Austria and Prussia appeared to signal a return to the policy of close co-operation. However, relations between Prussia and Austria were far from close. Many Prussians blamed Austria for the humiliation of the 'Capitulation of Olmutz'. Some were determined that Prussia should one day dominate a united Germany. Austria clearly stood in the way. In 1856 an emerging Prussian statesman, Otto von Bismarck, commented:

> Germany is clearly too small for us both ... In the not too distant future we shall have to fight for our existence against Austria ... it is not within our power to avoid that, since the course of events in Germany has no other solution.

Austrian economic and financial problems

In 1849 Schwarzenberg, realising the political implications of Prussia's economic success, proposed establishing a *Zollunion*, an extended customs union, between Austria and the *Zollverein* (see pages 15–16). This move failed. So too did Schwarzenberg's efforts in 1851 to establish an alternative customs union to include Austria and those German states still outside the *Zollverein*. Thus, while Austria clung to its political leadership of the Confederation, it was effectively isolated from the Prussian-dominated economic coalition of the German states.

Despite industrial expansion and rising exports, Austrian government finances were in difficulties. Taxation was not sufficient to finance the central administration or to maintain an efficient army. By the end of the **Crimean War** Austria was economically and financially vulnerable, crippled by the cost of keeping large armies mobilised during the war, and in no state to cope with the depression which swept across Europe in the late 1850s.

Key term

Crimean War
This was a war fought by Britain, France and Turkey against Russia. Most of the fighting was in the Crimea – a southern part of Russia. The war, lasting from 1854 to 1856, ended with Russia's defeat.

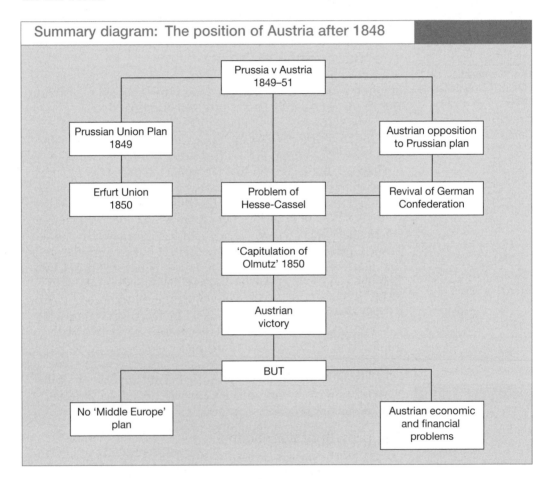

Summary diagram: The position of Austria after 1848

Prussia v Austria 1849–51

Prussian Union Plan 1849

Austrian opposition to Prussian plan

Erfurt Union 1850

Problem of Hesse-Cassel

Revival of German Confederation

'Capitulation of Olmutz' 1850

Austrian victory

BUT

No 'Middle Europe' plan

Austrian economic and financial problems

2 | The Position of Prussia After 1848

Prussian economic success

Although Prussia had suffered a serious political setback in 1850–1, economically the story was different. In the 1850s the Prussian economy boomed. Industrial production, railway building and foreign trade more than doubled.

Key question
What were the main developments in Prussia in the years 1850–62?

The Krupp works in Essen in 1866.

The reasons for Prussia's success are complex. Scholars may have ascribed too much influence to the *Zollverein*. It did not provide protection for Prussian industries. Nor did it create a unified German economy. Other factors may have been equally or more important:

- Prussia had a good education system at various levels, from primary schools to university level.
- There was a plentiful supply of coal, iron and chemicals.
- Prussia had a good system of communications.
- A number of key individuals like Alfred Krupp, the great iron and steel magnate, played an important role.
- Historians disagree about the role played by the Prussian state. Some think it helped economic development. Others think it hindered it.

For whatever reasons, by the mid-1850s Prussia was economically strong. Its ability to finance a full-scale war (against Austria) was increasing year by year.

The growth of liberalism

Despite repressive and reactionary policies after 1848–9 (see page 42), Prussian liberalism grew in strength. It was supported by an increasingly self-confident middle class. Professors, teachers, civil servants, Protestant pastors, businessmen and lawyers joined the great national liberal associations and subscribed to liberal journals.

Nevertheless, for much of the 1850s there was general political apathy in Prussia: few people bothered to make use of their franchise and politics was the concern of a small élite – for the most part lawyers and civil servants. Right-wing liberal politicians, traumatised by the experience of 1848, which showed how easily mass involvement in politics could descend into revolution, remained suspicious of full democracy. They were less concerned with strengthening Parliament than with ending the dominant influence of the aristocracy and the army over the government. However, left-wing liberals still argued in favour of universal suffrage and insisted that the masses could be trusted to vote for men of substance and culture. There was one thing on which both liberal wings could agree: that was that national unity was the absolute priority.

Conservative reform

During the 1850s, Minister-President Manteuffel was prepared to accept limited change as long as it did not lead to any extension of parliamentary influence. He had a particular hatred of the liberal, professional class, considering them to be arrogant, cowardly and godless. Nevertheless, he realised that he had to have a degree of popular support. He believed the best way to stabilise society and reduce the chance of revolution was to improve the living conditions of peasants and workers.

Reform in the countryside

Manteuffel was especially concerned to help the peasants. He believed that they were the basis of popular support for the monarchy.

- All the peasants were freed from their feudal obligations to their landlords.
- Special low-interest government loans were available to enable peasants to buy their land; 600,000 did so.
- In some parts of Prussia, where peasants had moved away to the towns looking for work, there was underpopulation in the countryside, but elsewhere there was overpopulation and great pressure on land. Where this was the case the government gave peasants financial help to move to less populated areas of the country.

Reform in the towns

- In towns the government set out to help factory workers.
- Payment of a standard minimum wage was encouraged.
- Financial help was given to industry.
- Inspectors were appointed to improve working conditions in factories, and children under 12 were forbidden to do factory work.
- Industrial courts were set up to help in the settlement of disputes.

Political reaction

Manteuffel believed that ministers had a duty to govern well, and that this meant governing in the best interests of all the people. At the same time he had no time for democracy and governed without Parliament for the whole of his time as Minister-President (1850–8). In other ways he was equally reactionary, imposing strict censorship and restrictions on the freedom of political parties to hold meetings. Prussia in the 1850s was a curious mixture; politically reactionary and repressive, socially reforming and economically prosperous.

The international situation

Key question
Why did the Crimean War help Prussia?

Key date
William I became King of Prussia: 1861

Key term
North Italian War
In 1859 French Emperor Napoleon III supported Piedmont against Austria. Piedmont was seeking to increase its influence in northern Italy – at Austria's expense. Austria was defeated.

Prussia, despite being a growing economic power, seemed to be a second-rate player in the 1850s. Having avoided military conflict with Austria in 1850, it then played no role in the Crimean War. However, by remaining strictly neutral, Prussia benefited politically as well as economically. It managed to keep on good terms with the other European powers, especially Russia.

Austria also remained neutral, but gained little respect because of its wavering diplomacy, sometimes siding against Russia, sometimes against Britain and France. By 1856 Austria had lost the friendship of Russia without obtaining that of Britain and France.

Prussia might have profited from the **North Italian War** in 1859 if it had supported Piedmont and France against Austria. However, popular feeling in Prussia, as in most German states, was anti-French. Prussia tried to benefit by offering Austria help in exchange for conceding Prussian primacy in Germany.

King William I of Prussia 1797–1888.

Austria's speedy defeat (an underfinanced and ineptly led army was defeated at the battles of Magenta and Solferino by French troops) and willingness to make peace with Napoleon III prevented Prussia's aims being realised. But, at least the war had been a severe blow to Austrian prestige. Austria lost Lombardy (in northern Italy) to Piedmont. Moreover, the cost of the war had a terrible effect on Austria's already strained finances.

William I

Frederick William, whose mental balance had always been precarious, became more and more unstable, until, in 1858, he was declared insane. His brother William became **regent**, and when Frederick William died in 1861, William succeeded to the throne as William I of Prussia.

William, already 63 when he became king, was to reign for another 27 years. A soldier by training and a conservative by instinct, William was practical, hard-headed and inflexible – the complete contrast to Frederick William. Only Bismarck, his chief minister for nearly the whole of his reign, was ever able to make him change his mind. A devout Protestant, he believed that he was answerable only to God, which made it difficult to argue with him. He was prepared to listen to advice from ministers, but not necessarily to act on it. At heart he was an absolutist.

On becoming regent, he dismissed Manteuffel, replacing him with a ministry containing both liberals and conservatives. The atmosphere of comparative freedom led people to talk of a 'new era'. The 1858 elections gave the moderate liberals a small majority in Parliament. They hoped to play a significant role in government. William had no intention that they should.

Reform of the army

The strengthening of the army was one of William's main concerns. He believed it was the key to the future greatness of Prussia. Little had been done to reform or increase the size of the Prussian army since 1815. The mobilisation of the Prussian army during the North Italian War in 1859 had been a disaster. The war was over before it could be organised into some degree of readiness. The delay meant William lost the opportunity to achieve some political advantage.

As a result of this ignominious failure, William appointed a new Minister of War, General Roon. In 1860 Roon, an administrative genius and an extreme conservative, introduced a bill to reform the army. This aimed to:

- double the regular army's size
- increase the period of **military service** from 2 to 3 years
- reduce the role played by the inefficient *Landwehr*
- re-equip the troops.

Roon's bill touched a number of sensitive points as far as the liberal majority in Prussia's Parliament was concerned. The liberals feared that the government might use the expanded

Key question
In what ways was William I different from Frederick William?

Key question
Why was there a constitutional crisis in Prussia between 1860 and 1862?

Regent
A ruler invested with authority on behalf of another.

Military service
The requirement for young men to serve in the army.

Landwehr
A middle-class reserve force that could be called up for service in an emergency. Many of its officers were old and poorly trained.

General Albrecht von
Roon 1803–79.

army, not for the defence of Prussia from foreign attack, but
against its own people as had happened in 1848–9 (see page 42).
Moreover, the civilian *Landwehr*, despite its military shortcomings,
was popular with liberals. While there was some room for
compromise on detail, both sides believed that important
principles were at stake:

- William was determined that army matters should be kept
  above parliamentary approval.
- Liberals believed that Parliament should have financial control
  over army expenditure. Without such a right it had very little
  power.

Constitutional crisis 1860–2

The army bill thus led to a constitutional crisis. In 1860
Parliament would agree only to approve the increased military
budget for a year and would not agree to extend the term of
military service to 3 years.

In June 1861, radical liberals formed the Progressive Party. The
Progressives were committed to a popular rather than a royal
army. In the newly elected Parliament in December 1861 the
Progressives became the largest party. Parliament would not pass

the money bill for the army and William would not accept
2 years' military service.

William again dissolved Parliament and replaced his liberal
ministers with conservatives. The May 1862 elections were a
disaster for the King and a triumph for the Progressives who, in
alliance with the other opposition groups, now had an overall
majority in the lower house.

In September, Parliament again refused to pass the army bill.
Some Prussian conservatives hoped that this would lead to a royal
coup and the overthrow of the constitution. Instead, William,
fearing civil war in Prussia, contemplated abdication. However, on
22 September on the advice of Roon, he appointed Otto von
Bismarck as Chief Minister. This was one of the most momentous
occasions in Prussian, German and European history.

The constitutional crisis solved

Bismarck's appointment as Chief Minister was seen as a deliberate
affront to the Prussian liberals. They regarded him as a bigoted
reactionary. Given that he had no ministerial experience, he was
not expected to last long in power. On 30 September 1862, in his
first speech to the Prussian Parliament, Bismarck declared:

> Germany does not look to Prussia's liberalism, but to its power. …
> It is not through speeches and majority decisions that the great
> questions of the day are decided. That was the great mistake of
> 1848–9. It is by iron and blood.

This phrase, afterwards reversed to 'blood and iron', became
almost synonymous with Bismarck. In truth, the speech was not
his greatest effort. What he had meant to say was that if Prussia
was to fulfil its role in leading Germany towards greater unity, it
could not do so without an efficient army, which the King's
government was seeking to build. His speech, aimed at winning
liberal support, badly misfired. To most liberal nationalists such
blood-curdling talk from a notorious reactionary was seen as a
deliberate provocation. Bismarck thus failed to build any bridges
to his political opponents.

In the end he solved the problem of the military budget by
withdrawing it, declaring that the support of Parliament for the
army bill was unnecessary as the army reforms could be financed
from taxation. To liberal suggestions that the people refuse to pay
taxes, Bismarck replied that he had 200,000 soldiers ready to
persuade them.

Parliament declared his actions illegal, but he ignored it. The
taxes were collected and the army was re-organised as if
Parliament did not exist. For 4 years and through two wars, he
directed Prussian affairs without constitutionally approved budgets
and in the face of fierce parliamentary opposition. New elections
in 1863 gave the liberals 70 per cent of the parliamentary seats.
'Men spat on the place where I trod in the streets', Bismarck
wrote later. But he rightly judged that his opponents would avoid
an appeal to force: few wanted a repeat of 1848.

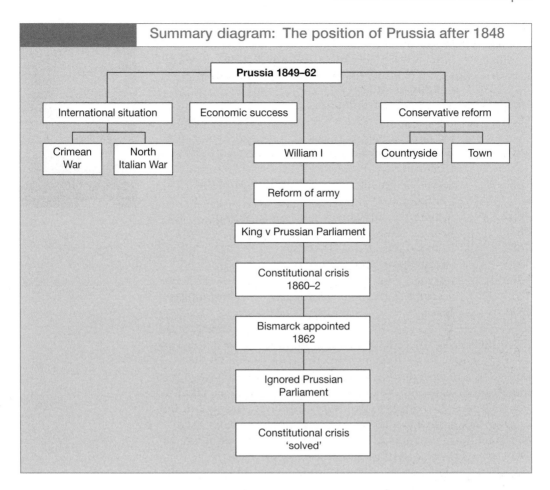

Summary diagram: The position of Prussia after 1848

3 | Bismarck: The Man and his Aims

Bismarck's early life

Key question
What were the main influences on the young Bismarck?

Key date

Bismarck became Prussia's Chief Minister: 1862

Bismarck's father was a moderately wealthy *Junker*. The *Junkers* were the landowning nobility, with their own rules of conduct based on an elaborate code of honour, devotion to the military life, a strong sense of service to the Prussian state and an even stronger sense of their own importance. Most were deeply conservative. Bismarck was proud of his *Junker* descent and all his life liked to present himself as a *Junker* squire. However, he was too clever, too enterprising and too non-conformist to be a typical *Junker*.

Bismarck's mother came from a middle-class family of Hamburg merchants. Many of her relatives were civil servants, university professors or lawyers. Most were politically liberal. Bismarck seems to have been ashamed of this side of his family, often speaking of them in a disparaging way. He did not get on well with his mother, but from her he inherited his intelligence and determination.

At his mother's insistence, he was sent away to school in Berlin, where he proved resistant to education, although he later became a good linguist, fluent in French, English and Russian. He was an

Profile: Otto von Bismarck 1815–98

1815	– Born, the son of a *Junker*. At university he developed a reputation as an accomplished duellist (one year fighting 25 duels)
1836	– Entered the civil service
1839	– Disliking civil service work, he returned to manage the family estates
1847	– Became an ultra-conservative deputy in the Prussian United *Diet*
1851–9	– Served as Prussia's delegate at the *Diet* of the Confederation
1859	– Appointed Prussian ambassador to Russia
1862	– Became Minister-President
1864	– Initiated war against Denmark
1866	– Initiated war against Austria
1870–1	– Initiated Franco-Prussian War
1871–90	– Served as Chancellor of the new German Empire
1898	– Died

After 1862 Bismarck became a man of imperious and dominating temperament with an unquenchable thirst for power. He saw himself as a man of destiny, convinced that he would have a great impact on Europe and the world. Nevertheless, he once admitted: 'I am all nerves; so much so that self-control has always been the greatest task of my life and still is'. He smoked 14 cigars a day, consumed huge amounts of alcohol and ate enormous meals. In 1883 his weight reached 114 kilograms.

Given to melancholy, he suffered from periods of laziness. He was also an inveterate womaniser and gambler. Aggressive and emotional, his relations with William I were stormy; their meetings sometimes degenerated into slanging matches. Bismarck once pulled the handle off the door as he left the room, so great were his feelings of tension. Ruthless, vindictive and unscrupulous in getting his own way, he could also be charming and witty, a delightful companion and entertaining conversationalist.

excellent sportsman, a crack shot and an expert fencer. He went on to university, where he wasted a good deal of time and money, drank too much and got into debt. Managing to pass his law examinations, he won entry to the Prussian civil service and spent 4 years as a less than committed civil servant. A year of military service followed, enjoyed neither by Bismarck nor by the army.

On his mother's death in 1839, he retired to help run the family estates. Country life soon bored him, and he found entertainment chasing after peasant girls and playing wild practical jokes on his neighbours. By the time he was 30, Bismarck had achieved little. Then in 1847 two events occurred to change the direction of his life. First, he married and secondly he got involved in Prussian politics.

His wife Johanna von Puttkamer was deeply religious: 'I like piety in women and have a horror of female cleverness', Bismarck wrote. Johanna satisfied both his requirements. Providing a stable background to his life, she brought up their numerous children and overlooked his continued infidelities.

Bismarck's political career 1847–62

In 1847 Bismarck was elected to the Prussian United *Diet*. It marked his entry into public life. During the March days of the Berlin riots in 1848 (see page 40), he involved himself in counter-revolutionary plots. He was excessively anti-liberal. 'Only two things matter for Prussia', he said, 'to avoid an alliance with democracy and to secure equality with Austria.'

In December 1850 he spoke in the Erfurt Parliament in defence of Frederick William's 'surrender' to Austria at Olmutz. He argued that a state should fight only in its own interest – what he called 'state egoism' – and war for Hesse-Cassel would have been foolish.

> Gentlemen, show me an objective worth a war and I will go along with you … woe to any statesman who fails to find a cause of war which will stand up to scrutiny once the fighting is over.

This speech led to Bismarck becoming Prussian envoy to the revived *Diet* of the Confederation at Frankfurt, where, apart from a short time in Vienna as Prussian ambassador, he remained until 1859. During his years at Frankfurt, it became his overriding concern to oppose Austria. He therefore moved away from the views of his conservative Prussian associates who had sponsored his appointment to Frankfurt. They thought the fight against revolution was still the priority and that it required the solidarity of the conservative powers Russia, Austria and Prussia. As he became increasingly anti-Austrian, he became convinced that war between Prussia and Austria was unavoidable. He believed that such a conflict would eventually lead to a divided Germany with a Protestant north and a Catholic south. By 1858 he was arguing that Prussia should seek support among German nationalists and a year later that Austria should be driven out of the Confederation and a *Kleindeutschland* established under Prussian control.

By the early 1860s he had a reputation as a tough, ambitious and ruthless politician. Although viewed (mistakenly) as a conservative reactionary and (correctly) as a loyal supporter of the monarchy, he was also seen (with some justification) as an unpredictable maverick. However, he was also a realist.

Bismarck's aims

Key question
What were Bismarck's aims in 1862?

Initially, Bismarck's main aim was Prussian domination of north Germany rather than full national unity. He was essentially a Prussian patriot rather than a German nationalist: his loyalty was to the Prussian King – not to the German people. Liberal nationalists viewed him with disfavour in the early 1860s, seeing him not as a potential unifier but as an anti-liberal reactionary. In the late 1840s and early 1850s Bismarck had shown little but contempt for nationalism. However, by the late 1850s his views began to change. Aware of the popular appeal of German nationalism, he realised that the movement might be manipulated in the interests of enhancing Prussian power. Indeed, he tended to see Prussian and German interests as one and the same. He said in 1858 there was 'nothing more German than the development of Prussia's particular interests'.

Convinced that great issues are decided by might not right, he was determined to make Prussia as mighty as possible. Prussian leadership in Germany would ensure Prussian might in the future. While he was determined to end Austrian primacy in the Confederation, he was not necessarily committed to war. A diplomatic solution, in his view, was a preferable option.

Realpolitik characterised Bismarck's political career from first to last. He had contempt for idealism and idealists. While he was a sincere Protestant, he was able to divorce personal from political morality. What was good for Prussia was good. In his view, the end justified the means. He recognised that a conservative regime could no longer operate without popular support, not least that of the liberal bourgeoisie whose power was growing. He hoped to achieve conservative ends by means that were far from conservative. His unscrupulous methods occasionally brought him into conflict with William I and the Prussian military and political élites. But while many distrusted his tactics, most respected his judgement. Indispensable to the Prussian monarchy for nearly thirty years, he made the difficult unification process appear, with hindsight, easy.

Realpolitik
The term is used to describe the ruthless and cynical policies of politicians, like Bismarck, whose main aim was to increase the power of a state.

Key term

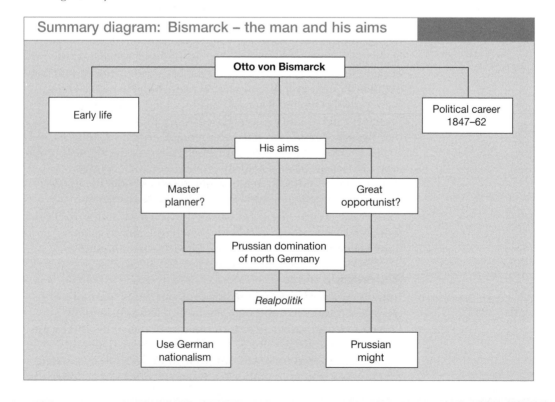

Summary diagram: Bismarck – the man and his aims

4 | Austro-Prussian Conflict

Key question
Why did Austria and
Prussia go to war
against each other?

Relations between Austria and Prussia, cool before 1862, became
much cooler after Bismarck's appointment. In December 1862 he
warned Austria that it was inviting catastrophe unless it recognised
Prussia as an equal in Germany. It should be said that in 1862–3
the prospect of Bismarck defeating Austria and bringing about a
Prussian-dominated Germany was highly unlikely. Bismarck's own
position in Prussia seemed vulnerable. Prussian (and German)
liberals regarded him with hostility and contempt. Prussia's
position in Germany seemed similarly vulnerable. Its territories
straddled across central Europe. Austria had a population almost
twice that of Prussia and had a larger army. Most German states
had no wish to be dominated by Prussia.

The Polish Revolt

Key dates
Austria and Prussia
fought Denmark: 1864

The Danish War: 1864

In the late eighteenth century Prussia, Russia and Austria had
divided Poland between them. Relations between Prussia and her
Polish citizens had been uneasy and Poles had been blamed,
without much evidence, for some of the disturbances of 1848.
Bismarck thought they were troublemakers.

In 1863 when the inhabitants of Russian Poland rose in revolt,
Bismarck viewed the situation with concern. The revolt might
escalate into a general Polish uprising. Tsar Alexander II ordered
the revolt to be suppressed. France, Austria and Britain protested
and offered mediation. Bismarck took the opportunity to gain
Russian friendship by offering military assistance. The Tsar,
confident he could defeat the Poles unaided, rejected the offer,
but agreed to a Convention by which Prussia would hand over to
the Russians any Polish rebels who crossed the border.

Prussian liberals, who hated autocratic Russia, protested at
Bismarck's action. So too did France, Britain and Austria.
Bismarck found himself isolated. In an attempt to improve his
diplomatic position, he claimed that the Convention did not exist
because it had never been ratified. This angered the Tsar and
Prussia was left completely friendless.

The Polish rising was finally suppressed in 1864. Prussia
emerged from the affair less disastrously than Bismarck expected.
Given that the Tsar had been deeply offended by Austrian and
French criticism, it was likely that Russia would remain neutral in
the event of Prussia going to war with Austria or France.

The problem of Schleswig and Holstein

Key question
Why did Prussia and
Austria go to war with
Denmark?

In November 1863 the childless King Frederick VII of Denmark
died. Frederick had also been the ruler of the Duchies of
Schleswig and Holstein that had been under Danish rule for 400
years. The population of Schleswig was mixed Danish and
German, while that of Holstein was almost entirely German.
Holstein was a member of the German Confederation; Schleswig
was not. There had often been trouble over the Duchies. In 1848
the Holsteiners had rebelled against Denmark and Prussian
troops had marched to their aid with the support of the Frankfurt

Parliament, until Russian intervention had forced the Prussian army into retreat.

A treaty signed in London by the Great Powers in 1852 had agreed that Frederick would be succeeded as ruler of Denmark and of the Duchies by Christian of Glucksburg, who was heir to the Danish throne through marriage to the King's first cousin. Schleswig and Holstein contested his claim on the grounds that inheritance through the female line was forbidden in the Duchies. Schleswig-Holsteiners put forward their own claimant, the Prince of Augustenburg. He, however, did not object to being passed over in the treaty, having been well paid to agree, although he never formally renounced his rights.

When Christian became King of Denmark in November 1863, government officials in Holstein refused to swear allegiance to him, and the son of the Prince of Augustenburg now claimed both duchies on the grounds that his father had not signed away his rights to them. This move was passionately supported by German nationalists. King Christian immediately put himself in the wrong by incorporating Schleswig into Denmark, thereby violating the 1852 Treaty of London. In December 1863 the smaller states of the German Confederation, condemning Christian's action as tyrannical, sent an army into Holstein on behalf of the Duke of Augustenburg, the Prince of Augusteburg's son. The Duke became the most popular figure in Germany, a symbol of nationalism, uniting both liberals and conservatives.

Bismarck's aims

Bismarck was not influenced by German public opinion. However, he did see that the crisis offered splendid opportunities. He hoped to annex the two duchies, strengthening Prussian power in north Germany and winning credit for himself into the bargain. He had no wish to see the Duke of Augustenburg in control of another independent state in north Germany. Nor did he care at all about the rights of the Germans within the duchies. 'It is not a concern of ours', he said privately, 'whether the Germans of Holstein are happy'.

Austrian–Prussian co-operation

Bismarck first won Austrian help. Austrian ministers had very different aims from Bismarck. Austria, while supporting the Augustenburg claim, was suspicious of rampant German nationalism. Anxious to prevent Bismarck from allying Prussia with the forces of nationalism, Austria was happy to pursue what appeared to be the traditional policy of co-operating with Prussia. Bismarck, implying that he too supported Augustenburg, kept secret his own expansionist agenda. Agreeing to an alliance, Austria and Prussia now issued an ultimatum to Denmark threatening to occupy Schleswig unless it withdrew the new constitution within 48 hours. Denmark refused. Thus, in January 1864 a combined Prussian and Austrian army advanced through Holstein and into Schleswig.

Denmark, failing to win the support of Britain, France or Russia, agreed that the Schleswig-Holstein matter should be resolved by a European conference. However, the London Conference (April–June 1864) failed to reach agreement. Counting on Britain's support, Denmark refused to make concessions and fighting recommenced. Despite British Prime Minister Palmerston's boast that 'if Denmark had to fight, she would not fight alone', there was little Britain could actually do. Denmark thus had little choice but to surrender in July 1864.

Key question
What were the results of the Danish War?

The Results of the Danish War

By the Treaty of Vienna in October 1864, the King of Denmark gave up his rights over Schleswig and Holstein which were to be jointly administered by Austria and Prussia.

As Bismarck probably intended, the question of the long-term fate of the Duchies now became a source of severe tension between the two German powers. Public opinion in Germany and the Duchies expected that Augustenburg would become Duke. However, Bismarck proposed that he be installed on conditions that would have left him under Prussia's power. This was totally unacceptable to Austria and to the Duke, who refused to become a Prussian puppet. Austria turned to the *Diet*. A motion calling for the recognition of the Duke of Augustenburg easily passed. But Prussia ensured nothing was done. Thus, by the summer of 1865 the future of the Duchies was still not settled, and relations between Austria and Prussia were poor. Austria continued to support Augustenburg's claim while Prussia worked for annexation.

The Convention of Gastein

In truth, neither Austria nor Bismarck wanted war at this stage. Austria, almost financially bankrupt, regarded war as too expensive a luxury. Bismarck was aware that William I was reluctant to fight a fellow German state. Nor was he convinced that the Prussian army was yet ready to fight and win. While Bismarck and William I were 'taking the waters' at the fashionable Austrian spa town of Bad Gastein, an Austrian envoy arrived to open negotiations. As a result of this meeting it was agreed in August l865, by the Convention of Gastein, that:

- Holstein (the Duchy nearer to Prussia) would be administered by Austria.
- Schleswig would be administered by Prussia.
- The two powers would retain joint sovereignty over both Duchies.

Bismarck knew he could now pick a quarrel with Austria over Holstein at any time he wanted.

Bismarck's motives

Bismarck's motives in dealing with the Schleswig-Holstein affair remain a subject of debate. Had he used the Duchies, as he later claimed, as a means of manoeuvring Austria into open confrontation with Prussia? Or did he (whatever he said later) have no clear policy at the time except to 'allow events to ripen'? Historian A.J.P. Taylor thought that he 'may well have hoped to manoeuvre Austria out of the Duchies, perhaps even out of the headship of Germany, by diplomatic strokes ... . His diplomacy in this period seems rather calculated to frighten Austria than to prepare for war'.

Key question
What were Bismarck's motives?

The meeting at Biarritz

The particular problem of the Duchies temporarily was solved, but the more general problem of rivalry between Prussia and Austria remained. While Bismarck may not have wanted war at this stage, he realised that it was a distinct possibility. He therefore did all he could to strengthen Prussia's international position. Confident that Britain and Russia would not support Austria, his main fear was France.

In October 1865 Bismarck met the French Emperor Napoleon III at Biarritz in the south of France. Historians continue to debate what occurred. Almost certainly nothing specific was agreed if only because neither man wanted a specific agreement. Bismarck was not prepared to offer German territory in the Rhineland in return for France's neutrality. Napoleon, calculating that a war between the two German powers would be exhausting and inconclusive, intended to remain neutral and then to turn this to advantage by mediating between the two combatants, gaining a much greater reward in the process than anything Bismarck could presently offer. Given Napoleon's anti-Austrian stance, it took little skill on Bismarck's part to secure the Emperor's good wishes.

War with Austria

Over the winter of 1865–6 Prussian-Austrian relations deteriorated. Austria now determined on a policy of confrontation with Prussia. It did so from a weak position:

- It had no allies.
- It was on the verge of bankruptcy.
- Holstein was sandwiched between Prussian territory.

In February 1866 at a meeting of the Prussian Crown Council Bismarck declared that war with Austria was only a matter of time. It would be fought not just to settle the final fate of the Duchies, but over the wider issue of who should control Germany.

Bismarck carefully laid the groundwork for war. A secret alliance was made with Italy in April 1866, by which Italy agreed to follow Prussia if it declared war on Austria within 3 months. In return Italy would acquire Venetia from Austria when the war ended.

Key question
Why did Austria and Prussia go to war in 1866?

Table 3.1 Prussian, Austrian and French strengths

	Population (millions)		Relative share of world manufacturing output		Key outputs in 1870	
	1840	1870	1830	1860	Coal	Steel
Prussia	14.9	19.4	3.5	4.9		
Germany	32.6	40.8			23.3	0.13
Austria-Hungary	30 [est.]	34.8	3.2	4.2	6.3	0.02

	Austria	France	Prussia
Military			
1850	434,000	439,000	131,000
1860	306,000	608,000	201,000
1866	275,000	458,000	214,000[a]
1870	252,000	452,000	319,000[b]

Railways (kilometres in operation)			
1850	1,579	2,915	5,856[c]
1860	4,543	9,167	11,089
1870	9,589	15,544	18,876

[a] In 1866 Italy, Prussia's ally, had an army of 233,000.
[b] By 1871 the German States under Prussia's leadership could mobilise 850,000 men.
[c] The figures are for the territory of the 1871 *Reich*.

Immediately after the treaty with Italy had been signed, Bismarck stoked up tension with Austria over Holstein and over proposals to reform the Confederation. Bismarck knew that these proposals, which included setting up a representative assembly elected by universal manhood suffrage, would be unacceptable to Austria.

The Austrians, afraid of a surprise attack, were forced to take what appeared to be the aggressive step of mobilising unilaterally in April 1866. Prussia mobilised in May, seemingly as a response to Austrian threats.

Britain, France and Russia proposed a Congress to discuss the situation. Bismarck felt compelled to agree: to do otherwise would put him in a weak position. But he was very relieved when Austria refused, making the Congress unworkable. The situation deteriorated further when, in early June, Austria broke off talks with Prussia and, in breach of previous promises, referred the problem of the Duchies to the *Diet*. Bismarck's response was to send a Prussian army into Austrian-controlled Holstein on 9 June. Austrian troops were permitted to withdraw peacefully.

To Bismarck's surprise and disappointment this did not immediately lead to war. To stir things up, he presented to the *Diet* an extended version of his proposals for a reform of the Federal Constitution:

- Austria was to be excluded from the Confederation.
- There should be a national parliament elected by universal suffrage.
- All troops in north Germany should be under Prussian command.

The next day Austria asked the *Diet* to reject Prussia's proposals and to mobilise for war. Censured by the *Diet*, the Prussians withdrew from the Confederation, declared it dissolved and invited all the other German states to ally themselves with them against Austria. However, most began mobilising against Prussia.

Bismarck now issued an ultimatum to three northern states, Hanover, Hesse-Cassel and Saxony, to side with Prussia or else to be regarded as enemies. When the ultimatums were rejected, Prussian troops invaded the three states on 15 June. Hesse-Cassel and Saxony offered no resistance; Hanoverian forces were quickly defeated.

The Seven Weeks' War

The future of Bismarck, Prussia and Germany lay with the Prussian army. Since the shambles of 1859, reforms had been successfully carried out and the army was now under the command of General Helmuth Moltke, a gifted military leader. Advance planning and preparation, particularly in the use of railways for moving troops, meant that mobilisation was much more efficient than that of the Austrian army.

Key question
Why did the Prussians win?

Key date
Start of the Seven Weeks' War: 1866

A contemporary illustration of the Battle of Sadowa, 1866.

Austria's position was far from hopeless:

- It had more soldiers: 400,000 to the Prussians' 300,000.
- Most of the other German states supported Austria.
- Austria had the advantage of a central position.
- Initially many Prussians were lukewarm about the war.

However, the Italians fulfilled their part of the secret treaty by following Prussia into the war. This meant that Austria was forced to fight on two fronts, in the north against Prussia and in the south against Italy.

The Italian army, weak and inefficient, was defeated by the Austrians on 24 June. To prevent the victorious Austrians in the south from linking up with their troops in the north, Moltke determined to invade Bohemia. One single-track railway ran from Vienna to Bohemia. By contrast, Prussia used five lines to bring its troops southwards. Moltke adopted the risky strategy of dividing his forces for faster movement, only concentrating them on the eve of battle. Fortunately for Prussia, the Austrian high command missed several opportunities to annihilate the separate Prussian armies.

The Battle of Sadowa

On 3 July 1866 the major battle of the war was fought at Sadowa (called Königgrätz by the Prussians). Nearly half a million men were involved, with the two sides almost equally balanced. The Austrians were well equipped with artillery, and used it effectively at the start of the battle, but they were soon caught in a Prussian pincer movement. The Prussians brought into use their new **breech-loading needle gun**. Its rate of fire was five times greater than anything the Austrians possessed, and it proved decisive. The Austrian army fled in disorder. Austria suffered 45,000 casualties, Prussia 9000. The Prussians had won the battle and with it the war.

The Austrian government recognised that further fighting would almost certainly lead to further defeats and might even result in a break up of the Austrian Empire. For Austria the priority was a rapid end to the fighting, at any reasonable cost. Prussia was now in a position to dictate terms as the victor. It was a personal victory for Bismarck, and put him in a position to dominate not only Prussia, but also the whole of Germany for the next quarter of a century.

Key date

Battle of Sadowa: July 1866

Key term

Breech-loading needle gun
This gun, which loaded at the breech rather than the barrel, could fire seven shots a minute.

Summary diagram: Austro-Prussian conflict

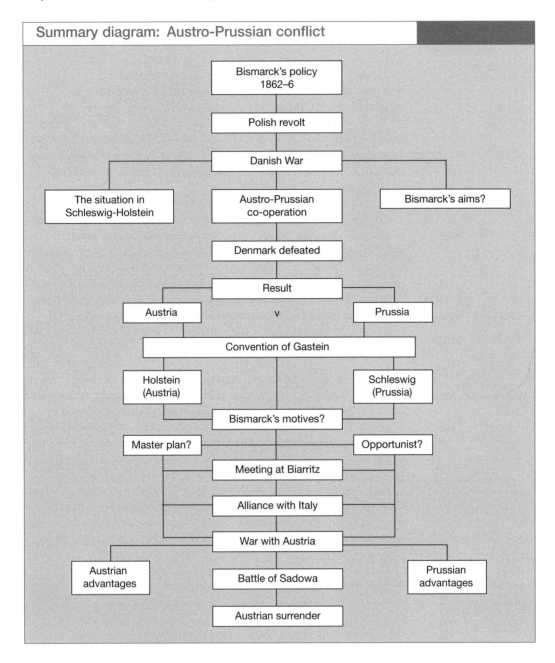

5 | Prussian Ascendancy

Bismarck returned to Berlin with the King and Moltke to a hero's welcome. A grateful Prussia presented him with a reward of £60,000, with which he bought an estate at Varzin in Pomerania. He was promoted to Major General in honour of the victory. It had been noticeable that at meetings of the war cabinet he had been the only one present wearing civilian clothes. Any uniform he was then entitled to would have marked him as an officer of lower rank than anyone else there, and he could not have borne that. Now he was a high-ranking officer he could flaunt his

Key question
What were the main results of the Seven Weeks' War?

uniform on an equal footing, and he never again appeared in public except in full dress uniform. He had earned his spurs and intended to wear them in a Prussia, and later a Germany, dominated by military power.

The aftermath of victory

The road to Vienna lay open after the victory at Sadowa. Austria was at the mercy of Prussia. William I, once reluctant to wage war on a fellow monarch, now proposed an advance on Vienna and a takeover of Austria. Bismarck, fearful that France and Russia might intervene, counselled caution. He wrote to William as follows:

> We have to avoid wounding Austria too severely; we have to avoid leaving behind in her unnecessary bitterness or feeling or desire for revenge. We ought to keep the possibility of becoming friends again. If Austria were severely injured, she would become the ally of France and of every opponent of ours … German Austria we could neither wholly nor partly make use. The acquisition of provinces like Austrian Silesia and part of Bohemia could not strengthen the Prussian state.

At a noisy and angry meeting of the war cabinet on 23 July, William I and his senior generals raged against Bismarck's policy of not annexing any Austrian territory, while Bismarck himself threatened suicide if his advice was not taken. In the end Bismarck got his way. The war was brought to a speedy end and a moderate peace concluded with Austria. The only territory lost by Austria as a result of the Seven Weeks' War (Holstein apart) was Venetia in Italy.

The Treaty of Prague

An armistice was signed between Prussia and Austria in July. This was followed by the Treaty of Prague in August. The terms of the treaty were mainly concerned with the remodelling of northern Germany:

- Prussia annexed a good deal of territory, including Schleswig and Holstein, Hesse-Cassel, Hanover, Nassau and Frankfurt.
- All other German states north of the River Main, including Saxony, were to be formed into a North German Confederation under Prussian leadership (see Map 3.1 on page 73).

Bismarck might have pressed for the unification of all Germany in 1866. However, as well as the threat of French intervention, he feared that if Prussia absorbed too much too soon, this might be more trouble than it was worth. The four Catholic states south of the River Main – Bavaria, Württemberg, Baden and Hesse-Darmstadt – thus retained their independence. Nevertheless, all four states agreed to sign a secret military alliance with Prussia, whereby, in the event of war, they would not only fight alongside

Key date

The Treaty of Prague: August 1866

Prussia, but also put their armies under the command of the King of Prussia.

The Treaty of Prague is usually seen as a milestone on the way to German unity. Ironically, the destruction of the German Confederation could be seen as dividing rather than uniting Germany. After 1866 Germans were separated into three distinct units:

- the North German Confederation
- the four South German states
- the Austrian Empire.

North Germany

Bismarck had shown a calculated moderation in his treatment of Austria. He showed neither of these to some of his fellow north Germans. Hesse-Cassel, Nassau, Hanover, Frankfurt and Schleswig-Holstein were not consulted about uniting with Prussia; they were just annexed. The King of Hanover was driven out and his personal fortune confiscated. (It came in useful to Bismarck later when it was used to bribe the King of Bavaria.)

Those north German states, such as Saxony, not annexed by Prussia, were left with some independence within the North German Confederation. Some historians have seen this as a trial run by Bismarck in North Germany for an eventual wider federation taking in all *Kleindeutschland*. They argue that he could easily have annexed the remaining northern states if he had so wished, but did not do so because he wanted to show those Germans south of the Main how advantageous membership of a Prussian-controlled federation could be. A more credible argument is that Bismarck saw no advantage to Prussia in too speedy a takeover of so many states at once. Such action would only lead to a dilution of Prussian culture and traditions. Instead of Prussia absorbing Germany, Germany would end up absorbing Prussia.

The North German Confederation

At the end of 1866 Bismarck began drafting the constitution for the North German Confederation. This was accepted by April 1867 and came into effect in July. The Confederation lasted only 4 years, but its constitution was to continue, largely unaltered, as the constitution of the German Empire. It was designed to fit the requirements of Prussian power and Bismarck's own political position.

Bismarck was always opposed to the idea of parliamentary government on the British model, which reduced the crown to symbolic status and put power in the hands of a parliament. His declared view of the political abilities of his fellow Germans was low:

> Considering the political incapacity of the average German, the parliamentary system would lead to conditions such as had prevailed in 1848, that is to say weakness and incompetence at the top and ever new demands from below.

Key date

North German Confederation created: 1867

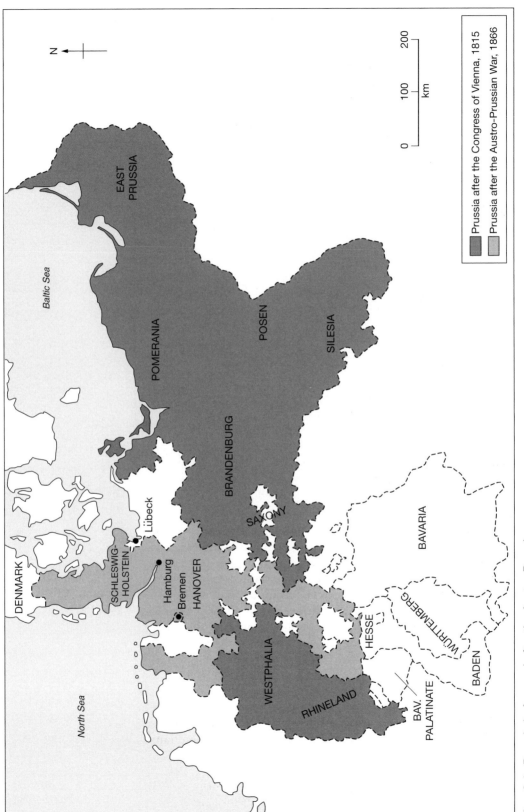

Map 3.1: Prussia before and after the Austro-Prussian war.

Prussia after the Congress of Vienna, 1815

Prussia after the Austro-Prussian War, 1866

km

EAST PRUSSIA

POMERANIA

POSEN

SILESIA

BRANDENBURG

SAXONY

Baltic Sea

North Sea

DENMARK

SCHLESWIG-HOLSTEIN

Lübeck

Hamburg

Bremen

HANOVER

WESTPHALIA

RHINELAND

HESSE

BAVARIA

WÜRTTEMBERG

BADEN

BAV. PALATINATE

THE STRUCTURE OF THE NORTH GERMAN CONFEDERATION

The King of Prussia was President of the North German Confederation and also the commander-in-chief, and had the power of declaring war and making peace. He appointed and could dismiss the Federal Chancellor.

The states, including Prussia, had substantial rights, keeping their own rulers and being governed by their own laws and constitutions with their own parliamentary assemblies. They had their own legal and administrative systems, and local taxation met the cost of government services.

The *Bundesrat* (the Federal Council) was the upper house of the Confederation's Parliament. Here the various states were represented by delegates who acted on the instructions of their governments. The number of delegates was fixed in relation to the size of the state: out of 43 votes, Prussia had 17, Saxony four and most of the others one each. Decisions were made by a simple majority vote.

The *Reichstag* was the lower house of the Confederacy's Parliament. It was elected by universal manhood suffrage – a seemingly giant step towards democracy. However, its powers were limited.

The Federal Chancellor (the Chief Minister) was the main driving force in the Confederation. He represented the Prussian King in the *Bundesrat*. He was not responsible to the *Reichstag* nor did he need majority support in it. He was responsible only to the President of the Confederation.

All laws needed approval of the *Reichstag*, the *Bundesrat* and the King of Prussia as President of the Confederation. They also needed the signature of the Chancellor.

Given his views, Bismarck's insistence on universal manhood suffrage in the election of the *Reichstag* is surprising. However, he believed that the traditional loyalties of peasants would preserve the conservative order in Germany. Nor did he intend the *Reichstag* to play a significant part in public life. Essentially, it was little more than an organ of public opinion. Speaking in confidence to a Saxon minister, he declared he was trying 'to destroy parliamentarianism by parliamentarianism'. In effect, he hoped that the activities of a weak *Reichstag* would help to discredit parliamentary institutions in German eyes. Certainly, the democratic manner of the election process did not compensate for the great weakness of the *Reichstag*, which was that ministers, including the Chancellor, were not members of it and were not responsible to it.

Popular support for Bismarck

On the same day as the battle of Sadowa, elections were held in Prussia. Patriotic war fever resulted in a big increase in the number of conservatives elected to the Prussian Parliament. The numbers jumped from 34 to 142, while the liberal parties were reduced from 253 to 148. Moreover, after Prussia's victory, many liberals changed their attitude to Bismarck. He was now acclaimed rather than maligned. This ensured an era of harmony between Bismarck and the Prussian Parliament. Only seven votes were cast against an Indemnity Bill introduced by Bismarck at the beginning of the new session. This Bill asked Parliament to grant an 'indemnity' for any actions taken by the government during the previous 4 years without Parliament's consent. Bismarck spoke of the need for the government to work jointly with Parliament to build a new Germany.

Both the left- and right-wing parties in Parliament split into new groupings. A large section of the old Liberal Party formed themselves into the National Liberal Party, pledged to support Bismarck in his nationalist policy, but equally pledged to maintain liberal constitutional principles against any government attempt to undermine them.

On the right, the *Junker* Party opposed Bismarck as a traitor to his class, whittling away at the royal prerogative and losing Prussia's identity in the new unified North Germany. Moderate conservatives formed a new party group, the Free Conservatives. They, together with the National Liberals, were to provide the support that Bismarck needed to carry out his policies.

The first *Reichstag*

The first *Reichstag* was elected in February 1867. The National Liberals were the largest single party in it and held the balance of power between Bismarck's conservative supporters and his various opponents. They were able to win a number of concessions from Bismarck, now the Federal Chancellor. These included the right to pass an annual budget. This financial control was very limited because it did not include control over the military budget, which accounted for about 90 per cent of the Confederation's spending. The Liberals and Bismarck struggled over the question of the military budget and eventually reached a compromise. It would remain outside the *Reichstag*'s control for 5 years, until 1872. Then the amount of money to be spent on the army would be fixed by law and for this the *Reichstag*'s consent would be required. Generally prepared to support Bismarck's policies, the *Reichstag* carried through an ambitious legislative programme including a range of unifying measures.

Bismarck and Germany

The Treaty of Prague brought huge gains to Prussia. Austria was now forced to withdraw from German affairs, leaving the field clear for Prussian influence to dominate. Two-thirds of all Germans, excluding German Austrians, were now part of the Prussian-dominated North German Confederation. Most north Germans quickly accepted the situation. For many liberal-nationalists there were no irreconcilable differences between Bismarck's Prussian policy and *Kleindeutsch* nationalism. Unification was happening, even if it was being carried out by force, and some liberals believed that the end justified the means. Indeed, after 1866 Bismarck found himself under nationalist pressure, north and south, to complete the process of unification. Recognising that union with the southern states would strengthen Prussia in relation to both France and Austria, Bismarck was not averse to the idea and was prepared to use the rhetoric and emotion of German nationalism to help to bring it about.

In 1866 the tide in south Germany in favour of union with the north seemed to be flowing strongly. Political parties were established in the southern states to work for unity. In 1867 the four southern states were incorporated into the new *Zollparlament* – a parliament elected to discuss the policy of the *Zollverein*. This was intended to encourage closer co-operation between north and south. However, by 1867 local loyalties in the south re-emerged. Many southern Catholics regarded Prussia with suspicion. The foreign minister of Baden described the North German Confederation as a 'union of a dog with its fleas'. In 1868 the southern states elected a majority of delegates (49 to 35) to the *Zollparlament* opposed to union with the north. National Liberals, who had hoped that the *Zollparlament* would be the motor for national unification, were bitterly disappointed. Bismarck was not too concerned. He believed that in good time, whether by war or simply as a result of evolution, the southern states would fall like ripe fruit into Prussia's basket.

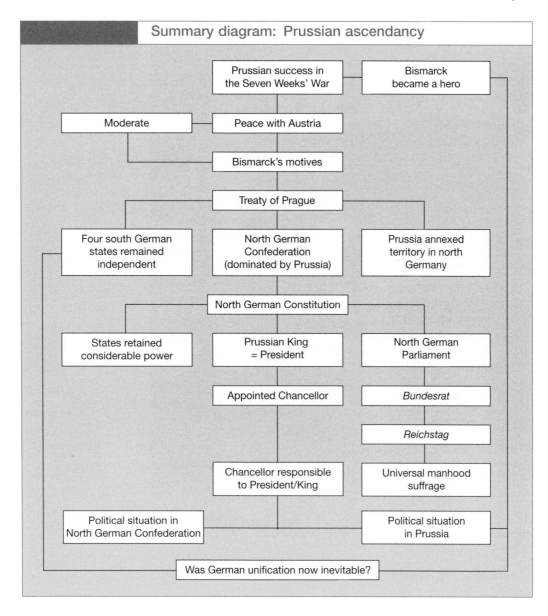

Key question
What factors helped
Bismarck?

6 | Factors Helping Bismarck

In 1869 Bismarck wrote:

> I am not so arrogant as to assume that the likes of us are able to
> make history. My task is to keep an eye on the currents of the latter
> and steer my ship in them as best I can.

He steered brilliantly. However, a variety of factors enabled him
to bring about German unification.

The Prussian army

German unification was the immediate result of three short wars –
against Denmark (1864), Austria (1866) and France (1870–1).

General Helmuth von Moltke – the 'brains' behind Prussian military success. Did Bismarck's success rest on Moltke's military achievements?

The Prussian army thus made Germany a reality. The fighting capacity of the Prussian army improved immensely in the early 1860s thanks to the efforts and ability of War Minister Roon and General Moltke, chief of the General Staff. Roon ensured that Prussian forces were increased, better trained and well armed. Under Moltke, the General Staff became the brains of the Prussian army, laying plans for mobilisation and military operations. In particular, Prussian military chiefs were quick to see the potential of railways for the rapid movement of troops.

Prussian economic success

Prussian economic growth in the 1850s and 1860s outstripped that of Austria and France. By the mid-1860s Prussia produced more coal and steel than France or Austria and had a more extensive railway network. In 1865 it possessed 15,000 steam engines with a total horsepower of 800,000. Austria, by contrast, had 3400 steam engines with a total horsepower of 100,000. The economic and financial strength of Prussia gave the military resources it needed to challenge first Austria and then France. A key industrialist was Alfred Krupp, whose iron foundries in the Ruhr produced high-quality armaments.

Economic unity and the *Zollverein*

The continued spread of the railway and the growth of an increasingly complex financial and commercial network helped to draw all parts of Germany into closer economic unity. So did the Prussian-dominated *Zollverein*, which by 1864 included virtually every German state except Austria. However, while the *Zollverein* ensured that Prussia had considerable economic influence in Germany, this was not translated into political domination. Many German states supported Austria politically to counter-balance economic subordination to Prussia. In 1866 most *Zollverein* states allied with Austria against Prussia.

German nationalism

The failure of the 1848 revolution was a serious blow to German nationalism. However, the idea of a unified state persisted in the hearts and minds of liberal-nationalists. In September 1859 the National Association was formed. Stimulated by the success of Italian nationalism, it promoted the idea that Prussia should lead the German cause (as the state of Piedmont had led the cause of Italian nationalism) and become more liberal in outlook. But gone was the romantic idealism of 1848. Many nationalists now accepted that nothing could be achieved without power. Only Prussia seemed to have that power. At its peak the National Association had only 25,000 members. However, it included many influential men and had close links with a range of other organisations, not least with liberal parties that won growing support in many states, including Prussia, in the early 1860s.

There is no doubt that nationalist sentiment was strong among middle-class Germans who, as a result of industrialisation, were growing in economic and social power. The middle classes tended to lead public opinion. Books and newspapers supported the idea of national unity. Moreover, fears of French expansion were still prevalent. Popular nationalism, strongest in the Protestant north, was a force that could not be ignored by Bismarck.

However, there is plenty of evidence to suggest that many Germans had little interest in national unity. There was certainly no massive sentiment in favour of a Prussian-dominated Germany.

The weakness of Austria

Austria was a power in decline after 1848–9:

- The Austrian economy was largely agricultural with pockets of industry confined largely to the western regions.
- Austria faced the growing problem of minority nationalism (especially in Italy).

- Austria had mounting financial problems.
- The Crimean War weakened Austria's diplomatic position.
- Defeat in the North Italian War (1859) was a serious blow to Austrian prestige.
- Austrian leaders displayed a lack of political and diplomatic skill.

The international situation

The fact that Prussia was regarded as a second-rate power in 1862 helped Bismarck. He was able to achieve supremacy in Germany without arousing the hostility of Prussia's neighbours:

- In the 1860s Britain adopted a non-interventionist posture towards continental affairs. The prevailing view was that Britain had nothing to fear from Protestant Prussia and that a strong Germany would be a useful bulwark against France or Russia.
- Russia, concerned with reform at home, showed little interest in central Europe. Its sympathies lay with Prussia. Russia had still not forgiven Austria for its policy during the Crimean War.

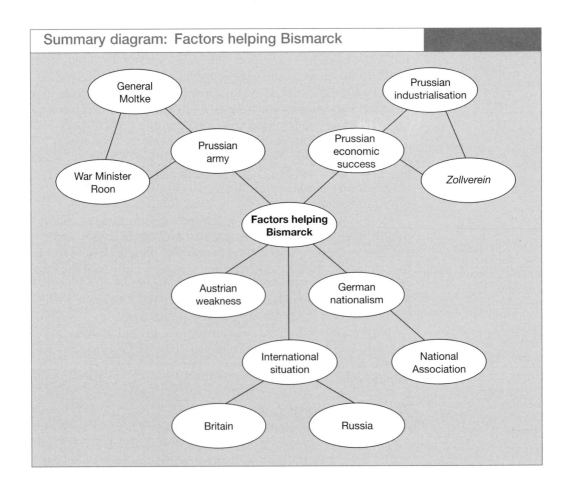

Summary diagram: Factors helping Bismarck

Study Guide: AS Question

In the style of Edexcel

How far was Bismarck's diplomatic skill responsible for bringing about the defeat of Austria in 1866?   (30 marks)

Source: Edexcel, May 2004

Exam tips

The cross-references are intended to take you straight to the material that will help you to answer the question.

Resist the temptation simply to record what Bismarck did. The need for focus and pointing of your material is essential. In dealing with the four bullet points which follow, try to bring out both Bismarck's diplomatic skill and how Austria was weakened in the process:

- the situation in 1862 (page 63)
- the Polish revolt (page 63)
- the Danish War (pages 64–5)
- worsening relations between Prussia and Austria 1865–6 (pages 65–8).

You will also need to stress that Bismarck's diplomatic skill, in itself, was not responsible for Austria's defeat. There were other important factors:

- Austrian weaknesses and mistakes (pages 79–80)
- Prussian military strength (pages 77–8)
- Prussian economic strength (pages 78–9)
- the favourable international situation (page 80).

Reach a conclusion. How significant was Bismarck's role?

Prussia and France 1862–71

Key dates

1867		The Luxemburg crisis
1868–70		The Hohenzollern candidature crisis
1870	July	The Ems telegram
		Start of Franco-Prussian War
	September	Napoleon III surrendered at Sedan
	October	Surrender of the French army at Metz
1871	January	German Second Empire proclaimed at Versailles
		France accepted an armistice
	May	Treaty of Frankfurt

1 | Franco-Prussian Relations 1866–70

The international situation in 1866 was far better than Bismarck might have expected:

• Britain generally welcomed Prussia's dominant position in central Europe, regarding it as a welcome counter-weight to both France and Russia.

Key question
What had been the state of relations between Bismarck and Napoleon pre-1866?

- Russia was pleased that it had a reliable partner against Austria.
- Austria, absorbed with the problem of dealing with its various subject nationalities, especially the Hungarians, was not in a position to mount a war of revenge.

The only real threat was France, unpredictably led by Emperor Napoleon III. Bismarck knew that Napoleon was likely to oppose the establishment of a powerful German state that would dominate Europe east of the Rhine and pose a threat to French security.

Napoleon III

The motives behind Napoleon III's foreign policy are difficult to determine. He seems to have wanted simply to restore France to a position of influence in Europe, through peaceful means if possible. But the difficulty he had in making a decision and sticking to it made him appear inconsistent and unpredictable. Unlike his uncle, Napoleon I, he lacked the ruthlessness and the will to carry things through to their logical conclusion. This put him at a marked disadvantage when dealing with a man as devious and determined as Bismarck, who was likely to outplay him at his own game.

Relations between Bismarck and Napoleon III pre-1866

Bismarck and Napoleon had first met in Paris in 1855. The meeting was a successful one on a personal level, and the two men parted on friendly terms. They met again at Biarritz in October 1865 (see page 66). Historians have speculated ever since on what passed between them. Perhaps Bismarck made a deal with Napoleon by agreeing on territorial or other rewards for French neutrality in the event of an Austrian-Prussian war. More likely he suggested that an opportunity might arise for French expansion, perhaps in the Rhineland, after a Prussian victory over Austria. Almost certainly there was no commitment on either side, but there probably were protestations of good will and general support.

The situation in 1866

Napoleon III remained neutral in the Austrian-Prussian War. He had hoped to turn his neutrality to good advantage by mediating between the combatants and by threatening to join in the war to persuade them to make peace on his terms, which would include territorial gains for France. The speed and scale of Prussia's victory (see pages 69–71) dashed Napoleon's hopes. When he attempted to mediate after the Battle of Sadowa, the offer was declined by Bismarck, who instead sent the Prussian ambassador in Paris to inform Napoleon that Prussian expansion would be limited to north Germany, and that the south German states would remain independent. The division of Germany was presented to Napoleon as a reward for his neutrality during the war. Bismarck realised that Napoleon would regard a united

Germany as a potential threat to France and feared that the Emperor might march to Austria's assistance.

The threat of German unity

After 1866 Napoleon was concerned by the situation in Germany. Prussia now controlled more than two-thirds of Germany and it was unrealistic to suppose that the remaining third could or

---

Profile: Louis Napoleon 1808–73

1808		– Born, son of Louis Bonaparte, King of Holland and brother of Emperor Napoleon Bonaparte
After 1815		– Lived in south Germany and Switzerland: he developed a deep sense of destiny, believing that he would restore his family's fortunes
1836		– His attempt to provoke a rebellion in support of the **Bonapartist** cause in Strasbourg ended in farce: he was arrested and forced into exile (in the USA, Switzerland and Britain)
1840		– A second attempt to raise a rebellion at Boulogne was unsuccessful: he was sentenced to life imprisonment
1846		– Escaped from prison and fled to Britain
1848		– Elected President of the new French Republic, following the overthrow of King Louis Philippe
1852		– Became Emperor Napoleon III
1859		– Defeated Austria in northern Italy
1870	July	– Led France into the Franco-Prussian War
	September	– Forced to surrender at Sedan
1873		– Died in exile in England

Many of those who have written about Napoleon III have been less than flattering. He can be seen as promising much but achieving little. He can be criticised for replacing a democratic republic with an authoritarian regime. Some see the disastrous Franco-Prussian War as the fitting finale to a corrupt, incompetent regime.

But Napoleon III has his admirers. Arguably the catastrophe of 1870–1 obscured many of his achievements. He can be seen as a far-sighted and pragmatic leader, keen to reconcile the desire for liberty and democracy with the principle of order. As a champion of the principle of nationality he had a significant impact on the re-shaping of mid-nineteenth century Europe. It was somewhat ironic that the forces of German nationalism destroyed him in 1870.

Bonapartist Supportive of the Bonaparte family. Although Napoleon Bonaparte had been defeated in 1815, many French people regarded his rule with great nostalgia. They hoped that a member of his family might again rule France.

Key term

would continue an independent existence indefinitely. After the Treaty of Prague Bismarck extended the *Zollverein* to include the four south German states and involved them in the new *Zollparlament* (see page 76). Although it was nominally concerned only with economic affairs, it seemed that the *Zollparlament* would be a further step towards full German unity.

The south German states

The four south German states did not present a united front, for they distrusted each other as much as they distrusted Bismarck. In addition, they distrusted Napoleon – with good reason. They believed – correctly – that he had had designs on part of their territory as his reward for French neutrality during the Seven Weeks' War. In July 1866 the French ambassador in Berlin had presented detailed plans to Bismarck for France to acquire part of the Rhineland belonging to Bavaria and Hesse. This idea was firmly rejected by Bismarck, who did not want to give away any German territory to France. But nor, in mid-1866, did he want to alienate Napoleon. He therefore suggested that France should look for expansion, not in the Rhineland, but further north in the French-speaking areas of Belgium and Luxemburg.

Key question
Why did Franco-Prussian relations deteriorate after 1866?

Key date
The Luxemburg crisis: 1867

The Luxemburg crisis

Having missed the chance to check Prussia's growth of power in 1866, Napoleon needed a diplomatic and territorial success to prove that France remained Europe's greatest power. Luxemburg seemed to provide an opportunity for Napoleon.

Bismarck's policy on the Luxemburg question is difficult to unravel. He began by helping Napoleon to 'persuade' the King of the Netherlands, who was also Duke of Luxemburg, to relinquish the Duchy. The King, short of money and with no real interest in Luxemburg, readily agreed. However, Prussia also had certain rights in Luxemburg, in particular to garrison the fortress. This right dated from the Vienna Settlement of 1815, which had made the fortress part of the German Confederation.

By the end of 1866 Bismarck was feeling much less need to be friendly towards Napoleon, who was stirring up demonstrations in Luxemburg against 'the hated domination of Prussia'. Partly in response to this and partly to encourage nationalist sentiment, Bismarck now began to refer to Luxemburg as German, and announced that its surrender to France would be 'a humiliating injury to German national feelings'. He declared: 'If a nation feels its honour has been violated, it has in fact been violated and appropriate action must ensue … . We must in my opinion risk war rather than yield.' Anti-French sentiment increased throughout Germany.

Why did Bismarck encourage this nationalist hysteria? It seems unlikely that he wished to start a war with France at this stage. The Prussian army needed time to recover from the Austrian War and the North German Confederation was still fragile. Perhaps his intention was to start a campaign of provocation to drive

Napoleon into war in due course. Perhaps, rather than leading, he was himself partly led by German nationalists who he knew he could not afford to alienate.

Napoleon v Bismarck

In March 1867 Bismarck released texts of the secret military alliances he had made with the south German states. These showed that the North German Confederation and the four southern states were not as independent of each other as had been assumed.

Napoleon and Bismarck now met head on in a series of diplomatic battles. Napoleon began new negotiations with the King of the Netherlands, playing on the King's fears that Prussia was after a slice of Dutch territory, and offering to protect the Netherlands in return for Luxemburg. From Napoleon's point of view the King wrecked the scheme by agreeing to sell Luxemburg for 5 million guilders, subject to approval by the King of Prussia. This, he must have known, was not likely to be given. Indeed, Bismarck used the patriotic German fervour he had encouraged as an excuse to threaten the King of the Netherlands not to give up Luxemburg.

Bismarck now appealed to the Great Powers to settle the Luxemburg question. At a conference in London it was agreed that:

- the Prussian garrison should be withdrawn
- Luxemburg's independence and neutrality would be guaranteed by the Great Powers.

While the outcome of the London conference seemed like a compromise, the fact that there was no territorial gain for France was a heavy blow for Napoleon.

The results of the Luxemburg crisis

The Luxemburg crisis seriously damaged Franco-German relations. Nevertheless, the years 1867–70 were peaceful. Bismarck was still keen to avert war. Fearful of French military strength, he was also concerned that Napoleon might find allies. Austrian Emperor Franz Joseph, hankering after regaining influence in Germany, twice met Napoleon in 1867 to see whether it was possible to reach agreement. Fortunately for Bismarck, these efforts came to nothing. There was no real basis for agreement. Franz Joseph was aware that most German Austrians totally opposed a pro-French and anti-Prussian policy.

The Luxemburg crisis has been seen as the point at which Bismarck stopped being a Prussian patriot and became a German one. However, there is no evidence that Bismarck himself thought this. He stirred up and used German national feelings quite cynically as a means to increase Prussian influence over the rest of the German states, as well as a weapon against France. He now wanted a united Germany (under Prussian control) but knew that this was unlikely to happen overnight. Only a war with France, which raised national consciousness and brought all Germans together, was likely to speed up the process.

Bismarck's peaceful intentions?

In a long interview which Bismarck gave to a British journalist in September 1867 he spoke of his wish for peace:

> There is nothing in our attitude to annoy or alarm France ... there is nothing to prevent the maintenance of peace for 10 or 15 years, by which time the French will have become accustomed to German unity, and will consequently have ceased to care about it.

In this interview Bismarck presented himself as a man of peace. He wanted to allay British fears about Prussian warlike intentions and to reduce the chance of a British alliance with France. He made use of such methods to present himself and his policies in a favourable light. He understood very well the value of a good public relations system. This makes it difficult to judge his true intentions from his public utterances. He did not always believe what he said, or say what he believed.

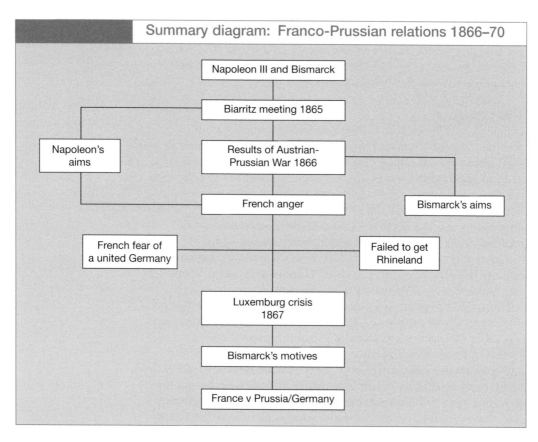

Summary diagram: Franco-Prussian relations 1866–70

2 | The Road to War

The Hohenzollern candidature

In 1868 the Queen of Spain, Isabella, was driven out of the country by a revolution. The Spanish government made efforts to find a new monarch among the royal houses of Europe. In February 1870 an official offer was made to Prince Leopold of Hohenzollern by the Spanish government. Leopold's father referred the request to William I, who as King of Prussia, was head of the Hohenzollern family. William left to himself would have refused consent. He knew that to proceed would provoke French hostility, for Napoleon would see it as a threat to 'encircle' France, with Hohenzollern monarchs in Berlin and Madrid pursuing anti-French policies simultaneously.

William was persuaded to change his mind by Bismarck, who sent him a strongly worded memorandum: 'It is in Germany's political interest that the house of Hohenzollern should gain in esteem and an exalted position in the world'. In the end the King gave his consent, provided that Leopold himself wished to accept the throne. As Leopold did not want to do so, the affair appeared to be at an end.

However, Bismarck had secretly sent envoys to Spain, with large sums of money as bribes, to push Leopold's candidacy. He also put pressure on the Hohenzollern family, as a result of which Leopold decided to accept after all. In June William gave his unconditional consent.

The crisis

Bismarck had planned that the document giving Leopold's acceptance would arrive in Spain, be immediately presented to the *Cortes* for ratification, and then the news be announced amid general rejoicing. However, the message, relayed in code through the Prussian embassy in Madrid, suffered an unforeseen mix-up of dates due to a cipher clerk's error. As a result the *Cortes* was not in session when the document arrived and before it could be recalled the secret of Leopold's acceptance leaked out.

The news reached Paris on 3 July 1870. Napoleon and his new aggressive Foreign Minister Antoine Gramont regarded Leopold's candidature as totally unacceptable. Moreover, they hoped to strengthen Napoleon's position at home by a resounding victory, diplomatically or otherwise, over Prussia. An angry telegram was sent to Berlin asking whether the Prussian government had known of Leopold's candidacy and declaring that 'the interests and honour of France are now in peril'. Count Benedetti, the French ambassador in Berlin, was instructed to go to the spa town at Ems, where William I was taking the waters, to put the French case that Leopold's candidacy was a danger to France and to the European balance of power, and to advise William to stop Leopold leaving for Spain if he wanted to avoid war.

William, who had no wish for war, assured the ambassador of Prussia's friendship for France, and on 12 July Leopold's father withdrew his son's candidacy. The affair appeared to have been

Key question
Who was most to blame for the Franco-Prussian War?

Key date

The Hohenzollern candidature crisis: 1868–70

Key term

Cortes
The Spanish Parliament.

settled, with the diplomatic honours going to France. Bismarck, in Berlin, spoke of humiliation, and threatened resignation. He was saved from having to make good his threat by Napoleon.

Goaded by Gramont, the French Emperor now overplayed his hand. Leopold's renunciation had been announced in a telegram from his father to the Spanish government. Now France demanded an official renunciation from William I, on behalf of Leopold, for all time, and the French ambassador was ordered to see the King again and obtain his personal assurance. They met on 13 July. William found this deeply insulting and refused to give the assurances demanded since he had already given his word. Even so, his reply was conciliatory. As a matter of course he instructed one of his aides to notify Bismarck, in Berlin, of the day's events in a telegram. He also gave Bismarck permission to communicate details to the press.

The Ems telegram

Key question
To what extent did the Ems telegram cause war?

That evening, in Berlin, Bismarck, dining with Generals Moltke and Roon, received the telegram from Ems. Having read it, Bismarck, 'in the presence of my two guests, reduced the telegram by striking out words, but without adding or altering anything'. The shortening of the text had the effect of making the King's message to the French ambassador appear to be an uncompromising response to the French demand to renounce support for the Hohenzollern candidature for all time.

Bismarck in his *Memoirs*, written in the 1890s, described his actions:

> After I had read out the concentrated version to my two guests, Moltke remarked. 'Now it has a different ring, in its original form it sounded like a parley; now it is like a flourish in answer to a challenge'. I went on to explain: 'If in execution of His Majesty's order, I at once communicate this text … not only to the newspapers but by telegraph to all our embassies it will be known in Paris before midnight … and will have the effect of a red rag on the French bull. Fight we must if we do not want to act the part of the vanquished without a battle. Success, however, depends essentially upon the impression which the origination of the war makes upon us and others: it is important that we should be the ones attacked'.

Key dates
The Ems telegram: July 1870

Start of Franco-Prussian War: July 1870

Bismarck ensured that the amended text of the Ems telegram was published in newspapers in Berlin. Prussian embassies received copies of the text by telegraph with instructions to communicate the contents to foreign governments. When William saw the published version he is said to have remarked with a shudder, 'This is war'.

The outbreak of war

As Bismarck had anticipated, the publication of the amended Ems telegram caused eruptions in France. French newspapers, convinced that French honour was at stake, demanded war.

Napoleon, urged on by his wife, his ministers, the Chamber of Deputies and public opinion, declared war on Prussia on 19 July.

It seems likely that Bismarck was prepared to fight a war against France from 1866 onwards, as long as it could appear to be a defensive war, brought about by French aggression. Such a war would almost certainly bring the south German states into the Prussian fold. All that he needed was a suitable opportunity. This occurred with the Hohenzollern candidature crisis, and Bismarck took full advantage of it.

However, there is little evidence that he was set on war from 1866 or even in 1870. He certainly did not control the whole Hohenzollern affair. Nor was it simply opportunism on his part that led to war. Equally important was a series of French diplomatic blunders. Moreover, the French Emperor and people in 1870 were ready to fight before the Ems telegram was published. If Bismarck set a trap for France, it was largely one of France's own making.

Bismarck, claiming that France was the aggressor who had 'committed a grievous sin against humanity', called on the south German states for support in accordance with the terms of their military alliances with Prussia. Convinced that the Fatherland was in danger, they agreed to support Prussia.

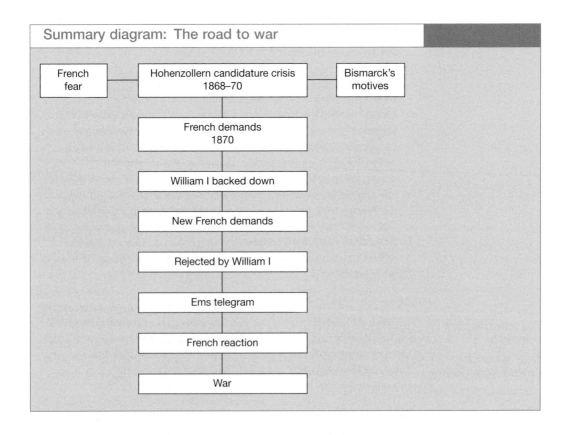

Summary diagram: The road to war

French fear — Hohenzollern candidature crisis 1868–70 — Bismarck's motives

French demands 1870

William I backed down

New French demands

Rejected by William I

Ems telegram

French reaction

War

Key question
Why was Bismarck in
a strong diplomatic
position?

3 | The Franco-Prussian War 1870–1

Historians are not in agreement about what to call the war –
should it be Franco-Prussian (the usually accepted name) or
Franco-German? In different ways it was both. The war was so
dominated by Prussian expertise that, in many ways, it was little
more than an extended Prussian military enterprise. Bismarck
and General Moltke organised the German war effort and
Prussian troops outnumbered all other troops in the army.
Nevertheless, the war was also the first genuinely German war, in
which all the German states fought. At the beginning some
support, particularly in the southern German states, was less than
enthusiastic. But by the end of the war this had changed. All
Germans were proud of, and wished to be associated with,
Germany's triumph. Moreover, by 1871 all Germany was united
by a blind hatred of France and all things French. This was
brought about by government propaganda, and particularly by
Bismarck's speeches, letters and newspaper articles.

The diplomatic situation in 1870

- Russia had promised to fight alongside Prussia if Austria joined
  France: this was enough to keep Austria neutral.
- Denmark toyed with the idea of supporting France in the hope
  of recovering Schleswig (see page 65), but in the end did nothing.
- Italy made such outrageous demands on France as the price of
  support, that Napoleon would not accept them.
- Long mistrustful of Napoleon's ambitions, Britain was
  unwilling to come to France's assistance, particularly after
  Bismarck made it appear as if the French Emperor was about
  to invade Belgium in defiance of the longstanding British
  guarantee of Belgian independence. He did this by publishing
  in *The Times* draft documents given to him by the French
  ambassador in 1867, when they were discussing possible
  'compensation' for French neutrality during the Seven Weeks'
  War. Bismarck appears to have kept these documents carefully
  for use in just such circumstances as arose in July 1870.

Key question
Why did Prussia win?

Early German success

The Prussian army, with troops from the other German states, was
quickly mobilised. Mobilisation had been well planned, and
nearly 500,000 troops had been moved by train to the borders of
Alsace (see Map 4.1 on page 92) by the beginning of August. Six
German railway lines ran to the French–German frontier: France
had only two. The German soldiers were under the command of
the brilliant General Moltke. French mobilisation was slower and
not complete by the time Napoleon III arrived at Metz to take
supreme command at the end of the month.

  The first battles of the war took place at the beginning of
August. Moltke's grand strategy was initially bungled by the
mistakes of his field commanders. French troops, armed with the
chassepot **rifle** and with elementary machine guns (the
mitrailleuses), fought well in the first battles. However, the

Key term

Chassepot **rifle**
A breech-loading
rifle, named after
the man who
invented it.

firepower of the Prussian Krupp artillery proved decisive and the German forces were victorious in the early battles in the French province of Lorraine.

Metz

The early German victories had a catastrophic effect on Napoleon and his chief commander Marshall Bazaine. They went on the defensive, withdrawing 180,000 men into the fortress of Metz. On 14 August, German armies crossed the Moselle river at several points and advanced beyond Metz to cut off the French escape route to Paris. Two days later the French army in Metz attempted to escape northwards but was defeated in a fierce battle and forced to retreat back into the fortress. There it remained besieged until it finally surrendered at the end of October. The decision to remain in Metz was fatal to the French cause for it meant that the bulk of Napoleon's finest troops were out of action.

Sedan

Napoleon had left Metz when the fighting began, and reached the Marne river, where a new French army was hurriedly collected under the command of General MacMahon. MacMahon set off with 130,000 men to rescue the army that was supposed to be breaking out of Metz. German troops intercepted MacMahon's forces and drove them back in confusion towards Sedan, near the Belgian border.

On 1 September the most important battle of the war began, watched from a hilltop by William I, Moltke, Bismarck and a selection of German princes. MacMahon refused to consider a

Key date

Napoleon III surrendered at Sedan: September 1870

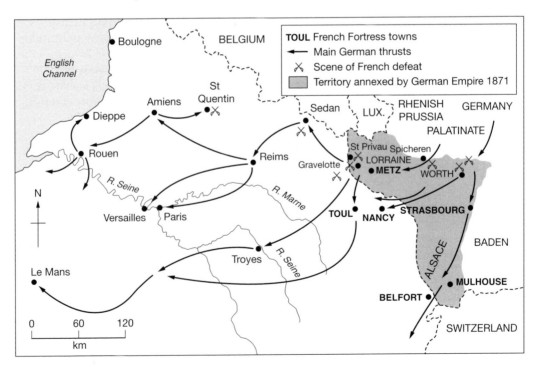

Map 4.1: The Franco-Prussian War.

retreat despite the severe battering his troops were receiving from the 600 German guns surrounding Sedan. 'We must have a victory', he said. It was a forlorn hope. French efforts to break out of Sedan failed. Napoleon rode round during the battle, looking hopefully for a bullet or shell that would spare him the disgrace of surrender. He did not find one.

That night Bismarck, Moltke and MacMahon met to discuss surrender terms. In a letter to his wife Bismarck described what happened next:

> Yesterday at five o'clock in the morning, after I had been discussing until one o'clock in the morning with Moltke and the French generals the terms of the capitulation, General Reille woke me to tell me that Napoleon wished to speak with me. I rode without washing and with no breakfast towards Sedan, and found the Emperor in an open carriage, with six officers, on the high road near Sedan. I dismounted, greeted him as politely as if we were in the Palace of the Tuileries in Paris … We sent out one of the officers to reconnoitre and he discovered a little villa a kilometre away in Frenois. There I accompanied the Emperor and there we concluded with the French General the capitulation, according to which forty to sixty thousand French – I cannot be more accurate at this time – with all that they had, became our prisoners. The day before yesterday and yesterday [1 and 2 September 1870] cost France one hundred thousand men and an emperor. … This has been an event of vast historic importance.

The day after the battle, under the terms of surrender, the Germans took prisoner 84,000 men, 2700 officers, 39 generals and one emperor. Later additions brought the total number of prisoners to over 104,000. Napoleon remained a prisoner until 1872 before going into exile in England. When news of the defeat and the Emperor's capture reached Paris on 4 September, Napoleon was deposed by a revolutionary government. The Second Empire was abolished and the Third French Republic was proclaimed in its place.

The end of the war

The war should have finished at this point. There were few French troops available to continue the fighting; most of them either had surrendered at Sedan or were still besieged in Metz (which finally surrendered in October 1870). Little stood in the way of a German advance on Paris. To everyone's surprise the war was to last for another 6 months.

The German forces surrounded Paris by mid-September, and settled down to starve the city into surrender. The government of the new Republic struggled to raise an army in the south of France to relieve the siege of Paris. The result was a large, undisciplined, enthusiastically patriotic mob, which proved no match for the experienced German army.

By January 1871 Parisians, desperately short of food, were also subject to bombardment by German guns. On 28 January 1871 the French government finally agreed to accept an armistice.

Key dates

Surrender of the French army at Metz: October 1870

France accepted an armistice: January 1871

Napoleon III (left) and Bismarck (right) on the morning after the battle at Sedan.

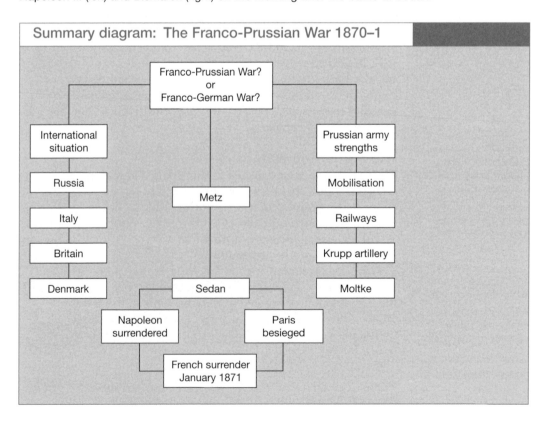

Summary diagram: The Franco-Prussian War 1870–1

4 | The Results of the War

Key question
What were the main
results of the war?

Key date
German Second
Empire proclaimed at
Versailles: January
1871

From the start of the war Bismarck was determined that King
William I of Prussia should become Emperor of Germany. This
was not an easy matter. The four southern German states had to
accept him. Moreover, William himself was reluctant to accept a
'German' title, which would take precedence over his Prussian
one. He was also determined that the offer of the Imperial crown
should come from the Princes, not from the German people, as it
had done in 1849 (see page 36).

The south German states

Bismarck was helped by the fact that the successful war against
France created a tidal wave of German patriotism. Popular
pressure in the four southern states for turning the wartime
alliance into a permanent union grew. This strengthened
Bismarck's negotiating hand with the south German rulers.

Seeking to preserve Prussian influence at the same time as
creating a united Germany, he was determined that the new *Reich*
would have a constitution similar to that of the North German
Confederation (see page 74). The south German rulers, by
contrast, wanted a looser system in which they retained more
rights.

Bismarck had to use all his diplomatic skill to get his way. His
trump card was the threat to call on the German people to

William proclaimed Emperor in the Hall of Mirrors at Versailles. Anton von Werner's famous
painting was completed 14 years after the event in 1885. Note Bismarck's position in the picture
(he is dressed in white). What type of people seem to have been present?

remove those rulers who stood in the way of unity. He also made some symbolic concessions, most of which meant little in practice. (Bavaria, for example, was allowed to retain its own peacetime army and a separate postal service.) King Ludwig II of Bavaria, who was particularly reluctant to co-operate, was finally won over by a secret bribe: Bismarck agreed to pay him a large pension to pay off his debts. He used the money confiscated from the King of Hanover (see page 72) in 1866.

In November 1870 separate treaties were signed with each of the four southern states by which they agreed to join the German Empire. The new *Reich* was to be a **federal** state: constituent states retained their monarchies and had extensive power over internal matters. But real power was to rest in the hands of the Emperor, his army officers and his handpicked ministers, of whom Bismarck, the new Imperial Chancellor, would be chief.

Key term

Federal
A government in which several states, while independent in domestic affairs, combine for general purposes.

The German Empire

Ludwig II, King of Bavaria agreed to put his name to a letter asking William to accept the title of Emperor. The other princes were then persuaded to add their names, and the document was sent to William. The appeal was seconded in December 1870, by a deputation to William from the North German *Reichstag*.

On 18 January 1871 King William I of Prussia was proclaimed Kaiser, or German Emperor, not in Berlin, but in the great French palace of Versailles just outside Paris. There was some difficulty about William's precise title. He had set his heart on 'Kaiser of Germany', but as part of a deal made with the King of Bavaria, Bismarck had agreed that the title should be 'German Kaiser'. The situation was saved by the Grand Duke of Baden, who neatly got round the problem by shouting out 'Long live his Imperial and Royal Majesty, Kaiser William'. William, gravely displeased, pointedly ignored Bismarck as the royal party left the platform. Bismarck, given his overall success, could afford to disregard William's displeasure.

The fact that William had been proclaimed German Emperor at Versailles was a bitter pill for the French to swallow, and added to the humiliation of the surrender which came 10 days later.

The Treaty of Frankfurt

The peace treaty between France and Germany was signed at Frankfurt in May 1871:

Key question
Was Bismarck right to impose a harsh treaty on France?

- German troops were to remain in eastern France until a heavy fine of £200 million had been paid.
- Alsace and the eastern half of Lorraine were annexed to Germany.

Key date

Treaty of Frankfurt: May 1871

These harsh terms caused consternation in France and were to lead to long-lasting enmity between France and Germany. 'What we have gained by arms in half a year, we must protect by arms for half a century', said Moltke. Why did Bismarck impose such a

humiliating treaty on France, so different from the one which
ended the war with Austria?

- A good ethnic case could be made for including Alsace in the
  German *Reich* (Strasbourg had been an imperial city in the
  days of the Holy Roman Empire). But Lorraine was very
  French and it might have been better not being annexed.
- Although Alsace and Lorraine were rich in iron ore and good
  agricultural land, Bismarck's interest in them was not
  essentially economic.
- There were good strategic reasons for taking both provinces.
  Bismarck believed that the French defeat, irrespective of the
  peace terms, turned France into an irreconcilable enemy. He
  thus wished to ensure that France was so weakened that it could
  pose no future threat to Germany. The fortresses of Metz and
  Strasbourg were crucial. Metz, in Moltke's view, was worth the
  equivalent of an army of 120,000 men.
- During the war, the German press had portrayed France as the
  guilty party. Justly defeated, most Germans now believed it
  needed to be punished. One way of doing this was to annex
  Alsace and Lorraine.

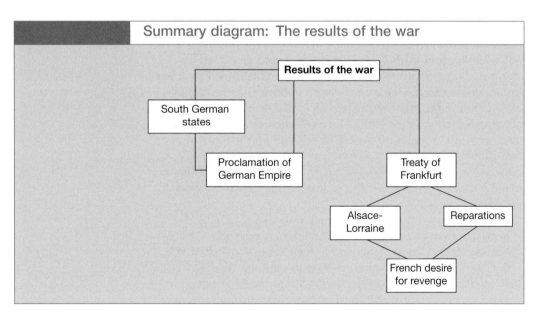

Summary diagram: The results of the war

5 | Key Debate

How skilful was Bismarck?

Bismarck was to be the chief architect of the German Empire. In
his memoirs, written in the 1890s, he depicted himself as a
statesman who foresaw events and brilliantly achieved his goals.
He left readers in no doubt that he was a veritable superman,
working from the start of his political career for German
unification. Some historians credit him with having a long-term

strategy to wage war on Austria and France in order to create a united Germany under Prussian control. As evidence, they cite the following words of Bismarck, allegedly spoken to future British Prime Minister Benjamin Disraeli in 1862:

> As soon as the army shall have been brought into such a condition to command respect, then I will take the first opportunity to declare war with Austria, to burst asunder the German Confederation, bring the middle and smaller states into subjection and give Germany a national union under the leadership of Prussia.

Other historians, like A.J.P. Taylor, are not convinced. They point out that the above quote was written down many years later by someone who was not present at the meeting. Taylor claimed that Bismarck was merely an opportunist, cleverly exploiting his enemies' mistakes and taking calculated risks which happened to be successful. Bismarck himself said: 'one must always have two irons in the fire'. He often had many more than two. In consequence, it is difficult to disentangle with any certainty his motives or the extent to which he planned ahead. Most historians think it unlikely that an unskilled statesman could have had so much luck. Nor is it likely that a skilled statesman had no plans. The general consensus is that Bismarck, at the very least, had a broad outline of what he wished to achieve in his mind from 1862. However, it is likely that he did not plan in any sense of mapping out a specific set of moves. He sought instead to reach his usually limited and clearly defined goals by taking advantage of situations either that he helped to create or that simply presented themselves to him. The exact means of achieving his aims were left to short-term decisions based on the situation at the time.

Was Bismarck a remarkable man or just a remarkably lucky man? Historian John Breuilly's view of Bismarck's skill is worth quoting:

> Many historians have exaggerated the extent of Bismarck's achievements in laying the groundwork for the war against Austria. Britain and Russia were always unlikely to intervene; Italy was anxious to use the Austro-Prussian conflict to secure Venice … Indeed, one could argue that any ordinary statesman in Berlin bent on war with Austria would not have done significantly worse.

This may be going too far. Historian David Blackbourn has a different view:

> There was no Bismarckian 'master-plan', only the firm determination to secure Prussia's position in north Germany and maintain the substance of the military monarchy. At the great-power level, Bismarck pressed for advantage when he saw it, but the chief characteristics of his policy were flexibility and the skilful exploitation of opportunities. He always tried to keep alternative strategies in play – in his own metaphor, to use every square on the

chessboard. Within that broad framework, Bismarck's policy towards Austria, for all its tactical twists and turns, was more single-mindedly bent on a particular outcome than his policy towards France or the southern states.

It is possible to argue that Bismarck did not make Germany: rather Germany made Bismarck. A variety of factors – German nationalism, Prussian economic growth, the international situation, the Prussian army – were such that Bismarck was able to gain the credit for bringing about a unification which may well have developed naturally, whoever had been in power. However, whatever view is taken about the 'inevitability' of German unification, it is clear that it happened as it did and when it did largely as a result of Bismarck's actions. Perhaps his main skill as a diplomat lay in his ability to isolate his enemy.

Some key books in the debate

D. Blackbourn, *The Fontana History of Germany 1780–1918* (Fontana, 1997).

J. Breuilly, *The Formation of the First German Nation-State 1800–1871* (Macmillan, 1996).

W. Carr, *The Origins of the Wars of German Unification* (Longman, 1991).

A.J.P. Taylor, *The Struggle for Mastery in Europe 1848–1918* (Clarendon Press, 1965).

5 Bismarck's Germany 1871–90

POINTS TO CONSIDER

Otto von Bismarck dominated Germany for the two decades after 1870. His prestige as the creator of the new Empire was enormous. What were Bismarck's aims after 1871 in both domestic and foreign policies and how successful was he in achieving them? To what extent was he the 'Iron Chancellor' – a man who was determined and ruthless in pursuit of his goals? This chapter will examine these questions through the following themes:

- The German Empire in 1871
- Bismarck's domestic policy 1871–90
- Bismarck's foreign policy 1871–90
- Bismarck's fall

Key dates

1871		German Empire proclaimed
1872–3		May Laws
1873		Three Emperors' League
1875		Start of Balkan crisis
1878	June–July	Congress of Berlin
	October	Anti-Socialist law passed
1879	July	German Tariff Act
	October	Dual Alliance between Germany and Austria-Hungary
1881		Three Emperors' Alliance
1882		Triple Alliance
1883		Sickness Insurance Act
1884		Accident Insurance Act
1885–6		Bulgarian crisis
1887		Reinsurance Treaty between Germany and Russia
1888		Death of William I
1888		William II became Kaiser
1889		Old age pensions introduced
1890		Kaiser Wilhelm II dismissed Bismarck

1 | The German Empire in 1871

The German Constitution

The **Second German Empire** was proclaimed on 18 January 1871 in the palace of Versailles (see page 96). King William I of Prussia became the new German Emperor (Kaiser) with Bismarck as his Imperial Chancellor. The constitution of the Empire incorporated the main provisions of the constitution of the North German Confederation, drawn up by Bismarck in 1867 (see page 74):

- Germany was to be a federal state.
- Powers and functions were divided between the central government and 25 state governments.
- While no longer sovereign or free to secede, the states preserved their own constitutions, rulers, parliaments and administrative systems (see Figure 5.1).

The German political system defies classification. Historians have variously described it as a military monarchy, a Prussian autocracy, a semi-autocracy or a constitutional monarchy. The complex system can be seen (positively) as creating a delicate equilibrium with the key institutions keeping each other in check. It can also be seen (negatively) as creating major tensions, not least between monarchical and parliamentary claims to power, and between federal and state power:

- As German Emperor, the Prussian King was head of the imperial executive and civil service and supreme warlord of the *Reich*'s armed forces.
- Prussia possessed 60 per cent of Germany's population and two-thirds of its territory. Prussia returned 235 deputies out of a total of 397 in the **Reichstag**. It could block any unwelcome constitutional amendments in the **Bundesrat**.
- Prussian and imperial institutions were so intertwined that they could hardly be distinguished. The Prussian minister of war was also the imperial minister of war. Imperial secretaries of state worked closely with Prussian ministers.
- Prussia, with its House of Peers and a Parliament elected by a three-class system, was dominated by the aristocracy, the rich, the military and a conservative civil service. This hindered the development of parliamentary democracy in Germany as a whole.
- Not surprisingly, the Prussian aristocracy enjoyed a dominant position in the political, military and administrative structure of the Empire.

However, for all the complaints about a 'Prussianisation' of Germany, the identity of 'old Prussia' was significantly diluted by its integration into the *Reich*. Prussia could no longer be governed without consideration of the wider interests of Germany. Prussian influence was slowly undermined by the need to make concessions to the states. Non-Prussians soon held important posts in government both in the *Reich* as a whole and

Key question
Who held control in the *Reich*?

German Empire proclaimed: 1871

Key date

Key terms

Second German Empire
The first Empire was the Holy Roman Empire, established by Charlemagne. The second Empire was the one established by Bismarck.

Reichstag
The National Parliament, elected by all males over 25 years of age.

Bundesrat
The Federal Council, comprising 58 members nominated by state assemblies. Its consent was required in the passing of new laws.

Emperor
• Always the King of Prussia
• Could appoint and dismiss the Chancellor
• Could dissolve the *Reichstag*
• Controlled foreign policy
• Could make treaties and alliances
• Commanded the army
• Could declare war and make peace
• Supervised the execution of all Federal laws
• Possessed the right to interpret the constitution

Chancellor
• Chief Minister of the *Reich*
• Not responsible to *Reichstag*, only to the Emperor
• He decided upon *Reich* policy outlines
• Chaired sessions of the *Bundesrat*
• Could 'hire and fire' State Secretaries responsible for the various government ministries
• Could ignore resolutions passed by the *Reichstag*
• Office was normally combined with the Minister-Presidency of Prussia

Federal
Centralised government with specific responsibilities for the *Reich* as a whole, e.g. foreign affairs, defence, civil and criminal law, customs, railways, postal service

Reich government

State
Regional government with specific responsibilities for individual states, e.g. education, transport, direct taxation, police, local justice, health

Bundesrat
• The Federal Council
• Comprised 58 members nominated by State assemblies
• Consent was required in the passing of new laws
• Theoretically able to change the constitution
• A vote of 14 against a proposal constituted a veto
• Prussia had 17 of the 58 seats
• Bavaria had six seats and the smaller states one each
• In theory, it had extensive powers. In practice it usually rubber stamped the Chancellor's policies

Reichstag
• The national parliament
• Elected by all males over 25 years of age
• Could accept or reject legislation, but its power to initiate new laws was negligible
• State Secretaries were excluded from membership of *Reichstag* and not responsible to it
• Members were not paid
• Could approve or reject the budget
• Elected every 5 years (unless dissolved)

Figure 5.1: How Germany was ruled.

in Prussia. It was the new *Reich*, not Prussia, that now engaged the loyalties of most Germans.

Key question
Why was Bismarck so powerful in Germany after 1871?

Bismarck as Imperial Chancellor

After 1871 Bismarck was Prussian Prime Minister and Foreign Minister and Imperial Chancellor. As such, he exercised most of the powers ascribed to the crown in the constitution. His influence over William gave him an immensely strong position, which he exploited.

Loathing the existence of any rival authority, he ensured that other ministers were little more than senior clerks, carrying out

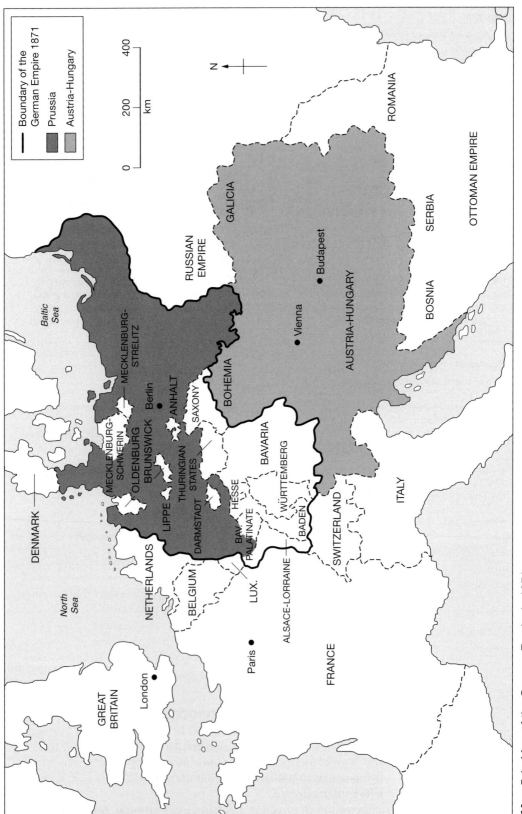

Map 5.1: Map of the German Empire in 1871.

Otto von Bismarck in 1871.

his orders. There was nothing that resembled an imperial cabinet. Bismarck dominated the secretaries of state and made sure that they did not confer with the Kaiser without his permission. His mistrust of potential rivals encouraged him to rely more and more on his son Herbert, who was Secretary of State of the Foreign Office from 1886.

While Bismarck exerted a tight grip over all aspects of policy, foreign and domestic, in the *Reich* and in Prussia, there were practical and theoretical limitations to his power, especially in domestic affairs:

- The fact that Germany was a federal state reduced his influence.
- The *Reichstag* was a major constraint.
- His long absences from Berlin (he liked to spend time on his country estates) and his poor health (often stomach troubles arising from overeating and drinking too much) reduced his control of day-to-day decision-making.

Many contemporaries viewed him with awe – a legend in his own lifetime. Recent historians have often been less impressed. They have represented him as more a lucky opportunist than a master-planner. They have also drawn attention to his less desirable attributes: his vindictiveness, his intolerance of criticism, and his frequent use of bullying to get his way. It should be said that these methods did not always succeed. After 1871 he was persistently thwarted in his efforts to shape the domestic developments of the *Reich*.

The weakness of the *Reichstag*

Bismarck was anxious for political power in Germany to remain in traditional hands – in those of the Emperor, his army officers, his ministers – and particularly in his own. Arguably the constitution gave little opportunity for the exercise of democracy. Bismarck regarded the *Reichstag* with some disdain – as a collection of squabbling politicians who did not reflect popular opinion.

Characteristically, he was ready to work with the *Reichstag* only on condition that it accepted his proposals or some compromise acceptable to him. If agreement could not be reached, he usually dissolved the *Reichstag* and called for fresh elections. He was prepared to use all the means at his disposal, not least the exploitation of international crises, to swing public opinion in elections to secure the passage of contentious legislation.

Reichstag politicians have often been criticised by historians for failing to do more to exploit their potential power. However, they faced a difficult task. The balance of power was tilted sharply in favour of the monarchy and most Germans remained deeply respectful of authority, believing that it was right and proper that the Emperor, or his Chancellor, should rule. There was no widespread conviction that power should be in the hands of the political party which happened to have a majority of seats in the *Reichstag*.

Even members of the more extreme left-wing parties did not expect the *Reichstag* to exercise much control over government. The most that they hoped for was that it would have some influence on government decisions.

The (potential) strength of the *Reichstag*

The Socialist leader August Bebel claimed that the *Reichstag* was the 'fig-leaf of despotism'. However, in reality, the *Reichstag* had more power than Bebel suggested and Bismarck had envisaged:

- The Second Empire needed a vast number of new laws and no bill could become a law until it passed the *Reichstag*. The government also needed more money, which only the *Reichstag* could provide. Bismarck, therefore, was forced to negotiate deals and grant concessions.
- The *Reichstag* was an open forum of debate whose members enjoyed parliamentary immunity. Debates were widely reported in the press. The Chancellor and the ministers of state could be questioned and embarrassed.
- Universal male suffrage promoted the development of mass political parties with popular appeal (see Table 5.2 on page 110). While these parties were in no position to form governments, Bismarck could not afford to ignore them. Although under no constitutional obligation to adopt policies approved by the *Reichstag*, he did need to secure support for his own legislative proposals.
- What is striking is how troublesome the *Reichstag* was for Bismarck, criticising and often thwarting his plans. Indeed,

Key question
How democratic was Germany?

historians may have overemphasised the way that the *Reichstag* bowed to Bismarck and not emphasised enough the way that he bowed to *Reichstag* pressure. On several occasions in the 1880s he explored the possibility of changing the constitution – proof of the *Reichstag*'s influence.

The *Reichstag* was thus neither an all-powerful Parliament nor simply a pliant instrument under Bismarck's control. It was something in between. It certainly acquired a genuine popular legitimacy and became a focal point for those whom Bismarck saw as 'enemies of the state': Poles, Catholics and Socialists.

The role of the army

The army played an important role in the *Reich*, as it had done in Prussia. It was essentially Prussian. The Prussian army was by far the largest of the four armies that comprised the German armies. Although the three other contingents owed allegiance to the kings of Bavaria, Saxony and Württemberg, respectively, they all came under the Emperor's command in time of war and followed the Prussian lead in organisation, instruction and weaponry.

Prussian-German generals had a huge influence on government policy. Officers owed personal loyalty to the Emperor, not the state. The system of conscription ensured that all German men served for 2–3 years in the army. This gave the officers ample opportunity to build on the values already inculcated at school: discipline, pride in military institutions and love of the Fatherland.

As the creator of the *Reich*, the army had a special place in the minds of most Germans. After 1871 it was taken for granted that the army's needs must always come first and that the highest virtues were military ones. Uniforms encouraged respect and obedience and both Bismarck and the Kaiser always wore military uniform in public.

Given that the military budget was not subject to annual approval, the army was virtually independent of *Reichstag* control. Many army officers were hard-line conservatives. They had little time for the *Reichstag* and even less for liberals and socialists. Indeed, some army officers were as much concerned with the 'enemy' within as they were with Germany's enemies beyond the borders of the *Reich*. If called upon, they were ready to disperse demonstrations, break strikes and crush any attempt at revolution.

Key question
How united was Germany?

German disunity

The new *Reich* was far from united:

- Each state had its own traditions. Each also had powers over education, justice, agriculture, religious matters and local government.
- Over 60 per cent of the population were Protestant, but Catholicism was strong in Alsace-Lorraine, in south-west Germany, in the Rhineland and among the Poles.

- Ten per cent of the *Reich*'s population were non-German minorities.
- There were economic and social divisions – between rich and poor, and between the industrialising north and west and the predominantly rural south and east.

Thus, a major problem was to unite Germany in fact as well as in theory.

German economic development

Key question
What were the main economic and social developments in Germany between 1871 and 1890?

The results of the war against France stimulated the German economy. Alsace-Lorraine, for example, contained Europe's largest deposits of iron ore and production increased rapidly after 1871. The injection of the French indemnity payments into the German economy (see page 96) helped to cause a spectacular, if short-lived, boom. The boom assisted German banks, which, in turn, provided capital for new railways and new industries such as electricity and chemicals. Between 1871 and 1890 coal production soared, steel production increased by some 700 per cent and the railway network doubled.

Table 5.1: German production: 1870–90

	1870		1890
Population (millions)	41	Germany	49
	32	Britain	38
	36	France	38
Coal (millions of tonnes)	38	Germany	89
	118	Britain	184
	13	France	26
Steel (millions of tonnes)	0.3	Germany	2.2
	0.6	Britain	3.6
	0.08	France	0.6
Iron ore (millions of tonnes)	2.9	Germany	8
	14	Britain	14
	2.6	France	3.5

German society

German society, despite all the economic changes, remained divided along traditional class lines. What mobility there was tended to be within a class rather than movements between different classes. The higher levels of the civil service and the army remained predominantly the preserve of the nobility. The most direct threat to the nobility's supremacy came from wealthy industrialists who tried to emulate, rather than supersede, the nobles.

While the middle classes were expanding, most Germans were agricultural or industrial workers. For many farm labourers life was hard and industrial employment seemed an attractive option. Thus, there was a drift to the cities, even though the living and working conditions of the proletariat remained poor.

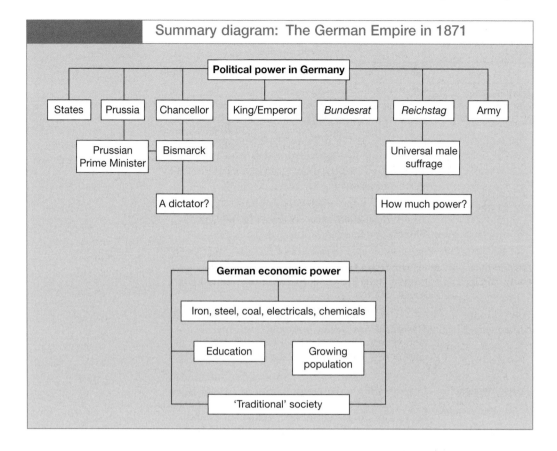

Summary diagram: The German Empire in 1871

2 | Bismarck's Domestic Policy 1871–90

The liberal era 1871–9

Key question
How effectively did
Bismarck work with
the National Liberals?

After 1871 Bismarck, who claimed to stand above party or
sectional interest, needed a parliamentary majority. Although he
was by no means a true liberal, he had little alternative but to
work with the National Liberals – the strongest party in the
Reichstag for most of the 1870s (see Table 5.2, page 110). In some
respects the National Liberals were ideal allies. Most of them
applauded Bismarck's success in creating a united Germany and
were eager to help him consolidate national unity. In the early
1870s, a great deal of useful legislation was passed:

Key term
Reichsbank
A national German
bank (like the Bank
of England).

- A national system of currency was introduced.
- A *Reichsbank* was created.
- All internal tariffs were abolished.
- There was much legal standardisation.

The National Liberals and Bismarck also united against the
Catholic Church.

Nevertheless, relations between Bismarck and the National
Liberals were always uneasy. Politically Bismarck did not agree
with their hopes for the extension of parliamentary government.
He became increasingly irritated as they opposed a number of his
proposals.

Table 5.2: Germany's political parties 1871–90

Party	Number of seats in Reichstag (1871–90)							
	1871	1874	1877	1878	1881	1884	1887	1890
The National Liberals	125	155	128	99	47	51	99	42
	The main support for this party came from the Protestant middle class. The party had two principal aims: (a) the creation of a strong nation-state and (b) the encouragement of a liberal constitutional state; the former in practice being the priority. Until 1878 the National Liberals were Bismarck's most reliable *Reichstag* allies.							
The Centre Party	58	91	93	94	100	99	98	106
	This party defended the interests of the Catholic Church.							
The Social Democratic Party (SPD)	2	9	12	9	12	24	11	35
	Having close links with the trade unions, this was predominantly a working-class party. It fought for social reforms.							
The German Conservative Party	57	22	40	59	50	78	80	73
	This party was mainly composed of Prussian landowners. Sceptical about the unification of Germany, it came to support Bismarck after 1878.							
The Free Conservatives	37	33	38	57	28	28	41	20
	Drawn from a wider geographical and social base than the German Conservatives, the party contained not just landowners, but also industrialists and professional and commercial interests. It offered Bismarck steady support.							
The Progressives	47	50	52	39	115	74	32	76
	A liberal party but one which, unlike the National Liberals, remained opposed to Bismarck's pursuit of a powerful nation-state at the expense of liberal constitutional principles.							
National Groups	14	30	30	30	35	32	29	27
	Reichstag members representing Alsatians, Poles and Danes.							
Guelphs	9	4	10	4	10	11	4	11
	Hanoverians who were supporters of the deposed King George.							

The army budget

The army budget was a particular bone of contention. In 1867 Bismarck and the National Liberals agreed that the military budget should remain at a fixed level outside *Reichstag* control until 1872. During the Franco-Prussian War the fixed budget was extended until 1874. In 1874 Bismarck presented a law that laid down that an army of over 400,000 men would be automatically financed by federal expenditure.

Given that 80 per cent of all federal expenditure was spent on the army, this threatened seriously to reduce the *Reichstag*'s monetary powers. The measure was thus opposed by the National

Liberals. Accusing them of trying to undermine German military strength, Bismarck threatened to call new elections. The National Liberals shrank from a constitutional conflict similar to that which had brought Bismarck to power in 1862 (see pages 57–8). A compromise was eventually reached. The military budget was fixed for 7 years at a time, rather than voted for annually or fixed permanently.

The *Kulturkampf*

Key question
Why did Bismarck support the *Kulturkampf*?

Key term

Kulturkampf
A struggle for culture or the struggle for civilisation. In Germany, the struggle was between the state and the Catholic Church.

Much of the 1870s was dominated by Bismarck's clash with the Catholic Church – the ***Kulturkampf***. There were a number of reasons for this clash:

- Two-thirds of Germans, mainly those in Prussia and the north, were Protestant. One-third were Catholic.
- In the late nineteenth century Church and State came into conflict in several countries. In 1864 Pope Pius IX's *Syllabus of Errors* had condemned as erroneous every major principle for which liberals stood (see page 9). In 1870 the Vatican Council laid down the doctrine of papal infallibility. This ruled that papal pronouncements on matters of faith and morals could not be questioned.
- These papal measures aroused great alarm in liberal circles. Many of Germany's most enlightened men believed that the future of mankind was at stake. It seemed certain that militant Catholicism would interfere in the *Reich*'s domestic affairs and support reactionary causes. The National Liberals, in particular, were determined to do battle with the Catholic Church in what they saw as a life and death struggle for freedom and progress against the forces of reaction.

The Centre Party

German Catholics formed their own party, the Centre Party, in 1870. In 1871 the Centre became the second largest party in the *Reichstag*. It was unique among German parties in drawing its support from all social strata. It favoured greater self-rule for the component states of the *Reich*. It also objected to state interference in the Church's traditional sphere of influence: the education system.

Bismarck and Catholicism

Bismarck, a sincere Protestant, had little affection for Catholicism and viewed the Catholic minority with suspicion. His greatest concern in domestic policy was to unify and consolidate the new *Reich*. Suspicious of those who opposed his creation, he saw plots and subversive activities everywhere. Many of the national minorities – the French in the west and the Poles in the east – who had no wish to be within the *Reich* were Catholic. So were Germans in the southern states, many of whom still tended to identify with Austria rather than with Prussia. So too were the Rhinelanders, some of whom still resented being 'Prussian' (despite being part of Prussia since 1815).

Bismarck saw the success of the Centre Party in 1871 as a grave danger to the Empire's unity. He thought that Centre politicians would encourage **civil disobedience** among Catholics whenever the policies of the state conflicted with those of the Church. His suspicions deepened when he observed how rapidly the party became a rallying point for opponents of the Empire.

Whether he really believed that the anti-Prussian political alignment in the *Reichstag* was a papal-inspired conspiracy of malcontents bent on destroying the *Reich* is debatable. But the *Kulturkampf* was widely understood at the time to be a war against internal opponents of unification.

It may be that the *Kulturkampf* was little more than a calculated political ploy on Bismarck's part: to put himself at the head of a popular, Protestant crusade. It certainly enabled him to work closely with the National Liberals in the 1870s.

The 'Old Catholics'

Some 5000 Catholics – they were known as 'Old Catholics' – refused to accept the decree on papal infallibility and broke with the Church. When Old Catholic teachers and professors were dismissed by Catholic bishops, Bismarck had an excellent excuse to attack the Catholic Church. Maintaining that the Prussian government was committed to the principle of religious toleration, he condemned the Catholic Church's actions in a series of newspaper articles in 1872. This marked the start of the *Kulturkampf*.

Actions against the Catholic Church

While the *Kulturkampf* was centred on Prussia and directed against the Catholics of the Rhineland and Poland, its effects were felt throughout the *Reich* and legislation against the Church was passed by the Prussian *Landtag*, by other state governments and by the *Reichstag*.

In 1872 Catholic schools were brought directly under the supervision of the state. In 1872 the *Reichstag* forbade the **Jesuit order**, whose members had always been supporters of Papal authority, to set up establishments in Germany and empowered state governments to expel individual Jesuits. In May 1873 Dr Falk, the Prussian Minister of Religion and Education, introduced a package of measures known as the May Laws. These aimed to bring the Catholic Church under state control:

- All candidates for the priesthood now had to attend a **secular** university before commencing training.
- All religious appointments became subject to state approval.
- In 1874 obligatory civil marriage was introduced in Prussia. Clergy could be fined, imprisoned and expelled if they failed to comply with the May Laws.

In 1875 the *Kulturkampf* reached a climax:

- Laws empowered Prussia to suspend subsidies to the Church in parishes where the clergy resisted the new legislation.
- All religious orders, except nursing orders, were dissolved.

Key terms

Civil disobedience Refusal to obey state laws and regulation.

Landtag The Prussian state Parliament.

Jesuit order A Catholic order of priests (the Society of Jesus), founded in 1534 by Ignatius Loyola.

Secular Non-religious and non-spiritual: civil, not ecclesiastical.

Key date

May Laws: 1872–3

The legislation was enforced vigorously in Prussia by Falk. By 1876 all but two of the 12 Prussian Catholic bishops were in exile or under house arrest and more than 1000 priests were suspended from their posts.

Key question
Why did the *Kulturkampf* fail?

The results of the *Kulturkampf*

The results of the *Kulturkampf* were not at all what Bismarck had hoped. Attempts to repress Catholicism met with considerable opposition. Pope Pius IX counter-attacked, threatening to excommunicate those who obeyed the oppressive laws. Only 30 out of 10,000 Prussian Catholic priests submitted to the May Laws. Catholic communities sheltered defiant priests and fiercely maintained their religious culture and identity.

Bismarck's hope of destroying the Centre Party backfired: the *Kulturkampf* strengthened rather than weakened his political opponents. In 1871 the Centre won 58 seats: in 1874 it won 91 seats. Bismarck's hope of leading a popular Protestant crusade also failed to materialise. Protestants opposed some of the *Kulturkampf* legislation because it limited the influence of the Protestant – as well as the Catholic – Church in education. Many on the left disliked the violation of fundamental civil rights, not least freedom of conscience.

The end of the *Kulturkampf*

By 1878 Bismarck accepted that the *Kulturkampf* had failed:

- He had underestimated the enemy: the Catholic Church had more popular support than he had bargained for.
- By opening up a rift between the *Reich* and its Catholic subjects, the *Kulturkampf* had increased disunity, not removed it.
- He was anxious to have the Centre Party on his side against a potentially worse enemy: socialism.

Bismarck was thus ready to cut his losses and end the *Kulturkampf*. His opportunity came with the death of Pope Pius IX in 1878. His successor Leo XIII was conciliatory and direct negotiations led to improved relations between Bismarck and the Church. Falk was symbolically dismissed in 1879 and some of the anti-Catholic measures were repealed: exiled clergy, for example, were allowed to return. However, the Catholic Church did not win a complete victory. Many of the May Laws remained in force: for example, civil marriage remained compulsory, Jesuits were forbidden to enter Germany, and the state continued to oversee all permanent church appointments.

Bismarck withdrew from a dangerous battlefield. Typically, he sought to turn failure to advantage, by henceforward harnessing Catholic political power in the *Reichstag* to the support of conservative, protectionist and anti-socialist measures.

Key question
Why did Bismarck come to support protectionist policies?

Economic protectionism

In the early 1870s Bismarck left economic matters in the hands of Delbruck, a capable administrator who continued the free-trade policies of the *Zollverein* (see pages 15–16). Support for free trade was an essential principle of most National Liberals. In 1879, however, Bismarck ditched both free trade and the National Liberals. Aligning himself with the Conservative and Centre parties, he supported the introduction of tariffs to protect German industry and farming. What were his motives? Perhaps he acted simply out of political opportunism. More likely he believed protectionism to be in the best economic interests of the *Reich*. As early as 1877 he had tried to persuade National Liberals to abandon their opposition to tariff protection.

Economic and financial factors

There were strong economic and financial reasons for introducing protective tariffs. In the late 1870s German agriculture suffered from the effects of a series of bad harvests and from the importation of cheap wheat from the USA and Russia. As the price of wheat fell, German farmers suffered. As a landowner himself, Bismarck understood the dangers of a prolonged agrarian depression. He also feared that if Germany was reliant on foreign grain, it would be seriously weakened in time of war. Protectionism would aid German self-sufficiency.

A slow-down in industrial growth after 1873 helped to produce a crisis of confidence in free trade. Industrialists and workers looked to the government to protect their interests and alleviate their distress. The adoption of protective tariffs by France, Russia and Austria in the late 1870s seemed to make it all the more desirable to follow suit.

Finally, the federal government's revenue, raised from customs duties and indirect taxation, was proving woefully inadequate to cover the growing costs of armaments and administration. In order to make up the deficit, supplementary payments were made by individual states, a situation that Bismarck found distasteful. He hoped that new tariffs would give the federal government a valuable extra source of income, ensuring that it was financially independent of both the states and the *Reichstag*.

Political factors

Bismarck realised there were political advantages in abandoning free trade. By the late 1870s landowners and industrialists were clamouring for protective tariffs. By espousing protectionist policies, Bismarck could win influential support.

Although he had worked with the National Liberals, he had never been particularly friendly with them. Their insistence on parliamentary rights and refusal to pass anti-socialist legislation irritated him. Moreover, in the 1878 elections, the National Liberals lost some 30 seats. The combined strength of the two Conservative parties was now sufficient to outvote them in the *Reichstag*. In pursuing the protectionist case, popular with the Conservatives, Bismarck saw his chance to break with the National Liberals and broaden his political support.

Key date

German Tariff Act:
July 1879

The 1879 Tariff Act

By 1879 protectionists, made up mostly of Conservatives and Centre Party members, had a majority in the *Reichstag*. Bismarck now introduced a general tariff bill. He addressed the *Reichstag* in May 1879 as follows:

> The only country [which persists in a policy of free trade] is England, and that will not last long. France and America have departed completely from this line; Austria instead of lowering her tariffs has made them higher; Russia has done the same … . Therefore to be alone the dupe of an honourable conviction cannot be expected from Germany for ever … . Since we have become swamped by the surplus production of foreign nations, our prices have been depressed; and the development of our industries and our entire economic position has suffered in consequence. Let us finally close our doors and erect some barriers … in order to reserve for German industries at least the home market, which because of German good nature, has been exploited by foreigners.

In July 1879 a tariff bill passed through the *Reichstag* and duties were imposed on imports. The political results were far-reaching. Bismarck had now firmly committed himself to the Conservative camp. The National Liberal party splintered. Those who still believed in free trade and parliamentary government broke away, eventually uniting with the Progressives (see page 110) to form a new radical party in 1884. Other National Liberals remained loyal to Bismarck but he was no longer dependent on their backing. In that sense the 'liberal era' was effectively at an end.

Historians continue to debate the economic effects of the abandonment of free trade. Arguably, protective tariffs consolidated the work of unification by drawing north and south closer together and accelerated the growth of a large internal market. Protection might have meant higher bread prices, but this did not mean that workers had lower living standards. Tariffs did serve to protect German jobs.

Bismarck and socialism

Key question
How successful was Bismarck in tackling the socialist 'threat'?

In 1869 Bebel and Liebknecht founded the Social Democratic Workers' Party, a Marxist party committed to the overthrow of the bourgeoisie. In 1875 moderate and revolutionary socialists united to form the Social Democratic Party (or SPD). The party's declared aim was the overthrow of the existing order. But it also declared that it would use only legal means in the struggle for economic and political freedom. The new party called for **nationalisation** of banks, coal mines and industry, and for social equality.

Key term

Nationalisation
Government
ownership.

The socialist threat

Bismarck was hostile to socialists, regarding them as revolutionary and little better than criminals. Rather than underestimating the enemy, as with the *Kulturkampf*, it may be that he overestimated the socialist threat. Socialists were not as strong or as revolutionary as he feared and they liked to appear.

However, Bismarck's fears were rational. Socialism was a threat to the kind of society he intended to maintain. Socialists did preach class warfare. Moreover, as Germany became more industrialised, swelling the ranks of the proletariat, socialist support increased. The SPD won two seats in the *Reichstag* in 1871: in 1877 it had 12 seats, winning nearly 500,000 votes.

Assassination attempts

In 1876 Bismarck tried to pass a bill preventing the publication of socialist propaganda. It was defeated. Other measures to prosecute the SPD also failed to get through the *Reichstag*.

In May 1878 an **anarchist** tried to assassinate Emperor William I. The would-be assassin had no proven association with the SPD, but Bismarck, like many of his contemporaries, drew no clear distinction between anarchism and socialism and saw the murder attempt as part of a 'red' conspiracy. However, his efforts to push through a bill against socialism were defeated by National Liberal members, concerned about civil liberties.

A week later there was a second attempt on William's life that resulted in the Emperor being seriously wounded. Again the failed assassin had no direct SPD link. Bismarck criticised the National Liberals for failing to pass the anti-socialist bill that might have protected the Emperor. Scenting political advantage, he dissolved the *Reichstag*.

His manoeuvre succeeded. The electorate, deeply shocked by the murder attempts, blamed the SPD and the National Liberals. The SPD vote fell from 493,000 in 1877 to 312,000 while the National Liberals lost 130,000 votes and 29 seats. Only by supporting anti-socialist legislation during the election campaign did they save themselves from a heavier defeat.

> **Key term**
>
> **Anarchist**
> A person whose ideal society is one without government of any kind. Late nineteenth-century anarchists often sought to bring about such a condition by terrorism.

> **Key date**
>
> Anti-Socialist Law passed: October 1878

Bismarck's actions against socialism

Bismarck now got his way in the new *Reichstag*. An anti-socialist bill, supported by Conservatives and most National Liberals, was passed in October 1878:

- Socialist organisations, including trade unions, were banned.
- Socialist meetings were to be broken up.
- Socialist publications were outlawed.

Between 1878 and 1890 some 1500 socialists were imprisoned and a great many emigrated. However, the Anti-Socialist Law, far from eliminating socialism, served to rally the faithful and fortify them in their beliefs. The SPD simply went underground. Moreover, the law, which was differently implemented in different German states, did not prevent SPD members from standing for election and speaking freely in both the *Reichstag* and state legislatures. After the dip in 1878, the SPD won increasing support. By 1890 it had over a million voters and 35 seats.

In short, Bismarck's attack on socialism was no more successful than his attack on the Church. His repressive measures may have helped to increase support for the SPD and ensured that moderate and revolutionary socialist factions remained united.

State socialism

Key question
Why did Bismarck
support state
socialism?

Bismarck not only used repression in his efforts to destroy socialism. He hoped to wean the working classes from socialism by introducing various welfare (state socialism) measures, designed to assist German workers. These measures may not have been as cynical as some of Bismarck's critics have implied. A devout Christian, Bismarck was conscious of a moral obligation to aid those in need. There was a strong tradition in Prussia and other parts of Germany, and a general belief, right and left, that one of the state's most important moral objectives was the promotion of the material well-being of its citizens.

Bismarck, however, also hoped to win the support of the workers, thus cutting the ground from beneath the feet of the SPD. In a speech to the *Reichstag* in 1881 he said:

> A beginning must be made with the task of reconciling the labouring classes with the state. A remedy cannot be sought only through the repression of socialist excesses. It is necessary to have a definite advancement in the welfare of the working classes.

Key dates

Sickness Insurance
Act: 1883

Accident Insurance
Act: 1884

Old age pensions
introduced: 1889

In 1883 the first of his proposals for state socialism became law. The Sickness Insurance Act provided medical treatment and up to 13 weeks' sick pay to three million low-paid workers. The workers paid two-thirds of the contribution and the employers one-third.

A worker who was permanently disabled or sick for more than 13 weeks was given protection by the Accident Insurance Act of 1884. This was financed wholly by the employers.

Finally in 1889 came the Old Age and Disability Act which gave pensions to those over 70, and disablement pensions for those who were younger. This was paid for by workers, employers and the state.

How successful was state socialism?

Bismarck's scheme was the first of its kind in the world and became a model of social provision for other countries. However, his hopes that the working class could be won over by state socialism were not fully realised. While some workers approved the measures, others thought them a 'sham', particularly as the government still opposed the formation of trade unions. Many workers continued to labour under harsh conditions and while such conditions persisted, the SPD was assured of a future. Bismarck, believing that employers must control their factories, opposed demands for state intervention to regulate working hours and limit child and female employment.

118 | The Unification of Germany 1815–1919

Treatment of the national minorities

Bismarck regarded the national minorities – the Danes, French and Poles – as potential 'enemies of the state'. He thus sought to reduce their influence:

- The Polish language was outlawed in education and law courts.
- Alsace-Lorraine was not granted full autonomy. Instead it became a special region under direct imperial rule with a governor and Prussian civil servants. The German language was imposed in schools and local administration.

However, Bismarck did not rely solely on repression. Those French people who were unhappy with German rule were allowed to leave (400,000 had done so by 1914). The German governors of Alsace-Lorraine made great efforts to conciliate the French-speaking provinces.

It does seem that the national minorities' alienation from the *Reich* probably lessened over the years. School, conscription and everyday experience 'Germanised' many minorities.

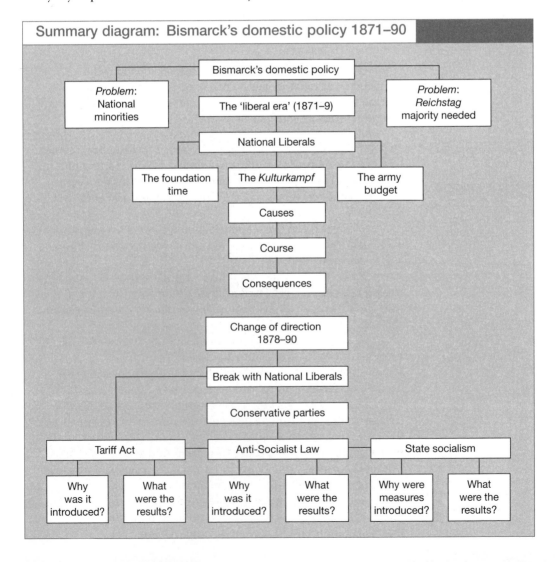

Summary diagram: Bismarck's domestic policy 1871–90

Key question
What were Bismarck's
main aims after 1871?

3 | Bismarck's Foreign Policy 1871–90

The creation of a united Germany in 1871 caused a revolution in the European balance of power. Overnight Germany became the strongest nation on the continent. It was conceivable that Bismarck might attempt further expansion. In fact, this was far from his intent. Aware that Germany was surrounded by potentially envious, resentful and anxious neighbours, he made it clear after 1871 that Germany was now a 'satiated power', with no further territorial ambitions. Consequently, he was not interested in attaching Austrian Germans to the new *Reich*. He believed that any attempt to extend Germany's frontiers further would unite the other powers against it. Convinced that further wars could only threaten the *Reich*'s security, his main aim was to maintain peace.

France seemed the main threat to peace. France would have resented its defeat in 1870–1 whatever followed. The loss of Alsace-Lorraine merely sharpened the edge of that resentment.

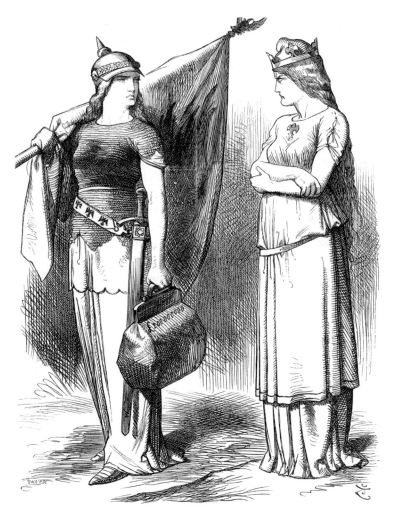

This cartoon was published in Britain in 1871. What point is the cartoonist trying to make?

"AU REVOIR!"

Many French people wanted revenge. However, France without allies did not pose a serious danger: Bismarck was confident that the German army could defeat it again if necessary.

Bismarck's main fear was that France might ally with either Russia or Austria. Germany might then have to fight a war on two fronts. He was determined to avoid this possibility by isolating France and remaining on good terms with both Russia and Austria. The main problem was that there was always the possibility of friction between Austria and Russia over the Balkans, where their interests were at variance.

The problem of the Balkans

The Balkans, the most troublesome area of Europe, presented major problems for Bismarck:

Key question
Why did the Balkans pose a serious problem for Bismarck?

- The Turkish government's authority in many Balkan areas was only nominal.
- Peoples of various races and religions co-existed in a state of mutual animosity.
- The **Slav** peoples were becoming fiercely nationalistic.

Russia sought to assist the Slavs to obtain independence from Turkey. As leader of the **Orthodox Church**, the Tsar felt a moral obligation to aid Christian Slavs if their Muslim rulers treated them too oppressively. Russia also sought to profit from Turkey's weakness. In particular, Russia hoped to win control of the **Straits**.

Austria was opposed to the expansion of Russian power so close to its territories. In addition, Russia's encouragement of Slav nationalism could serve as a dangerous example to national groups within the Habsburg Empire. Austria thus sought to maintain the **Ottoman Empire**. Austria feared that if the multinational Ottoman Empire collapsed, its own similarly multinational Empire might follow.

Bismarck had no territorial ambitions in the Balkans: he once remarked that the area was not worth 'the healthy bones of a single Pomeranian musketeer'. However, if Austria and Russia fell out over the Balkans, Germany might have to choose between them and the rejected suitor might find a willing ally in France.

Although Bismarck faced problems, he also had a strong hand:

- He enjoyed far more control in the handling of foreign affairs than in domestic matters.
- Germany was the greatest military power in Europe.
- His friendship was eagerly sought by Austria and Russia, in part because of their growing antagonism in the Balkans.
- It was unlikely that Tsarist Russia would seek alliance with **republican** France.
- Britain was reasonably friendly to Germany.

Key terms

Slavs
People who regard themselves to be of the same ethnic group and whose language is Slavonic. Slavs include Russians, Czechs, Serbs and Bulgarians.

Orthodox Church
The Greek or Eastern Christian Church.

The Straits
The Bosphorus and Dardanelles, which link the Black Sea with the Mediterranean Sea.

The Ottoman Empire
The Turkish Empire, which was ruled by the Ottoman family.

Republican
Of, or favouring, a government without a monarch.

The Three Emperors' League

Austria, fearing a German–Russian agreement, took the initiative in pressing for a Three Emperors' alliance. Following a meeting in 1872, the Emperors of Germany, Russia and Austria reached an agreement known as the Three Emperors' League or *Dreikaiserbund*. Given that the three powers found it hard to reach agreement on any concrete objectives, the terms were somewhat vague. The Emperors identified republicanism and socialism as common enemies and promised to consult on matters of common interest or if a third power disturbed Europe's peace.

Key date

Three Emperors' League: 1873

The 1875 war scare

After 1871 France made determined efforts to throw off the effects of defeat. Its rapid military reorganisation and the prompt repayment of the war indemnity, ensuring the end of German military occupation by 1873, alarmed Bismarck. In 1875 he reacted to French recovery and rearmament by provoking a diplomatic crisis. He prohibited the export of horses to France and the *Berlin Post* carried an article 'Is War in Sight?' Bismarck expected that the other powers would similarly put pressure on France, discouraging it from further military expansion. He miscalculated. Britain and Russia supported France, forcing Bismarck to offer assurances that Germany was not contemplating another war. The crisis thus ended in a diplomatic victory for France.

The Balkan crisis 1875–8

Key date

Start of Balkan crisis: 1875

In 1875 Christian peasants in Bosnia and Herzegovina revolted against Turkish rule. In April 1876 the revolt spread to Bulgaria and in July Montenegro and Serbia declared war on Turkey. Thousands of Russian volunteers joined the Serbian army amidst a wave of popular pro-Slav fervour. There was thus pressure for Russian intervention in the Balkans. It was likely that Austria would oppose anything that smacked of Russian expansionism. Determined to avoid taking sides, Bismarck had somehow to convince both Austria and Russia of Germany's goodwill and prevent them from quarrelling.

The situation in 1876

Bismarck was helped by the fact that Tsar Alexander II and his Foreign Minister Gorchakov had no wish to find themselves in a Crimean situation again – at war with Turkey and isolated. Gorchakov, recognising that Turkey's fate concerned all the great powers, preferred international discussion to unilateral action. Austrian Foreign Minister Andrassy, aware that German support was unlikely in the event of a clash with Russia, tried to collaborate with Gorchakov in an attempt to limit the effects of the crisis.

However, Turkish atrocities in 1876 in Bulgaria (some 10,000 Bulgarians were allegedly killed) changed the situation. The atrocities stirred public opinion in both Britain and Russia, with important effects:

- Britain was prevented temporarily from pursuing its traditional policy of supporting Turkey against Russia.
- In Russia the sufferings of the Bulgarians and the defeat of Serbian and Montenegrin forces enflamed **Pan-Slavist** sentiment to such an extent that the Tsarist government found itself under mounting pressure to intervene in the Balkans.

In November 1876 Alexander II declared that if his 'just demands' for the protection of Balkan Christians were not agreed to by Turkey, and the other great powers would not support him, then he was prepared to act independently.

Russian and Austrian policy was suddenly out of step and both turned to Germany for support. In December the Tsar asked for an assurance of German neutrality in the event of an Austro-Russian war. Bismarck was evasive. He similarly refused Andrassy's offer of an Austro-German alliance against Russia.

The Russo-Turkish War 1877–8

In January 1877 Russia managed to buy Austrian neutrality in the event of a Russo-Turkish war by agreeing that Austria would receive Bosnia-Herzegovina, and promising that no large state would be set up in the Balkans. In April Russia declared war on Turkey.

Courageous Turkish defence of the fortress of Plevna deprived Russia of a quick victory. It also caused British opinion to swing back in favour of the Turks. Plevna finally fell in December 1877 and the Russians were able to resume their advance. By January 1878 they threatened Constantinople.

The Treaty of San Stefano

In March Russia imposed the San Stefano Treaty on the Turks. This treaty significantly improved Russia's position in the Balkans:

- European Turkey was to be reduced to small, unconnected territories by the creation of a Big Bulgaria under Russian occupation.
- Serbia, Montenegro and Romania were to be fully independent of Turkey.
- There was no mention of Austria taking Bosnia-Herzegovina.
- The San Stefano Treaty confirmed Andrassy's worst fears that he had been duped. The proposal to create a Big Bulgaria was seen as a cynical Russian attempt to establish a Balkan **client state** with a strategically important Aegean coastline. Austria mobilised its army. Britain summoned troops from India and despatched the fleet to Turkish waters.

Faced with the threat of a major war, which it was in no economic or military state to fight, Russia agreed to an international conference to revise the peace terms. Bismarck, somewhat reluctantly, offered his services as the 'honest broker'. He realised that he was likely to be blamed by one or the other, or even by both, of his allies for their disappointments.

Key terms

Pan-Slavist
Someone who supported the union of all Slav peoples.

Client state
A country that is friendly with, and dependent on, a stronger country.

Map 5.2: The Balkans 1878.

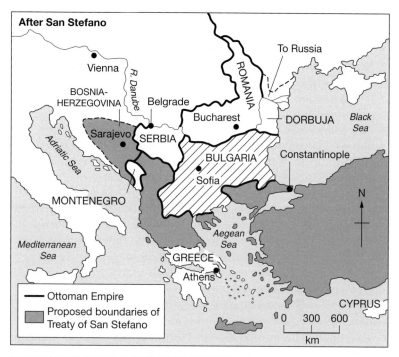

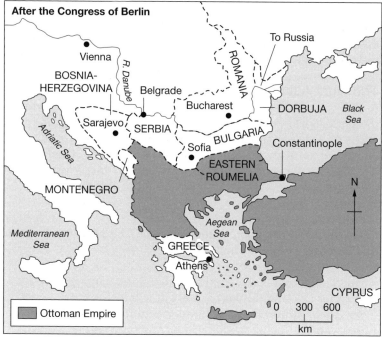

Key date

Congress of Berlin:
June–July 1878

The Congress of Berlin

The fact that the Congress – the most important meeting of the powers since 1856 – took place in Berlin was a sign of Germany's new power and Bismarck's prestige. Much negotiation had been done before the Congress met. Nevertheless, the Congress was not all plain sailing. At critical moments, only Bismarck's energetic intervention saved the day.

By the Treaty of Berlin:

- Big Bulgaria was divided into three.
- Bulgaria proper was granted complete independence under Russian supervision.
- The province of Eastern Roumelia was to have a form of self-government under nominal Turkish rule.
- Macedonia was returned to Turkish rule.
- Russia recovered southern Bessarabia from Romania.
- Austria was to occupy Bosnia-Herzegovina.
- Britain gained Cyprus.

For Bismarck the Congress was a mixed blessing. His main desire – that of keeping peace – had been achieved. However, Russia felt that it had suffered a humiliating diplomatic defeat. Russia had done all the fighting and then seen Britain and Austria get away with some major spoils. Russia blamed Bismarck for its diplomatic defeat. Alexander II described the Congress as 'a coalition of the European powers against Russia under the leadership of Prince Bismarck'. Russo-German relations quickly deteriorated. The introduction of German protective tariffs in 1879 (see pages 114–15) did not help matters, given Russia's dependence on wheat exports to Germany.

By 1878–9 the *Dreikaiserbund* was well and truly dead. Bismarck was now in a potentially dangerous position. There was suddenly the real possibility of a Franco-Russian alliance.

The Dual Alliance

In 1878–9 it seemed to Bismarck that Germany was faced with the stark choice: continuing Russian hostility or allying with it. An alliance would jeopardise his relationship with Austria and risk enmity with Britain. He had no wish to be isolated. His greatest fear was that somehow (and somewhat improbably) Russia, France and Austria would ally and that this would lead to Germany's destruction.

His response to the pressure from Russia was to put out feelers for an alliance with Austria. In October 1879 Bismarck and Andrassy agreed to the Dual Alliance:

- This committed both countries to resist Russian aggression.
- If either Germany or Austria were at war with a third power, the other partner would remain neutral unless Russia intervened.

The alliance was to last for 5 years. However, the option to renew the arrangement was taken up so that it became the cornerstone of German foreign policy, lasting until 1918. The Dual Alliance was something of a 'landmark'. Previous treaties had usually been concluded on the eve of wars. This was a peacetime engagement. It encouraged other powers to negotiate similar treaties until all Europe was divided into pact and counter-pact.

Key question
How important was the Dual Alliance?

Key date
Dual Alliance between Germany and Austria-Hungary: 1879

Emperor William, who regarded good relations with Russia as of vital importance, was reluctant to sign the alliance. In the end Bismarck forced the Emperor's hand by threatening resignation. Grudgingly William gave way.

Why did Bismarck agree to the Dual Alliance?

Bismarck claimed that the Dual Alliance was the fruition of a grand design cherished since 1866. There is, in fact, no evidence that he had it in mind before 1879. In reality he acted on the spur of the moment to deal with an emergency situation.

In 1879 the Dual Alliance provided Germany with an ally with whom it could weather the storm of Russian hostility. Bismarck chose to ally with Austria rather than Russia partly because he felt Austria would be easier to control and partly because an alliance with a fellow German power was likely to be more popular in Germany. In truth, however, the Dual Alliance was only a temporary expedient to preserve the precarious balance of power in the Balkans and to compel a more friendly Russian attitude towards both Austria and Germany. It was not a final choice between them. Bismarck never wavered in his belief that some form of *Dreikaiserbund* was Germany's best hope.

The Three Emperors' Alliance

Russia, alarmed at its isolation and not anxious to ally with France, soon turned back to Germany. However, more than 18 months elapsed before a new *Dreikaiserbund* was signed. This was partly due to problems arising from the death of Alexander II and the accession of Tsar Alexander III. Austria was also opposed to the entire project. However, Andrassy finally yielded to Bismarck's pressure and in 1881 the Three Emperors' Alliance, a secret treaty of 3 years' duration, was signed. It aimed at resolving Austro-Russian disputes in the Balkans and at reassuring Russia that it did not need to seek accommodation with France. The three powers agreed:

- that if Russia, Germany or Austria were at war with another power, the others would remain neutral
- to keep the entrance to the Black Sea closed to foreign warships
- to divide the Balkans into 'spheres of influence'; Russian interests were recognised in the eastern portion, Austrian interests in the western
- Austria acknowledged Russian ambitions to re-create a Big Bulgaria; Russia accepted Austria's right to annex Bosnia-Herzegovina.

Although Russia continued to resent the Dual Alliance, it was pleased with the new *Dreikaiserbund*. Russia's partners had written off half the Balkans and had committed themselves to Russia if it came to blows with Britain. Bismarck was also pleased. His confident assertion to Emperor William that Russia would return to the fold had come to pass and the conservative alliance was restored.

Key date

Three Emperors'
Alliance: 1881

The Triple Alliance

Bismarck, hoping to divert French attention away from Alsace-Lorraine, encouraged France to embark on colonial expansion in Africa and Asia. This had the added advantage of alienating France from Britain. In 1881, with Bismarck's support, France seized Tunis. This angered Italy, who had designs on the same territory.

In 1881 Italy made overtures to Austria aimed at securing an alliance. Austria had little interest in the Italian bid for closer ties but Bismarck, although having a poor opinion of Italy's strength, saw its potential. Bringing Italy closer to the Dual Alliance would secure Austria's vulnerable southern flank and deprive France of a potential ally. Accordingly, in 1882 the Triple Alliance was signed:

Key question
Why did Bismarck agree to the Triple Alliance?

Triple Alliance: 1882

Key date

- If any of the signatories were attacked by two or more powers, the others promised to lend assistance.
- If France attacked Germany, Italy would provide support to its partner.
- If Italy was attacked by France, both Germany and Austria agreed to back Italy.

Bismarck and colonies

In 1881 Bismarck declared that 'so long as I am Chancellor we shall pursue no colonial policy'. He knew that the acquisition of colonies was likely to be expensive. Moreover, it might well alienate Britain, the strongest colonial power. However, in 1884–5 Germany was suddenly to acquire an overseas Empire. Why did Bismarck change his mind?

Key question
Why did Bismarck support the acquisition of colonies in 1884–5?

- In the early 1880s colonialism became fashionable. Many European nations were interested in carving up Africa. Enthusiastic pressure groups sprang up agitating for colonies on economic grounds and as a sign of national greatness. The German Colonial Union, founded in 1882 with support from major industrialists, did much to interest German public opinion in overseas expansion.
- Within Germany there was concern about the consequences of protectionist policies. Trading companies were complaining of being squeezed out of parts of Africa by foreign rivals. Bismarck hoped that colonies might benefit the German economy by providing new markets and raw materials.
- Bismarck had a sharp eye for a new opportunity. In the mid-1880s he seriously considered the possibility of a lasting reconciliation with France. Active co-operation with France in the colonial field was the first step. By picking quarrels with Britain over German colonial claims, he aligned Germany on France's side.
- The absence of serious difficulties with either Russia or France enabled Bismarck to embark on an energetic colonial policy. Moreover, by putting pressure on Britain in the colonial field, Bismarck hoped to force her into adopting a more pro-German policy in European affairs.

- Bismarck had also good political reasons to support German colonialism. The 1884 elections were in the offing. He needed an issue that would weaken the liberal parties. Colonialism was a convenient way of rallying patriotic support.

The German overseas empire

In 1884 Bismarck deliberately picked quarrels with Britain over colonial claims in South-West Africa and sided with France in opposition to British plans in Egypt. The Franco-German entente reached its high water mark at the Berlin Conference of 1884–5, called to regulate the affairs of central Africa. Facing a Russian threat in central Asia, Britain had no wish to antagonise Germany and was not opposed to its acquiring colonies. Thus, between 1884 and 1885 Germany acquired South-West Africa, Togoland, the Cameroons, German East Africa and some Pacific islands – one million square miles of land in total (see Map 5.3).

However, Bismarck's interest in colonial matters was short lived. By 1887 he was resisting demands for further colonial expansion on the grounds of Germany's continental security. As German

Map 5.3: German colonies in Africa in 1890.

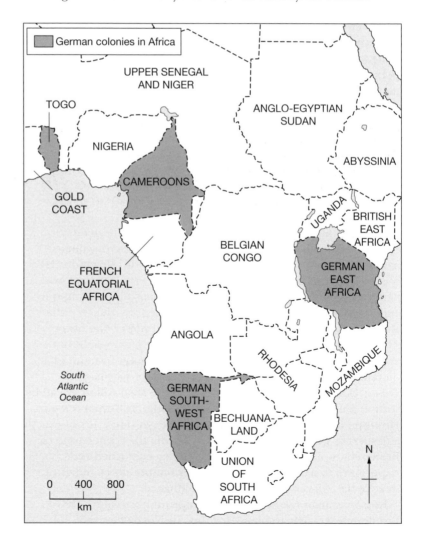

relations with France and Russia deteriorated (see below), he had no wish to alienate Britain. Thus, he made substantial concessions to Britain when East Africa was partitioned in 1889. A German official observed that a 'good understanding with England means much more to Bismarck than the whole of East Africa'.

The Bulgarian crisis

A crisis in Bulgaria in 1885–6 shattered the Three Emperors' Alliance, due for renewal in 1887. Austria and Russia again squared up against each other in the Balkans. Bismarck refused to take sides in the dispute. He warned the Austrians that Germany would not help them. He also warned Russia that he would not abandon Austria.

As Austro-Russian relations worsened, Bismarck's fears of France revived. In 1886 General Boulanger became French War Minister and talked of a war to recover Alsace-Lorraine. Franco-German relations quickly deteriorated. To make matters worse, Pan-Slav advisers, sympathetic to France and hostile to Germany, seemed to be exerting great influence in Russia. For domestic reasons, Bismarck may well have exaggerated the danger of war. However, he was clearly alarmed by the fear of a Franco-Russian alliance and felt that diplomatic precautions were needed to safeguard Germany.

In February 1887 the Triple Alliance was renewed on terms more favourable to Italy than those obtained in 1882. Bismarck persuaded Austria to promise to consult Italy on all matters affecting the Balkans, the Adriatic and the Aegean.

In March 1887, with Bismarck's full backing, Britain, Austria and Italy signed the First Mediterranean Agreement, committing themselves to the maintenance of the *status quo* in the eastern Mediterranean – an action that was clearly anti-Russian.

The Reinsurance Treaty

Events now turned in Bismarck's favour. France, suddenly cautious, avoided Russian feelers and conservative diplomats again won the upper hand in St Petersburg. Tsar Alexander III accepted their argument that an agreement with Germany was better than nothing. Bismarck jumped at the suggestion and in June 1887 the Reinsurance Treaty was signed. By this, if either Russia or Germany were at war with a third power, the other would remain benevolently neutral. The provision would not apply to a war against Austria or France resulting from an attack on one of these two powers by either Russia or Germany.

The Treaty, which did not contravene the Dual Alliance, can be seen as a masterpiece of diplomatic juggling on Bismarck's part. However, its importance should not be exaggerated. If not exactly a desperate stop-gap measure, it was hardly the cornerstone of Bismarck's system; indeed, he seems to have attached little importance to it. It was simply another temporary expedient to remove his fears of a Franco-Russian alliance.

Russo-German relations did not improve much after 1887. Bismarck was partly to blame for this. In November 1887 he

---

Key question
Why did Bismarck feel threatened in 1886?

Key date
Bulgarian crisis: 1885–6

Key question
Why did Bismarck sign the Reinsurance Treaty?

Key date
Reinsurance Treaty between Germany and Russia: 1887

denied Russia access to the Berlin money market for loans to finance industrialisation in order 'to remove the possibility that the Russians wage war against us at our cost'. In consequence, Russia simply turned to Paris where French financiers were eager to invest money in Russia.

Nor did the Reinsurance Treaty necessarily reduce the danger of a clash over the Balkans. Indeed, the Bulgarian situation continued to cause tension. Bismarck used all his influence to encourage Britain, Italy and Austria to sign the Second Mediterranean Agreement (December 1887), again guaranteeing the *status quo* in the east Mediterranean. In February 1888 he published the Dual Alliance, partly to warn Russia that Germany would stand by Austria if it came to war and partly to restrain Austria by making it clear that Germany's obligations were limited to a defensive war. The publication, coupled with rumours of the Mediterranean Agreement, persuaded Russia to hold its hand and the Bulgarian crisis finally fizzled out.

Summary diagram: Bismarck's foreign policy 1871–90

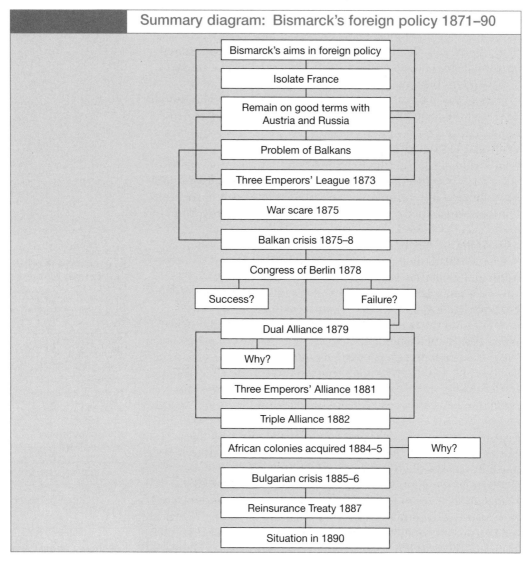

4 | Bismarck's Fall

By the late 1880s Bismarck's position seemed in jeopardy. Emperor William I was in his eighties. If William died, Crown Prince Frederick, a man of liberal views, would ascend the throne. It seemed likely that Frederick would dismiss Bismarck and appoint a liberal chancellor.

Key question
How did Bismarck fall from power?

Problems with the *Reichstag*

By 1887 Bismarck was at odds with the *Reichstag* over the renewal of the army grant or **Septennates**. The current Septennates were not due to expire until 1888, but the international situation alarmed the generals, who pressed for an early renewal. So, in late 1886 Bismarck asked the *Reichstag* to agree to substantial military increases. The *Reichstag* agreed, but only on condition that in future it was allowed to review military expenditure every 3 years.

Bismarck was furious: 'The German army is an institution which cannot be dependent on short-lived *Reichstag* majorities', he declared. Dissolving the *Reichstag*, he conjured up a picture of a revenge-seeking France, ready for war at any moment. Germany would remain in danger until the Septennates were passed and only the Conservatives and National Liberals could be relied on to pass them. Bismarck's electoral strategem worked. The Conservatives and National Liberals won an absolute majority in 1887 and the Septennates were passed.

Septennates
The arrangement whereby military spending was agreed for 7 years.

Key term

Wilhelm II and Bismarck

While William I lived Bismarck's hold on power was never in question. Their meetings were often stormy, emotional and noisy. They shouted, threw things and quarrelled for much of the time. But they understood each other. 'It is not easy to be the Emperor under such a Chancellor', William remarked, but he managed it successfully, mainly by letting Bismarck have his own way.

When William died (aged 90) in March 1888 he was succeeded by his son Frederick. Frederick, however, died from cancer only 3 months later. Frederick's 29-year-old son Wilhelm then became Emperor. He was a convinced German nationalist and was committed to the belief that he ruled by Divine Right of God. Wilhelm's character was complex (see page 141). On the positive side, he was intelligent, talented, cultured and energetic. On the negative, he was overbearing, arrogant and erratic.

After Frederick's death, Bismarck's position seemed secure again. He had cultivated Wilhelm's friendship for several years and in public the new Kaiser expressed his admiration for Bismarck. But a great gulf separated the two, not least age. Bismarck, assuming that Wilhelm would not involve himself much in matters of government, tended to treat him in a condescending manner. He underestimated the new Kaiser. Wilhelm was determined to rule as well as to reign, and resolved to dispense with Bismarck as soon as decently possible. 'I'll let the old boy potter along for another six months', he told his cronies, 'then I'll rule myself'.

Death of William I: March 1888

Wilhelm II became Kaiser: June 1888

Key dates

> **Note: William (or Wilhelm) II**
> This book will call the new Kaiser Wilhelm II – rather than William II. This will help to differentiate him from William I.

'The Dropping of the Pilot'. What does this 1876 *Punch* cartoon suggest was the main reason for Bismarck's dismissal?

Bismarck and Wilhelm in conflict

Wilhelm and Bismarck were soon at odds:

- Wilhelm questioned the need to maintain links with Russia.
- The two disagreed over social policy. Unlike Bismarck, Wilhelm was confident that he could win over the working class by a modest extension of the welfare system, including an end to child labour and Sunday working. Bismarck, by contrast, favoured further repression. Thus, in 1889 he proposed to make the anti-socialist law permanent. Wilhelm was not against renewing the law (he too feared socialism), but he wanted the measure watered down. Bismarck refused. He was then let

down by the *Reichstag*, which rejected his entire bill in January 1890. This was a sign that his political power was crumbling.

In February 1890, with new *Reichstag* elections underway, Wilhelm issued a proclamation promising new social legislation. The absence of Bismarck's counter-signature from this proclamation caused a sensation. The election was a disaster for Bismarck. His Conservative and National Liberal allies lost 85 seats while the Radicals gained 46 seats and the Socialists won 24 seats. The opposition was again in control of the *Reichstag*.

Bismarck was trapped between an Emperor bent on having his own way and a hostile *Reichstag*. In an attempt to recover his position he proposed an extraordinary scheme: the *Reichstag* would be asked to agree to a large increase in the army and a new and extremely repressive anti-socialist law. If, as was probable, they refused, an assembly of German Princes would meet, alter the constitution and drastically curtail the powers of the *Reichstag*. Wilhelm refused to support his plan and relations between the two men became even worse.

Bismarck dismissed

In March 1890 Wilhelm and Bismarck quarrelled about the right of ministers to advise the monarch. Bismarck had revived an old order first issued in 1852, which forbade ministers to approach the King (of Prussia) except through the Minister-President. Bismarck interpreted this to mean that all ministers must obtain permission from him as Chancellor, before they could discuss any government business with the Emperor.

Wilhelm II dismissed Bismarck: 1890 — Key date

Wilhelm was not prepared for such restrictions and commanded that the 1852 order be withdrawn. At a stormy interview Bismarck nearly threw an inkpot at Wilhelm and then enraged him by letting him see a letter from Tsar Alexander III very disparaging of his talents.

Wilhelm now sent Bismarck an ultimatum: resign or be dismissed. Three days later Bismarck sent a letter of resignation in which he justified his actions, claiming (wrongly) that the real difference between Wilhelm and himself lay in the Kaiser's pursuit of an anti-Russian policy. This letter was not made public until after Bismarck's death. The official announcement implied that he had resigned for health reasons and that Wilhelm had made every effort to persuade him to change his mind.

In reality Bismarck retired with ill grace to write his memoirs and innumerable newspaper articles, invariably critical of Wilhelm. Failing to exert any influence on policy, he was even heard to speak in favour of republicanism: kings, he said, were dangerous if they had real power. He died in July 1898. On his grave were the words, 'A faithful German servant of Kaiser William I'.

Bismarck in 1890.

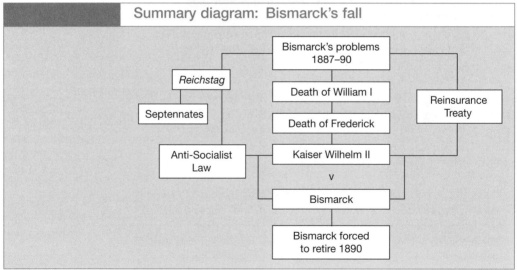

Summary diagram: Bismarck's fall

5 | Key Debate

How successful was Bismarck?

Although his body was laid to rest, Bismarck's spirit has continued to haunt German history. Historians have argued over his achievement, his motives and his methods. Innumerable books have been written about him. By 1895, 5 years after his resignation, there were already 650 biographies available. Twenty years later there were 3500 and the number has gone on increasing ever since.

When it comes to primary evidence the problem is not a lack of material but an excess, much of it conflicting. Bismarck left a wealth of letters, articles, speeches and official reports. There were also his voluminous *Reminiscences*, written long after the events and in a time of great bitterness. They are not entirely reliable, for fact was often embroidered with a little fiction.

During his time in office, Bismarck frequently made totally contradictory statements at the same time about the same events. Historians interpret this differently:

- Some see it as symptomatic of Bismarck's perversity of mind, a desire to confuse or mislead friends and enemies alike.
- Others see it as a lack of settled purpose and the inability to think clearly and coherently in abstract terms.
- Others see it simply as Bismarck's way of 'reasoning out loud', rehearsing a number of different arguments before reaching a decision.

Whatever the reason, it means that Bismarck's own evidence needs to be used with caution. A single letter or speech is not necessarily a true reflection of his policies or intentions at any given time. Therefore it is difficult to disentangle with any certainty Bismarck's motives, or to decide how far he planned ahead. 'Politics', he said, 'is not in itself an exact and logical science but is the capacity to choose in each fleeting moment of the situation that which is least harmful or most opportune.' He was the supreme opportunist, both before and after 1871. Accordingly, his policies can best be described as flexible.

Realpolitik characterised Bismarck's political career from his earliest days. In 1850 he declared that the only sound foundation for a great state is not idealism but 'state egoism' (national self-interest). Thirty years later, his beliefs had not changed. Defending himself against critics in the *Reichstag* who accused him of sudden changes of policy, he said:

> I have always had one compass only, one lodestar by which I have steered: the welfare of the state ... When I have had time to think I have always acted according to the question, 'What is useful, advantageous and right for my Fatherland and – as long as this was only Prussia – for my dynasty, and today for the German nation'.

Bismarck's critics

Bismarck had critics in his own time and has had many since. The main criticisms of his policies post-1871 are as follows:

- He was responsible for France remaining embittered.
- His elaborate alliance system was fragile – little more than a form of crisis management.
- The Dual Alliance, far from being a means by which Germany could control Austria, eventually dragged her into war in 1914.
- His acquisition of colonies had negative results. German colonial ambitions alienated Britain in the 1880s and more importantly thereafter when they became the basis for

Germany's claim to be a world power. The colonies proved to be an expensive financial burden.

- His style – his frequent use of bluster and blackmail – created a legacy of distrust.
- His influence is often exaggerated. Economic and military strength was the basis of German power – not Bismarck's diplomatic skill.
- The *Kulturkampf* was a major blunder.
- His attack on the socialists was ill-advised and unsuccessful.
- His inability either to delegate authority or to tolerate anyone who even approached his equality meant that he effectively ruled as a dictator.
- He left a flawed legacy. His strategies and tactics were responsible for **Wilhelmine Germany** and Nazi Germany.

Bismarck's admirers

In response, Bismarck's supporters can make the following claims:

- He was not the total reactionary of left-wing myth. He helped to promote the consolidation and modernisation of Germany.
- The national minorities, Catholics and socialists were a threat to the *Reich*. Although his campaigns against 'enemies of the state' were not successful, they were not total failures. Nor, in the context of the time, were his measures particularly repressive.
- For most of the 1870s he worked closely with the National Liberals, putting their – liberal – programme into place.
- He pioneered State Socialism.
- His policies assisted Germany's economic development.
- The fact that he remained in power for so long is testimony to his political skill.
- He was not a dictator. His powers were far from absolute.
- He brilliantly maintained peace from 1871 to 1890.

Overall, Bismarck's admirers have the best of the argument. Germany did not exist when he became Prussian Chief Minister in 1862. When he left office in 1890 it was Europe's strongest state. This did not happen by chance. It had much to do with his diplomatic prowess. He manipulated situations even if he did not always create them, and he worked hard and successfully to ensure the outcomes he desired. In so doing he won the trust of few but the respect of virtually everyone he encountered. It was unfortunate that after 1890 Germany was in the hands of less skilful men.

Key term
Wilhelmine Germany The period from 1888 to 1918 when Wilhelm II was Kaiser.

Some key books in the debate
L. Abrams, *Bismarck and the German Empire 1871–1918* (Routledge, 1995).
E. Crankshaw, *Bismarck* (Macmillan, 1981).
W.J. Momsen, *Imperial Germany 1867–1918* (Edward Arnold, 1995).
A.J.P. Taylor, *Bismarck: The Man and Statesman* (New English Library, 1974).
B. Waller, *Bismarck* (Blackwell, 1985).

Study Guide: AS Questions

In the style of AQA

(a) Explain why Bismarck was unsuccessful in his campaign against the Catholics in the period 1871–8. (12 marks)

(b) How successful was Bismarck in creating a strong and united German nation by 1890? (24 marks)

Exam tips

The cross-references are intended to take you straight to the material that will help you to answer the questions.

(a) You will need to refer to pages 111–13. Make a list of reasons why the *Kulturkampf* failed and then work out a logical order in which to address these. Was one more important than another? Are the reasons interlinked? In assessing Bismarck's failure you will need to take into consideration what he set out to achieve and you should also try to draw some broad conclusions to show judgement. Were his failures the result of his constitutional position, his unrealistic aims, political and/or economic circumstances or other factors outside his control?

(b) You will need to plan your answer carefully. You will need to identify the ways in which Germany was a strong and united nation by the time of Bismarck's fall and the ways in which it was not. Material that would suggest Germany was strong and united might include:

- The growth of German unity (page 118).
- The constitution, which allowed some elements of democracy (pages 102–7).
- Government stability for two decades (pages 109–18).
- The success of State Socialism (page 117).
- German economic strength (page 108).
- German military and diplomatic strength (page 135).

Material that would suggest Germany was weak and disunited might include:

- The problems of the constitution – not least the stunting of the *Reichstag* by Bismarck (pages 106–7).
- The tensions created by industrialisation and urbanisation (page 108).
- The challenge of the socialists (pages 115–17).
- The fact that many 'Germans' were not committed to the Reich (pages 107–8).
- The personality of Kaiser Wilhelm II (pages 130 and 141).

You also need to look over these factors and decide how far Bismarck was himself responsible for the various successes and failures. When you have made your decision about the degree of Bismarck's own success, you should be ready to begin writing. Don't forget your essay should be an argument and all your ideas will need supporting with relevant factual material. You should provide balance in your answer – looking at both sides – and should aim to reach a well-supported conclusion.

In the style of Edexcel

To what extent was the *Kulturkampf* a political misjudgement by
Bismarck?   (30 marks)

Source: Edexcel specimen paper Unit 1 F2, 2007

Exam tips

*The cross-references are intended to take you straight to the material
that will help you to answer the question.*

In planning your answer, you will need to identify aspects of the
Kulturkampf which could be seen as a misjudgement (and explain
why you think so). In order to respond to the 'to what extent' part of
the question, the examiner also expects you to identify aspects
which could be shown not to be a misjudgement (and explain why).
  Those elements which provide evidence of misjudgement are:
- The underestimation of opposition (page 113).
- The *Kulturkampf*'s effects in promoting political disunity
  (page 113).
- The strengthening of the challenge from the Centre Party
  (pages 111 and 113).
- Bismarck's public reversal of the policy (page 113).

The counter-evidence comes from the *Kulturkampf*'s political benefits
for Bismarck:
- It allowed him to put himself at the head of a popular Protestant
  crusade (page 112), but see the limitations to this (page 113).
- He was politically strengthened in the 1870s by his alliance with
  the Liberals (pages 111 and 112).
- His effective manipulation of the situation in 1878–9 allowed him
  to retain key elements of the policy, and allowed him to move
  towards harnessing Catholic political power in the *Reichstag*
  against socialism (page 113).

Your conclusion will depend on what weight you decide to attach to
the points on either side. What is your decision? Your answer will
flow better if you deal first with whichever set of points carries less
weight, so it is important to make up your mind before you start to
write. Your whole answer will also be more focused if you are clear
about where it is going. It is often a good aid to planning to draft a
conclusion first – try it and see if it helps.

6 Wilhelmine Germany 1890–1914

POINTS TO CONSIDER

Few Germans regretted Bismarck's retirement in 1890: most accepted that he had outlived his political usefulness. Germany turned to the future with confidence under the young emperor Wilhelm II. At the height of the diplomatic crisis in July 1914 which eventually culminated in the First World War, the Austrian Foreign Minister asked in frustration: 'Who actually rules in Berlin?' This was a pertinent question, not just in 1914, but throughout Wilhelm's rule. Who exactly exerted the decisive influence on policy and events? What were the objectives of that leadership?

This chapter will examine these questions through the following themes:

- The Wilhelmine political system
- Economic change
- Intellectual trends
- Domestic politics
- Foreign policy

Key dates

1890	March	Bismarck resigned; Caprivi became Chancellor
1894		Dual Alliance between France and Russia
1898		First Navy Law
1900	June	Second Navy Law
	October	Bülow appointed Chancellor
1904		Entente between Britain and France
1905–6		First Moroccan crisis
1906		Launch of the *Dreadnought*
1908–9		Bosnian crisis
1909		Appointment of Bethmann-Hollweg as Chancellor
1911		Second Moroccan crisis
1912		SPD became the largest party in the *Reichstag*
1914	June 28	Assassination of Franz Ferdinand
	July 5–6	Germany gave Austria the 'blank cheque'
	July 23	Austrian ultimatum to Serbia
	August 1	German declaration of war on Russia
	August 3	German declaration of war on France
	August 4	British declaration of war on Germany

1 | The Wilhelmine Political System

The Kaiser

According to historian Michael Balfour, Wilhelm was 'the copybook condemnation of the hereditary system'. This view may be over-harsh. Wilhelm did have some talents: a quick if not original mind, an excellent memory, and a charming manner. Unfortunately, his understanding of issues was often superficial and distorted by his own prejudices. He lacked powers of steady application and his moods and behaviour were liable to wild fluctuations. 'The Kaiser is like a balloon', said Bismarck, 'If you do not hold fast to the string, you never know where he will be off to'.

Arguably, Wilhelm's influence should not be exaggerated. His life was an endless whirl of state occasions, military manoeuvres, cruises and hunting trips. In the first decade of his reign he averaged 200 days per year travelling on official business or private recreation. His social and ceremonial duties meant that he was absent from Berlin for long periods and so he did not have command of the detail of the government's work. Accordingly, it is possible to claim that he did not really determine the course of German policy.

However, the German constitution did grant the Kaiser extensive powers. He alone had the right to appoint and dismiss the chancellor and his state secretaries – completely independent of the wishes of the *Reichstag*. Wilhelm claimed that 'there is only one Ruler in the Reich and I am he'. He believed that his accountability was to God alone. Given his constitutional powers, no major decision could be taken without his agreement. When he spoke, people, in and out of Germany, listened.

Key question
To what extent did Wilhelm's personality shape the history of imperial Germany?

The German Chancellors

There were four chancellors between 1890 and 1914:

- General Leo Caprivi (1890–4)
- Prince Chlodwig Hohenloe (1894–1900)
- Bernhard Bülow (1900–9)
- Theobold Bethmann-Hollweg (1909–17).

Given that none of them dominated the German political scene as decisively as Bismarck, they are often portrayed as lesser men. They may well have lacked Bismarck's talent; they certainly lacked his prestige and independence. William I had usually deferred to Bismarck, but Wilhelm II was determined to participate in the affairs of state. Political survival for the chancellors was essentially dependent on showing loyalty to Wilhelm and doing his will. This was far from easy when his personal involvement often amounted to little more than whimsical flights of fancy.

Profile: Kaiser Wilhelm II 1859–1941

1859 – Born, the eldest child of Crown Prince Frederick and Victoria, the eldest daughter of British Queen Victoria
1888 – Became Kaiser on the death of Frederick
1890 – Dismissed Bismarck: supported the 'New Course'
1897 – Supported a policy of *Weltpolitik*
1908 – Homosexual scandal at Wilhelm's court, involving his close friend Eulenburg
1914 – Germany entered the First World War
1918 – Abdicated and fled to the Netherlands
1941 – Died

Most historians are of the view that Wilhelm was arrogant, blustering, overtly theatrical – a neurotic braggart, a romantic dreamer, a man who frequently changed his mind. Many scholars, convinced that Wilhelm was, at the very least, deeply disturbed, have spent a great deal of time trying to explain his personality:

- Wilhelm's breech birth delivery resulted in the partial paralysis of his left arm and damage to the balance mechanism in his ear. These physical problems have prompted speculation about the possible psychological consequences for the young prince.
- Close attention has been paid to the strained relationship with his parents. During his adolescent years, he grew apart from them, opposing their liberal sympathies and preferring the company of his grandfather. He particularly enjoyed the regimental life of the military garrison at Potsdam. (His love of military ceremonial verged on the pathological.)
- Some have suggested that Wilhelm's self-assertive and erratic behaviour should be seen as symptoms of insanity, megalomania or sadism.
- More recently, he has been depicted as a repressed homosexual or a sufferer from attention deficiency disorder – a mental condition which reveals itself in volatile and irrational behaviour.

Key question
How powerful was the *Reichstag*?

The *Bundesrat*

The upper house of the national parliament, comprising men chosen by the various states, was essentially a conservative body. It had been at the centre of Bismarck's system. After 1890 it declined in influence. An increasing number of bills were first discussed by the main political parties and then introduced in the *Reichstag* rather than in the *Bundesrat*.

Table 6.1: *Reichstag* election results 1890–1912

Party	1890	1893	1898	1903	1907	1912
German Conservatives	73	72	56	54	60	43
Free Conservatives	20	28	23	21	24	14
National Liberals	42	53	46	51	54	45
Centre	106	96	102	100	105	91
Left Liberals	76	48	49	36	49	42
Social Democrats	35	44	56	81	43	110
Minorities	38	35	34	32	29	33
Right-wing splinter parties	7	21	31	22	33	19
Total	397	397	397	397	397	397

Table 6.2: Major political parties in the *Reichstag*

SPD *Sozialdemokratische Partei Deutschlands*. Social Democratic Party. The party of theoretical Marxism. Closely connected with the trade unions and supported by the working classes.

ZP *Zentrumspartei*. Centre Party. Formed in 1871 specifically to uphold the interests of the Catholic Church. Its appeal was therefore denominational rather than class-based. Despite the *Kulturkampf* it had become an influential political voice in the Reichstag.

DKP *Deutschkonservative Partei*. German Conservative Party. The party of the landowning farming community. Its outlook was ultra-conservative and hostile to the new forces of political and economic liberalism. Especially strong in Prussia.

RP *Reichspartei*. Free Conservative Party. Conservative in outlook, it was backed by both industrialists and landowners.

NLP *Nationalliberale Partei*. National Liberal Party. Traditionally the party of economic and political liberalism. A middle-class party, it was increasingly conservative in its policy.

DFP *Deutsche Freisinnige Partei*. German Free Thought Party (Left Liberals). Formed in 1884 following the secession of the more radical elements from the NLP. In 1893 it split into three factions and was only re-united in 1910 under the new name of the FVP (*Fortschrittliche Volkspartei*; Progressive People's Party).

National minorities
The independence parties of the ethnic minorities in Germany. Poles, Danes, French in Alsace-Lorraine and Guelphs (Hanoverians).

Right-wing splinter parties
There were a number of ultra-conservative parties, which were nationalistic, anti-socialist and often anti-Semitic.

The *Reichstag*

While the *Reichstag* could discuss, amend, pass or reject government legislation, its power to initiate new laws was negligible. No party or coalition of parties ever formed the government of the day. Even a vote of no confidence in the Chancellor had minimal effect. Thus, although Germany had universal manhood suffrage, the Kaiser's authority in many areas was impervious to popular control.

Marxist programme
The plan of those who supported the ideas of Karl Marx. Marxists believed that the leaders of the proletariat must work to overthrow the capitalist system by (violent) revolution.

Minimum programme
The name given to the plans of moderate socialists who were opposed to violent revolution.

Lobby groups
People who campaign to persuade politicians to pass legislation favouring particular interests.

The Pan-German League
Formed in 1893, the League was a right-wing nationalist movement. It supported German expansion both in Europe and world-wide.

Key question
How strong was the *Reich* government?

The right-wing parties

On most issues Wilhelm and his governments could rely on the backing of the right-wing parties: the Conservatives, the Free Conservatives and the National Liberals. However, after 1890 the voting strength of these parties was in decline. In 1887 they won 48 per cent of the popular vote: by 1912 their share of the vote was down to 26 per cent. Consequently, the imperial government had to find support from other parties if legislation was to be ratified.

The Centre Party

The Centre Party consistently won between 90 and 110 seats. This made it the largest party in the *Reichstag*, until 1912. Representing Catholics, it had a wide spectrum of sociopolitical views ranging from conservatism to progressive social reform. By 1900 it had emerged as the pivotal party, allying with either right or left as the occasion demanded.

The Social Democrat Party (SPD)

The Wilhelmine era saw the meteoric rise of the Social Democrat Party (SPD). Liberated by the lapse of the Anti-Socialist Law in 1890, the SPD appealed to Germany's growing industrial working class. In 1893 it won 25 per cent of the popular vote. In 1912 it won 35 per cent, becoming the largest party in the *Reichstag*.

The SPD was far from united. In 1891 it adopted an uncompromising **Marxist programme** to overthrow the Wilhelmine class system. However, many SPD members, who were committed to democratic socialism, favoured the party's so-called **minimum programme**. Given that most SPD deputies continued to talk in favour of revolution, most other political parties saw the SPD as a force for evil.

Interest groups

In the 1890s professionally led interest groups became powerful. Some were economic **lobby groups** like the Agrarian League and the League of German Industrialists. There were a huge variety of trade unions. There were also nationalist pressure groups. These included the **Pan-German League**, the Navy League and the Colonial Society. These organisations were a symptom of escalating political participation, especially on the part of the middle class.

The states

While the 25 federal states retained control over many domestic matters, imperial authority inexorably gained at the expense of that of the states. This happened not only because of Germany's greater role on the world stage, but because domestically the functions of the *Reich* government expanded, while those of the states remained static. The social insurance schemes (see page 117) were *Reich* measures. Tariffs were *Reich* issues. So were military and naval matters. Urbanisation, better communications, the influence of education and military service wore down provincial isolation and helped to bring about the beginnings of a German, as opposed to a Prussian or a Bavarian, identity. The great issues of the day were German, not just Prussian, issues.

Prussia

Prussia was easily the *Reich*'s largest state. Its state parliament, the *Landtag*, was elected on a system of indirect balloting, and a three-class male suffrage giving disproportionate political weight to the rich. The *Landtag* therefore remained a bastion of conservative interests. German chancellors, with the exception of Caprivi, were also prime ministers of Prussia. This dualism meant that, while as imperial chancellors they had often to pursue a liberal policy, as Prussian prime ministers they had to respond to a conservative majority.

The Army

Bismarck had fought hard to keep the military under political control. His successors found it increasingly hard to stand up to the military chiefs, who frequently had the support of Wilhelm. The civilian ministers were not consulted when the General Staff drew up its war plans. War, declared Count Schlieffen, head of the General Staff from 1891 until 1906, was too serious a business to be left to politicians. Schlieffen came up with a master-plan in the event of war – a plan which involved the invasion of France via Belgium. Most of Germany's civilian leaders were unaware of the Schlieffen plan (see page 178) and its implications.

By 1914 the German army was no longer so Prussian dominated or aristocratically led as it had been under Bismarck. Most of its officers now came from the middle class. Nevertheless, in 1913 over half the officers of rank of colonel and above were aristocrats. Officers were selected not by competitive examination, but by regimental commanders. They tended to pick men of like mind and background. Bourgeois officers aped the ways of their aristocratic brothers-in-arms. The army thus remained a right-wing force whose officers often regarded 'mere' civilians with contempt. Most civilians, by contrast, admired military virtues and had great faith in the army as an institution. The special status of the army was a major stumbling block to a modernisation of the political system.

The structuralist view

In the 1960s the 'structuralist' school of historiography, led by H.U. Wehler, emerged. It sought to explain history through a detailed examination of social, political and economic forces. Wehler and fellow structuralists believed that Wilhelm II lacked the strength of character to determine a coherent and co-ordinated policy. Given the power vacuum, other forces emerged to exert a dominating influence over German

Key question
How powerful were the élites?

affairs. Wehler identified these forces as Prussia's traditional élites:

- *Junkers*
- army officers
- leading civil servants and diplomats.

These traditional élites, thought Wehler, were determined to maintain their power against (what they saw as) the threat of mass democracy. This prompted them to seek an alliance with the newly emerging leaders of industry and commerce by offering them a stake in the system. The structuralists claim that the élites set about imposing anti-democratic and anti-modern values on German society from above. In Wehler's view, for example, Germany's decision in the 1890s to undertake *Weltpolitik* (see page 161) was 'social imperialism' – an attempt to buttress the position of the elites by diverting the masses away from social and political reform and towards a populist acceptance of the Kaiser and the *Reich*.

The anti-structuralist view

While the élites had a considerable influence in the Wilhelmine era, the structuralist interpretation is far too sweeping:

- It exaggerates the unity of purpose within the élites. The conception of the German nobility – or even the Prussian nobility alone – as a single class is nonsense.
- *Junker* influence was in decline, even in the army.
- *Weltpolitik* had little to do with social imperialism (see page 161).
- Although most members of the German bourgeoisie – academics, clergymen, doctors, lawyers, engineers, bankers, merchants – feared revolution and opposed full democracy, this does not mean they took their cue from the élite.
- Historians must always be careful with class conflict explanations for political activity. Political debate, then as now, often revealed a surprising lack of consensus within classes, neighbourhoods, even families.

A reactionary state?

Wilhelmine Germany can be seen as a reactionary state, in which the old élites still exerted huge influence and the Kaiser was an authoritarian ruler. However, Germany was rather more democratic than scholars once believed:

- The German press had considerable freedom and criticisms of the Kaiser were commonplace. Wilhelm's expressions of autocratic power, in particular, evoked storms of protest.
- By the early twentieth century, the *Reichstag* had an impressive legislative record and a central place in the popular imagination. Remarkable fairness characterised most election campaigns.
- Given the growth in political activity, Germany's leaders were often responding to, rather than manipulating, public opinion.

Study diagram: The Wilhelmine political system

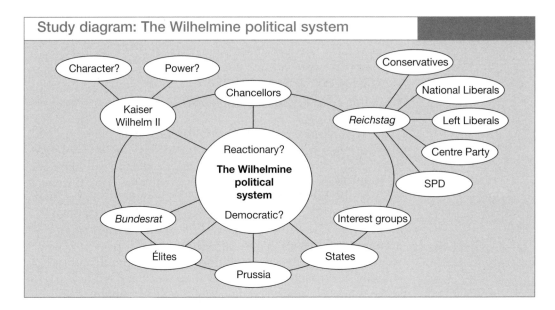

2 | Economic Change

British economist John Maynard Keynes claimed that the 'German Empire has been built more truly on coal and iron than on blood and iron'. German industry, strong by the mid-nineteenth century, forged ahead after 1871, profiting from political unity. Between 1870 and 1913, while the productive capacity of Britain doubled, that of Germany increased eightfold. Only the USA, among major producers, showed a faster rate of growth. By 1914 Germany had become Europe's industrial superpower. This was partly the result of continued increases in production in 'old' industries: coal, iron, heavy engineering and textiles. By 1914 Germany had almost caught up with Britain's level of coal production and exceeded its level of iron production. However, what really marked out the German economy was the expansion of newer industries: steel, electrical engineering, chemicals and motor construction:

Key question
Why was Germany so successful economically?

- German steel production increased nearly ninefold in this period. By 1914 German output was double that of Britain's.
- Two German firms, AEG and Siemens, dominated the world electrical industry. By 1914 nearly half of the world's electrical products originated from Germany.
- The German chemicals industry led the way in the production of fertilisers, dyes and pharmaceutical products.
- Daimler and Benz manufactured the world's first marketable automobile.

The standard of living

Not all Germans benefited from the booming economy. The mass of the population remained agricultural and industrial workers. For agricultural labourers life was particularly difficult. To many on the land industrial employment seemed an attractive option.

But living and working conditions in the industrial towns remained dismally poor for many. Nevertheless, the standard of living of most Germans was rising. Between 1885 and 1913 real wages rose by over 30 per cent. This was at a time when unemployment rarely exceeded three per cent and when the length of the average working week was falling.

Reasons for German economic success

There are several reasons for Germany's economic success:

- Germany's population continued to grow rapidly, from just under 50 million in 1890 to almost 68 million in 1914. This provided both the market and the labour force for an expanding economy. Internal migration continued unabated as Germans moved from the countryside into towns. In 1871, 64 per cent lived in the countryside: by 1910 this had fallen to 40 per cent.
- Germany possessed huge natural resources: coal from the Ruhr, Saar and Silesia; iron ore from Alsace-Lorraine and the Ruhr.
- Germany had an excellent railway system.
- Germany had an excellent education system. Its institutes of higher education led the world. As well as offering study in traditional subjects, they made increasing provision for those with technical skills. Between 1890 and 1914 German university enrolments increased from 28,000 to 60,000. A university degree came within the grasp of the lower middle classes.
- German industry encouraged scientific research. Many important discoveries, especially in the new industries, resulted from this policy.
- German banks pursued an adventurous policy of generous long-term credit facilities for industrial firms. Representatives of the big banks were often invited on to the board of directors of firms, thus cementing a close partnership between the banking and commercial sectors of the economy.
- The banks were instrumental in the development of a distinctly German feature of industrialisation: the growth of **cartels**. In Britain and the USA the idea of groups of businesses combining together to control prices, production levels and marketing was seen as being against the spirit of free enterprise and against the consumer's interests. In Germany, by contrast, cartels were seen as a sensible means of achieving economic planning, eliminating wasteful competition, and promoting efficient large-scale production. In 1875 there were only eight cartels in Germany. By 1905, 366 existed.
- In 1888 agriculture's share of Germany's **gross national product** had been about a half: by 1914 it had shrunk to less than one quarter. However, German agriculture was in no danger of disappearing. While those employed in agriculture dropped from 42 to 34 per cent between 1882 and 1907, this was still a large proportion: in Britain the proportion was under 10 per cent. Germany remained largely self-sufficient in terms of food supply.

Key terms

Cartel
An association of manufacturers who come to a contractual agreement about the level of production and the scale of prices and maintain a monopoly.

Gross national product
The total value of all good and services produced within a country.

Table 6.3: The development of the German economy

Population (millions)

Year	Total	Per cent in towns over 2000
1871	41.1	36.1
1880	42.2	41.4
1890	49.4	42.5
1900	56.4	54.4
1910	64.9	60.0

Output of heavy industry (millions of tonnes)

Coal

Year	Germany	Britain
1871	37.7	119.2
1880	59.1	149.3
1890	89.2	184.5
1900	149.5	228.8
1910	222.2	268.7

Steel

Year	Germany	Britain
1871	0.14	0.41
1880	0.69	1.32
1890	2.13	3.64
1900	6.46	4.98
1910	13.10	6.48

Index of industrial production (1913 = 100%)

Year	Per cent
1871	21.1
1880	49.4
1890	57.3
1900	61.0
1910	86.0
1913	100.0

Balance of payments (millions of marks)

Year	Imports	Exports	Visible balance	Invisible balance	Overall balance
1880	2814	2923	+109	+168	+277
1890	4162	3335	−827	+1249	+422
1900	5769	4611	−1158	+1566	+408
1910	8927	7475	−1452	+2211	+759

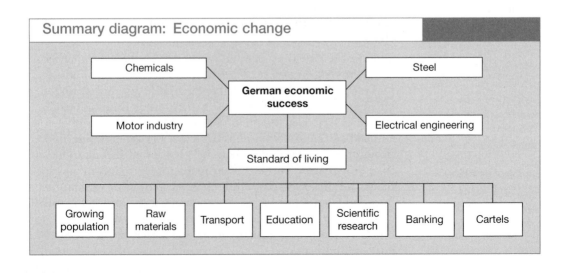

Summary diagram: Economic change

3 | Intellectual Trends

Religion

Key question
To what extent did German nationalism change in the late nineteenth and early twentieth centuries?

In rural and small-town life especially, the Church was – and was seen to be – firmly on the side of authority. Few Germans stood outside the religious establishment. Such a stance required personal courage or an alternative belief system such as Marxism.

Nationalism

In the mid-nineteenth century nationalism had been a progressive force that aimed to promote parliamentary government (see pages 9–10). By the end of the century this had changed. Most nationalists were now conservative, bent on maintaining the *status quo* in a militarised Germany.

German nationalism was not yet directed towards Germans living outside the frontiers of the *Reich* (for example, in Austria, Switzerland and Belgium). German nationalists were rather more concerned with the substantial number of non-Germans – Poles, French and Danes – who lived within the *Reich*. Nationalists wanted to create an ethnically and linguistically homogeneous nation-state. They had little respect for minority languages and culture. There was some discrimination against national minorities – particularly the Poles, who comprised five per cent of Germany's population. Prussia's language legislation in Poland gave rise to a political crisis of national proportions, including a mass strike by 40,000 Polish schoolchildren in 1906. Polish repression fuelled rather than dampened Polish nationalism.

Anti-Semitism

Key question
How strong was anti-Semitism in Germany?

Key term

Anti-Semitic
Someone who is anti-Jewish.

By the late nineteenth century many German nationalists were **anti-Semitic**. Before this time European anti-Semitism was based to a large extent on religious hostility: Jews were blamed for the death of Christ and for not accepting Christianity. While anti-Semitism did not disappear, hostility towards Jews in Germany was politically insignificant by the mid-nineteenth century. In 1871 the German Empire extended total civil equality to Jews.

Throughout the nineteenth century, thousands of Jews from eastern Europe moved west. Many of those who settled in Germany prospered, becoming doctors, bankers, lawyers and academics. Thus, by 1900 Jews played an active and visible part in the cultural, economic and financial life of Germany. Most saw themselves as loyal Germans. Many no longer identified with a separate Jewish community: some inter-married with Germans and became converts to Christianity. In 1910 the 600,000 practising Jews who lived in the *Reich* constituted about one per cent of the population.

Belief in race struggle

During the late nineteenth century, anti-Semitism became increasingly racial rather than religious. As early as the 1850s French Count Joseph Arthur de Gobineau argued that different races were physically and psychologically different. History, in Gobineau's view, was essentially a racial struggle and the rise and fall of civilisations was racially determined. He claimed that all the high cultures in the world were the work of the **Aryan** race and that cultures declined when Aryans interbred with racially 'lower stock'.

Charles Darwin's *The Origin of Species*, published in 1859, provided further ammunition for the race cause. Although Darwin said nothing about race, his theory of natural selection as a means of evolution was adopted – and adapted – by many scholars. 'Social Darwinists' soon claimed that races and nations needed to be fit to survive and rule. A number of writers claimed that the Germans had been selected to dominate the earth. They therefore needed more land: *lebensraum*. This would have to be won from other inferior races, most likely the Slavs. Such visions of international politics as an arena of struggle between different races for supremacy were commonplace by 1914.

Aryan
The Germanic or Teutonic race.

Lebensraum
Living space.

Key terms

The growth of anti-Semitism

Many late nineteenth-century European writers, by no means all German, extolled the virtues of the Germanic race. Militant German nationalists, who believed that the Germans were indeed the master race, were invariably hostile to – and contemptuous of – other races, especially the Jews. Jews came to stand for all that the nationalists loathed: liberalism, socialism and pacifism. Pamphleteers, newspaper editors and politicians presented anti-Semitic views to the German public. So did artists and musicians (like Richard Wagner, the famous composer). Among the most prominent anti-Semitic writers was Wagner's son-in-law Houston Stewart Chamberlain. Son of a British admiral and a German mother, Chamberlain published his most influential work – *Foundations of the Nineteenth Century* – in 1900. Chamberlain argued that the Jews were a degenerate race, conspiring to attain world domination and threatening German greatness. His book became a bestseller and even drew praise from Wilhelm.

Economic factors may have encouraged anti-Semitism. Those groups hit by economic and social change (peasant farmers and skilled workers) were easily persuaded that Jewish financiers were to blame. Anti-Semitic prejudice was also strong in the higher reaches of society: the court, the civil service, the army and the universities. Thus, anti-Jewish feeling permeated broad sections of German society. In the late nineteenth century anti-Semitic politicians contested elections. Right-wing parties, which espoused anti-Semitism, gained a majority in the *Reichstag* in 1893.

However, the strength of political anti-Semitism in Germany should not be exaggerated. The success of the nationalist parties in 1893 had little to do with anti-Semitism. Indeed, no major German political party pre-1914 was dominated by anti-Semites and after 1900 the anti-Semitic parties were in steep decline, running out of voters and money. Respectable opinion in Germany remained opposed to anti-Semitism. In 1914 German Jews seemed in less danger than Jews in France or Russia.

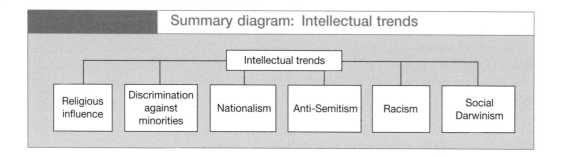

Summary diagram: Intellectual trends

4 | Domestic Politics

Caprivi's 'new course' 1890–4

Key question
How successful was Caprivi's 'new course'?

Key date
Bismarck resigned; Caprivi became Chancellor: March 1890

The new chancellor Leo Caprivi, a middle-aged soldier, had a good administrative record, but little political experience. He hoped to stand above parties and particular interests. Wilhelm had singled out Caprivi because he thought him an amenable character who would do what he was told. In fact, he soon displayed a will of his own. In his first speech to the Prussian *Landtag* he declared that he was ready to steer a 'new course' that involved a more consultative approach to government and a conciliatory attitude to previously hostile forces. He went out of his way in his first weeks as chancellor to make concessions to socialists, Poles and Centrists. For example, the anti-socialist laws were allowed to lapse and schools in Polish-populated Prussian areas were allowed to use the Polish language for instruction purposes.

Conciliation proved successful. Caprivi was thus able to rely on *Reichstag* support for government measures and in 1891 was able to push through a number of social measures:

- Sunday work was prohibited.
- The employment of children under 13 was forbidden.
- Women were forbidden to work more than 11 hours a week.
- Courts, with representatives from both sides of industry, were set up to arbitrate in industrial disputes.

Tariff reform

The most important single measure Caprivi put before the *Reichstag* was a bill to reform the 1879 tariff act (see pages 114–15). Prompted by short-term wheat shortages that had led to a rise in food prices, Caprivi negotiated a series of commercial treaties with Austria, Italy, Russia and a number of smaller states between 1891 and 1894. Germany agreed to reduce tariffs on agricultural goods in return for favourable rates for German manufactured goods.

The Agrarian League

Although most parties supported tariff reform, Conservatives opposed it. So did the Agrarian League, formed in 1893. The League soon had 300,000 members and became an effective and well-organised pressure group. An anti-Semitic, rabble-rousing movement, it won widespread support in eastern Prussia. It mounted a virulent anti-Caprivi propaganda campaign, denouncing him as a 'socialist' bent on ruining wheat producers. It agitated for subsidies, import controls and minimum prices to protect farmers.

The 1893 election

Caprivi angered the right further by reducing the period of military service from 3 to 2 years. He then alienated the left by introducing an army bill that increased the peacetime army strength by 84,000 men. When the army bill was defeated, Caprivi dissolved the *Reichstag*. In the 1893 election, the Conservatives and National Liberals improved their position and the new *Reichstag* passed the army bill.

Caprivi's fall

Wilhelm's enthusiasm for social reform barely survived Bismarck's fall. Conservative opposition to the 'new course' reinforced Wilhelm's growing doubts about Caprivi's political suitability. Worried by the SPD's success in 1893 (the party won 44 seats) and frightened by a series of anarchist outrages across Europe, Wilhelm pressed Caprivi to draw up new anti-socialist measures. Aware that the *Reichstag* would not tolerate a new anti-socialist law, Caprivi refused. Wilhelm and the Prussian Minister-President Count Eulenburg now devised a bizarre plan to change the constitution, increasing the Kaiser's power and reducing that of the *Reichstag*, and going on to crush socialism. Caprivi managed to talk Wilhelm out of such a course of action. However, having lost the Kaiser's confidence, Caprivi resigned in October 1894.

Prince Hohenlohe 1894–1900

Prince Chlodwig Hohenlohe-Schillingsfurst was a 75-year-old Bavarian aristocrat of mildly liberal views. Not the man to restrain Wilhelm, he was soon little more than a figurehead. The government was dominated by men who were more closely in tune with the direction of policy desired by the Kaiser.

In 1894–5 the governments in Germany and Prussia tried to take strong action against potential revolutionaries and subversives. In 1895 SPD offices in Berlin were ransacked and party leaders put on trial. Prussians suspected of sympathising with socialism lost their jobs. However, the *Reichstag* rejected all efforts to introduce an anti-socialist bill. By 1897 a state of deadlock existed between government and *Reichstag*, much as in the last years of Bismarck's rule (see pages 131–2). The government would not introduce legislation acceptable to the majority, and the majority refused to accept bills presented by the government. In conservative circles there was talk of the former chief of the General Staff, General Waldersee, staging a military coup and overthrowing the constitution. Nothing came of this.

The re-organisation of the government

In 1897 there were three new government appointees:

- Admiral Tirpitz became Navy Secretary
- Count Posadowsky-Wehner became Interior Minister
- Bernhard Bülow became Foreign Minister.

In addition, two long-serving figures began to assume even greater prominence:

- Friedrich Holstein, a senior official in the Foreign Office
- Johannes Miquel, Prussian Finance Minister.

The emergence of this new team coincided with a new policy: *Weltpolitik* (see page 161).

Chancellor Bülow 1900–9

Bülow exerted a strong influence as Foreign Minister before becoming Chancellor in 1900. A competent administrator, he kept the trust of Wilhelm and effectively handled the *Reichstag*. His main interest was foreign policy and he refrained from close contact with the various *Reichstag* parties, hoping not to become too involved in domestic issues.

Key question
What were the aims of Bülow?

Key date
Bülow appointed Chancellor: October 1900

Social reform

By 1900 it was clear that harsh measures to retard the growth of socialism had failed. Interior Minister Posadowsky resumed, in effect, the policy of the 'new course'. He hoped that by extending social welfare benefits the working class might be reconciled with the state. The new measures included:

- an extension of accident insurance (1900)
- a law making industrial courts compulsory in all large towns (1901)
- an extension of the prohibition on child labour (1903).

Tariffs

The renewal of Caprivi's commercial treaties was an issue of great controversy. While left-wing parties called for lower tariffs to reduce the price of bread, the Agrarian League demanded higher tariffs. Bülow worked successfully for a compromise. By a huge majority, the *Reichstag* restored tariffs to the pre-1892 level.

Chancellor Bernhard
von Bülow
(1849–1929),
with his distinctive
moustache.

When the treaties were renegotiated, Germany's partners
accepted the tariff increases, and its exports to these countries
were not greatly affected.

Popular opposition to higher tariffs helped the SPD to win
nearly a million extra votes and an additional 26 seats in 1903.
The Centre Party remained the largest party and continued to
hold the balance of power in the *Reichstag*.

Political problems

The mounting costs of maintaining the army, expanding the navy
and running the empire had resulted in a large budget deficit. In
1905 Bülow proposed a two-pronged attack on the deficit by
proposing an increase in **indirect taxes** and an inheritance tax.
The Centre Party and the SPD voted down the indirect taxes,
which would have hit the ordinary German hard. The
Conservatives and the Centre Party weakened the inheritance tax
so as to make it financially insignificant.

Meanwhile Bülow's government was criticised for its handling
of a revolt in the colony of South-West Africa in 1904–5. The
revolt was crushed but subsequent revelations of brutality,
corruption and incompetence in the administration of the colony
encouraged the Centre Party to ally with the SPD and others to

Indirect taxes
Taxes placed on the
sale of goods rather
than those collected
directly from the
taxpayer (like
income tax).

Key term

vote against the government's proposal to provide extra money for colonial administration.

In 1907 Bülow, determined to bring the unreliable Centre Party to heel, dissolved the *Reichstag*. In the ensuing **Hottentot election**, pro-government parties gained a good result by campaigning on a nationalistic, anti-socialist and anti-Catholic ticket. The Conservatives, Free Conservatives, National Liberals and Left Liberals came together in a coalition known as the 'Bülow Bloc'. Bülow removed ministers objectionable to the Bloc. Posadowsky, 'the red count', was dismissed and replaced by Bethmann-Hollweg, a conservative bureaucrat. The Bloc, however, was always fragile. Most Conservatives preferred to co-operate with the Centre Party than ally with the Left Liberals with whom they had little in common.

The *Daily Telegraph* Affair

A major crisis occurred in the autumn of 1908 following an article in Britain's *Daily Telegraph* newspaper in which Wilhelm expressed his wish for closer relations with Britain. *Reichstag* deputies questioned Wilhelm's right to make such important policy statements and there was suddenly clamour for constitutional changes to reduce the Kaiser's power. Bülow, who had cleared Wilhelm's article before publication, was in a difficult position. Caught between loyalty to Wilhelm and the demands of the *Reichstag*, he secured a promise from the Kaiser that constitutional formalities would in future be properly respected.

Wilhelm's declaration mollified the opposition and the crisis ended without leading to constitutional change. However, Wilhelm's trust in Bülow had been fatally weakened. He determined to be rid of him.

He did not have long to wait. As naval and colonial expenditure continued to mount, the budget deficit increased. To cover the deficit, Bülow introduced a finance bill increasing indirect taxation (opposed by the SPD) and the inheritance tax (opposed by Conservatives). The Centre, determined to have its revenge on Bülow for 1906, supported the Conservative stand. When the budget proposals were rejected in 1909 Wilhelm secured Bülow's resignation.

Chancellor Bethmann-Hollweg

Theobald Bethmann-Hollweg now became Chancellor. His position was weakened by the fact that he had little support in the *Reichstag*. His essential conservatism aligned him to the right-wing parties. Search for broader *Reichstag* support only alienated his natural supporters. The elections of 1912 further increased Bethmann's difficulties since there was a distinct shift to the left with the SPD and a united group of Left Liberals winning 110 and 42 seats, respectively. The new *Reichstag* was no longer dominated by the Conservative–Centre Party alliance. Thus, Bethmann found it very difficult to push government bills through the *Reichstag*.

Theobald von Bethmann-Hollweg 1856–1921.

Serious budgetary problems continued. In 1912–13 the problems of imperial finance and defence came to a head. Both the army and navy submitted major expenditure plans. Fortunately for Bethmann the inheritance tax was finally accepted. Ironically, the tax was still opposed by the Conservatives – who supported the military measures – and supported by Socialists – who disliked military spending but were keen to set the precedent of a property-based tax.

The new tax did not solve the fiscal crisis. By 1914 the *Reich* debt reached five billion marks. Given that indirect taxes were unpopular with the left and direct taxes unpopular with the right, there was no easy solution.

The Prussian Constitution

Although Conservatives were losing support in the *Reichstag*, in the Prussian *Landtag* their position was virtually unassailable. They controlled the upper chamber and usually had a

Key question
What were Germany's main domestic issues in the years 1909–14?

Key date
Appointment of Bethmann-Hollweg as Chancellor: July 1909

majority in the lower house, which was still elected by the outmoded three-class system (see page 42). In 1908 the SPD won 23 per cent of the vote in the Prussian elections but won only seven seats. The Conservatives, with 16 per cent of the vote, won 212 seats. This glaring injustice led to increasing demands for reform.

The SPD

Key date

SPD became the largest party in the *Reichstag*: January 1912

In 1912 the SPD became the largest party in the *Reichstag*. However, its deputies remained divided between orthodox Marxists, who maintained their revolutionary agenda, and moderates who believed that the party's role was to fight for the improvement of conditions by peaceful means within the framework of capitalism (see page 143).

Significantly, in 1913 SPD deputies supported the new taxes that Bethmann introduced to cover increased defence expenditure. While they might resent the injustice of the Prussian franchise, indirect taxes, which hit the poor proportionately more than the rich, and above all the high price of food, SPD deputies were aware that most SPD voters were patriotic and concerned about the perceived threat from Russia, France and Britain.

Nationalist Associations

After 1912 the various nationalist associations (for example, the Pan-German League and the Navy League) became more vocal in their criticism of the German government for what they regarded as its weakness at home and abroad. By 1914 many extreme German nationalists were anti-socialist, anti-Semitic and anti-parliamentarian. Many believed in Aryan superiority and the need for *lebensraum*. They dreamed of a new Bismarck who would be strong and ruthless, unafraid to pursue aggressive policies against enemies at home and abroad. 'The political maelstrom of radical ideologies out of which Nazism would eventually emerge was already swirling powerfully well before the First World War', says historian Richard Evans.

The Zabern Affair

Relations between Alsace-Lorraine and the rest of Germany were poor. There was considerable friction between the local populace and garrison troops. At Zabern, a small town in Alsace, a young officer made contemptuous remarks about Alsatian recruits that aroused indignation and led to several demonstrations. During one disturbance, in November 1913 the commanding officer ordered his men to clear the streets. In the ensuing mêlée 28 citizens were detained overnight in the barracks. This led to public and official protests: only civilian courts and the police could interfere with the liberty of citizens; the army was acting above the law.

Rather than punish the soldiers concerned, Wilhelm ordered them to be sent away on manoeuvres. The affair rumbled on. The minister of war and Bethmann rejected criticism of the army on the grounds that commanding officers were responsible only to the Kaiser and certainly not to the *Reichstag*. The political opposition was so intense that there was a massive vote of no confidence in Bethmann. This had little effect. While the Zabern affair underlined the power of the Kaiser, it also showed that he could not altogether ignore public opinion.

Conclusion

Key question
Was Germany set to become more democratic?

In 1914 Germany was still in many respects an authoritarian monarchy. Wilhelm's power to appoint the chancellor enabled him to set the general tenor of government, and he did so, particularly in the period from 1897 to 1908. This coincided with the political supremacy of Bülow, who recognised that his own position depended on catering to Wilhelm's personal whims.

However, the Kaiser's political power was within a constitutional framework. German governments could not ignore the *Reichstag* and had to patch up working majorities in order to pass legislation. The *Reichstag*, with its ever-increasing SPD presence, extended its right to debate government policy. Nor was Wilhelm able to take firm action against his critics. All Wilhelm's more repressive schemes were defeated in the *Reichstag*. While he might dream of using his army to strike against the SPD he did not dare do this in reality.

It may be that Germany was on the way to evolving into a thoroughly democratic state. Certainly many Germans desired the creation of a genuine parliamentary democracy in which the imperial government was responsible to the *Reichstag*. However, the forces of conservatism were strong. The middle classes, backbone of the empire, were solidly on the side of the Establishment. While most *Reichstag* deputies favoured constitutional change, the vast majority had great respect for the monarchy. In short, while there was political tension and frustration in Germany – as elsewhere in 1914 – revolution seemed less likely than elsewhere.

Summary diagram: Domestic politics 1890–1914

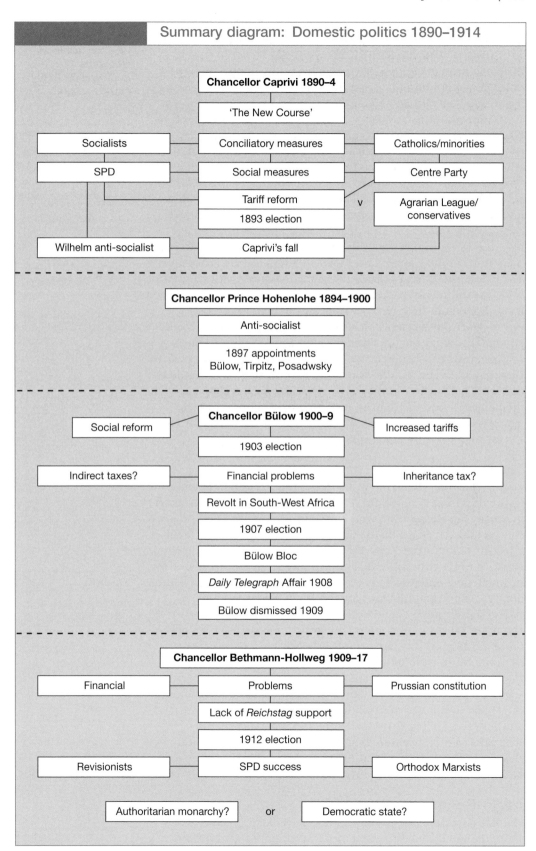

Chancellor Caprivi 1890–4

'The New Course'

| Socialists | Conciliatory measures | Catholics/minorities |

| SPD | Social measures | Centre Party |

| Tariff reform | v | Agrarian League/ conservatives |
1893 election

| Wilhelm anti-socialist | Caprivi's fall |

Chancellor Prince Hohenlohe 1894–1900

Anti-socialist

1897 appointments
Bülow, Tirpitz, Posadwsky

| Social reform | **Chancellor Bülow 1900–9** | Increased tariffs |
1903 election

| Indirect taxes? | Financial problems | Inheritance tax? |
Revolt in South-West Africa
1907 election
Bülow Bloc
Daily Telegraph Affair 1908
Bülow dismissed 1909

Chancellor Bethmann-Hollweg 1909–17

| Financial | Problems | Prussian constitution |
Lack of *Reichstag* support
1912 election

| Revisionists | SPD success | Orthodox Marxists |

| Authoritarian monarchy? | or | Democratic state? |

5 | Foreign Policy

The end of the Bismarckian system

Bismarck's resignation was a crucial event in German foreign policy. By upholding the Triple Alliance (see page 126), seeking friendship with Britain and signing the Reinsurance Treaty (see page 128) with Russia, Bismarck had ensured the isolation of France. After 1890 there was an important re-orientation of policy. Wilhelm was determined to be his own man in foreign affairs. However, his anti-Russian prejudice and pro-British sympathies did not amount to a coherent policy. Caprivi had little experience in foreign policy. Thus, Baron Holstein, permanent head of the political department in the foreign office, exerted considerable influence. A protégé of Bismarck, Holstein tried to copy the tortuous diplomacy of his mentor, with far less success.

In March 1890 Caprivi and Holstein allowed the Reinsurance Treaty to lapse. They believed it was incompatible with Germany's other commitments, especially to Austria. They feared that if the terms leaked out then Austria, Italy and Britain would be estranged from Germany. Moreover, Wilhelm hoped to ally with Britain, a country that was traditionally anti-Russian. In fairness to Germany's new leaders, cracks had already begun to appear in Bismarck's alliance system. Russo-German relations had cooled markedly before his dismissal. Nevertheless, Bismarck thought the failure to sign the Reinsurance Treaty an act of criminal stupidity, which pushed Russia towards friendship with France. Events were to prove him right.

The Dual Alliance

Germany assured Russia that it still desired friendly relations, but Caprivi's refusal to entertain further written agreements aroused misgivings in Russia. Annoyed by the growing friendship between Austria and Germany, Russia was positively alarmed by Wilhelm's attempts to ingratiate himself with Britain. Fear of isolation drove Russia into the arms of France. In August 1891 the two countries negotiated an **entente**. This was followed by a military convention in 1892, which laid the basis for the Dual Alliance in 1894.

The significance of the Dual Alliance was not immediately apparent. Wilhelm, worried by the growth of socialism, quickly regretted his anti-Russian attitude. He was soon on excellent personal terms with his cousin Tsar Nicholas II. In 1894 the *Reichstag* approved a commercial treaty with Russia, which did something to restore Russian confidence in Germany. For most of the 1890s Germany's position in Europe seemed secure. Austria and Italy were allies. Russia, absorbed in Asia, was friendly. Relations with France were better than they had been under Bismarck. However, the Dual Alliance meant that Germany now faced the prospect of a war on two fronts.

Anglo-German relations 1890–8

Germany's diplomatic position would have been greatly strengthened if it had reached an understanding with Britain.

Key question
Was the failure to renew the Reinsurance Treaty a major mistake?

Dual Alliance between France and Russia: 1894 — Key date

Entente A friendly agreement. — Key term

However, German advances to Britain in 1894 came to nothing. Indeed, in 1896 Anglo-German relations deteriorated following Wilhelm's congratulatory telegram to President Kruger for upholding the independence of the Transvaal after the **Jameson Raid**. In a muddled fashion, Wilhelm and his advisers hoped that by bringing pressure to bear on Britain they could draw it closer to the Triple Alliance. The Kruger telegram was an inept diplomatic manoeuvre. Condemned as a piece of unwarranted meddling, it simply aroused indignation in Britain.

Weltpolitik

> **Key question**
> How and why did *Weltpolitik* emerge as government policy?

Bismarck thought of Germany as a continental European power. While he had no objection to overseas colonies, he did not regard them as a priority and had no desire to alienate Britain. Bülow and Tirpitz, both of whom were appointed in 1897, had a different vision of Germany's future. This vision, supported by Wilhelm and large numbers of ordinary Germans, was *Weltpolitik*. The decision to pursue *Weltpolitik* in 1897 was a vital moment in German history.

> **Key term**
> **Jameson Raid**
> In December 1895 Dr Jameson, administrator for the British South African Company, led a force of 470 men into the Transvaal, hoping to spark a revolt which would overthrow President Kruger's Boer government. The raid was a total failure.

Structuralist historians (see pages 144–5) think that the ruling class embarked on *Weltpolitik* hoping to rally support around the Kaiser and divert attention away from the socialist threat at home. (In 1898 the SPD won 27 per cent of the vote in the national elections.) However, the view that *Weltpolitik* was simply a manoeuvre in domestic politics is too simplistic. There were powerful forces at work in Germany that contributed to the new policy:

- Industrialisation had created economic demands for the acquisition of raw materials and markets beyond Europe.
- Social Darwinist ideas stressed the struggle between nations and races. Some believed that Germany's survival as a leading nation necessitated a more active world policy.
- In the 1890s radical nationalists formed pressure groups like the Pan-German League and the Navy League. These popularised the message of *Weltpolitik*. They also exerted pressure on the government to pursue the policy to the full.

In reality, *Weltpolitik* was a deliberate attempt to make Germany into a world power on par with Britain. This meant expanding Germany's navy, creating a large colonial empire and supporting Germany's economic interests across the globe. Wilhelm declared that henceforward no major colonial issue must be decided without Germany having a say in it.

Anglo-German rivalry

> **Key question**
> Why was *Weltpolitik* seen as a threat to Britain?

Bülow proclaimed the new aims in his first speech to the *Reichstag*: 'We want to put no-one in the shade, but we too demand our place in the sun'. Tirpitz was given the task of building the navy (see below). The navy, in Tirpitz's view, was to be a direct challenge to Britain – the lever with which it would be forced to respect Germany. This was a serious miscalculation.

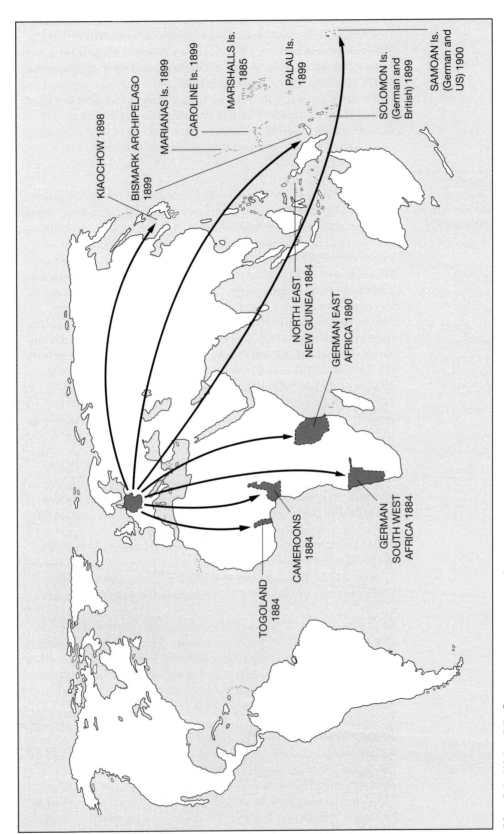

Map 6.1: *Weltpolitik*: German overseas expansion.

KIAOCHOW 1898

BISMARK ARCHIPELAGO 1899

MARIANAS Is. 1899

CAROLINE Is. 1899

MARSHALLS Is. 1885

PALAU Is. 1899

SOLOMON Is. (German and British) 1899

SAMOAN Is. (German and US) 1900

NORTH EAST NEW GUINEA 1884

GERMAN EAST AFRICA 1890

TOGOLAND 1884

CAMEROONS 1884

GERMAN SOUTH WEST AFRICA 1884

Key dates

First Navy Law: 1898

Second Navy Law: June 1900

Britain felt threatened, but was not prepared to be intimidated. Nor would Britain allow Germany to be its equal. Britain's navy and colonies were the basis of its political and commercial power. It seems not to have occurred to Wilhelm or Tirpitz that:

- Germany needed British support against the threat from Russia and France.
- Britain might look for support elsewhere.

Ironically, German policy set about antagonising Britain at a time when British opinion, at all levels, was pro-German.

Naval expansion

The decision to expand the German navy was of central importance to *Weltpolitik*. Wilhelm believed passionately that Germany's future lay on the high seas. He was dissatisfied with a fleet only seventh in size in the world when Germany's foreign trade was almost equal to Britain's. Tirpitz's appointment as Secretary of State for the Navy was crucial. Recognising the importance of gaining *Reichstag* support for naval expansion, he was instrumental in the creation in 1898 of the Navy League. Supported by the financial aid of key industrialists, like Krupp,

Admiral Alfred von Tirpitz (1849–1930), with his distinctive beard.

who had an obvious interest in the construction of a big navy, it soon dwarfed all the other nationalist groups, with a membership in excess of 300,000. The League drummed up popular support for naval expansion. This, in turn, put pressure on the *Reichstag*.

The 1898 Naval Bill, which proposed building 16 major ships, was finally carried by 212 votes to 139. The bill was opposed by some on the right and some on the left: the right thought the money would be best spent on the army: the left opposed any increase in military spending. In 1900 a second bill, which proposed building three battleships a year for the next 6 years, was passed by a larger majority than the first.

Germany and Britain 1898–1905

Bülow assumed that Britain would be unable to patch up its differences with France (over African territories) and with Russia (over central Asia). Between 1898 and 1901 Britain, concerned at its less than **splendid isolation**, made several approaches to Germany, hoping for some kind of agreement. Germany's reaction was negative. Bülow thought that Britain was seeking cheap insurance in the shape of a continental ally to save it from the effects of its rivalry with Russia. German interests, it was thought, were best served by remaining on good terms with Russia. The **Boer War** did not help matters. Most Germans sympathised with the Boers. Thus, instead of an alliance, there was a gradual distancing between Britain and Germany.

What German policy-makers had not envisaged was the possibility that Britain would allay its fears of isolation by signing an alliance with Japan (1902), a power eager to challenge the Russian colossus. Worse followed. In 1904 Britain signed an entente with France. The entente was not a firm alliance, but merely an understanding to settle colonial differences. Lord Lansdowne, who concluded the entente, conceived it as in no way anti-German. But this was not the way it was seen by vocal sections of British public opinion and the press.

In 1904 the **Russo-Japanese War** broke out. Germany's hopes that Britain would be dragged into war were soon dashed. Britain and Russia had no wish to fight each other. The war, which seriously weakened Russia, was not altogether bad news for Germany. Given that Russia (temporarily) was no threat, Germany adopted a more aggressive policy.

The First Moroccan crisis

Hoping to break the Anglo-French entente, Germany provoked a crisis in Morocco. Morocco was seen as being within the French sphere of influence. In March 1905 Wilhelm landed at Tangiers, and assured the Sultan of Morocco that Germany considered Morocco an independent nation, a state of affairs that he intended to support with all his might.

This was a deliberate challenge to France. Bülow hoped to humiliate France and reveal the flimsy nature of Britain's loyalty to the entente. He miscalculated. At the international conference at Algeciras in January 1906 Britain, France and Russia

Key question
How skilful was German diplomacy between 1897 and 1907?

Entente between Britain and France: 1904

Splendid isolation
For much of the late nineteenth century, Britain had not allied with any major power. Its great naval strength meant that it seemed to be in no danger of invasion.

Boer War
The conflict in South Africa (1899–1902) between Britain and the Boer republics of the Transvaal and the Orange Free State. Britain eventually triumphed.

Russo-Japanese War
This conflict, caused by the conflicting imperial ambitions of Japan and Russia in Asia, was fought in 1904–5. Japan won.

Key dates

First Moroccan crisis: 1905–6

Bosnian crisis: 1908–9

supported French influence in Morocco. So, too, did Italy, Germany's erstwhile ally. Germany, not France, found itself diplomatically isolated. The Anglo-French entente had stood firm; indeed, thanks to German pressure, had been strengthened. British leaders were now convinced that Germany represented a major threat to European stability and to the security of the British Empire. The Morocco crisis ended disastrously for Germany.

The Anglo-Russian entente

In 1907 Britain signed an entente with Russia. This was essentially a colonial agreement, settling differences over Tibet, Persia and Afghanistan: it was not directed at Germany. Nevertheless, the threat of the German navy and resentment at Germany's blustering diplomatic methods played a part. Moreover, the very fact of the agreement emphasised Germany's isolation.

The situation by 1907

From 1897 to 1907 *Weltpolitik* had achieved little. Germany had added only the Chinese port of Kiaochow (1897) and a few islands in the Pacific (1899) to its small empire. The diplomatic and strategic consequences of *Weltpolitik* were huge. Maladroit German diplomacy had resulted in Britain aligning itself with France and Russia. German newspapers complained of the ring closing round Germany. There was little substance in the 'encirclement' accusation: the **Triple Entente powers** were not banded together to destroy Germany. Nevertheless, Germany's strategic position was much weaker by 1907 than it had been in 1890.

Key term

Triple Entente powers
Britain, France and Russia.

Key question
Why did Anglo-German rapprochement fail?

The years from 1907 to 1911

The 1909 Bosnian crisis

The deterioration in Germany's international standing made it increasingly dependent on one loyal ally, Austria. In Bismarck's day, Germany had restrained Austria from adventurous policies in the Balkans. Under Bülow Germany began to underwrite the efforts of Austria to preserve its unstable empire. This was apparent in 1908–9.

In October 1908 Austria decided to annex the province of Bosnia-Herzegovina, which it had administered since 1878, even though it had remained nominally under Turkish rule. This move was opposed by Turkey and – more importantly – Serbia, which hoped to incorporate Bosnia in its own state. Russia supported Serbia, a fellow Slav state.

Germany, keen to improve relations with Turkey, did not altogether approve of Austria's move. Nevertheless, Bülow assured the Austrian Foreign Minister Aehrenthal that Germany would support whatever action Austria considered appropriate against Serbia. In January 1909, when Hotzendorf, chief of the Austrian General Staff, asked his German equivalent Helmuth Moltke (son of the great Moltke) what help Austria could expect if

Map 6.2: The Balkans 1908–13.

it attacked Serbia and Russia intervened, Moltke replied that Germany would mobilise. Aehrenthal seriously considered a war against Serbia. Only second thoughts in Vienna prevented German involvement in a major war over Bosnia.

Russia tried to get Austria to the conference table. Austria refused to attend unless the powers accepted the annexation. Germany supported this defiant stand, declaring bluntly in March 1909 that if Russia did not recognise the annexation it must take full responsibility for the subsequent course of events. Russia, not ready to risk war over Bosnia, gave way. The annexation was recognised by the Great Powers and the crisis ended. Germany's diplomatic victory was dearly bought. Russia, deeply resentful of its humiliation, drew closer to Britain and France.

Anglo-German naval rivalry

In 1906 Britain launched HMS *Dreadnought*, a vessel that rendered all existing ships obsolete. Tirpitz and Wilhelm grasped

Launch of the
Dreadnought: 1906

Key date

HMS *Dreadnought* leaving Portsmouth harbour in October 1906.

eagerly at the possibility of building on what seemed to be a position of equal terms with Britain. Two German naval laws in 1906 and 1908 threatened Britain's naval supremacy. In 1908 the British government, facing massive pressure from public opinion, agreed to build an extra eight 'Dreadnoughts'. Britain and Germany had thus become enmeshed in an expensive naval race, which worsened relations between the two countries.

Bethmann recognised that an agreement with Britain to limit naval construction would not only reduce his budget difficulties, but might also loosen Britain's ties to the Triple Entente. However, negotiations with Britain between 1909 and 1911 ended in failure. Wilhelm and Tirpitz refused to make any serious concessions and Britain was determined to preserve its naval supremacy.

The Second Moroccan crisis

Key date

Second Moroccan crisis: 1911

In 1911 France, in clear violation of the Algeciras agreement, looked set to establish a full protectorate over Morocco. Germany was prepared to accept this, but only in return for being given French territory elsewhere in Africa as compensation. France, conscious of the weakness of its position, started negotiations with Germany.

German Foreign Minister Kiderlen, hoping to secure substantial compensation, sent the gunboat *Panther* to the Moroccan port of Agadir, ostensibly to protect German nationals, but in reality to remind France that Germany must not be ignored. He increased the tension further by demanding the whole of the French Congo. Britain stood by France in the face of

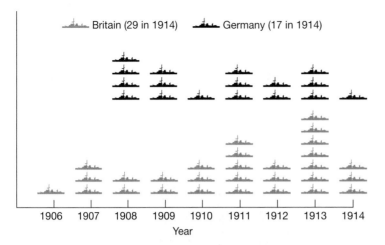

Britain (29 in 1914)   Germany (17 in 1914)

1906   1907   1908   1909   1910   1911   1912   1913   1914

Year

Figure 6.1: The relative numbers of 'Dreadnoughts' built by Germany and Britain 1906–14.

perceived German bullying. Lloyd George, Chancellor of the Exchequer, warned Germany that Britain was ready for war and the British fleet prepared for action. Germany now backed down, accepting a narrow strip of the French Congo as compensation for the French protectorate in Morocco. Kiderlen's blustering diplomacy had succeeded only in heightening tensions and confirming Entente suspicions of Germany.

The years from 1911 to 1914

The last 3 years of peace have been the focus of considerable historical analysis. German historian Fritz Fischer thought that the 'excitement and bitterness of nationalistic opinion over what was seen to be the humiliating outcome of the [Moroccan] crisis were profound and enduring'. He believed that after 1911 there existed a clear continuity of German aims and policies that culminated in war in 1914 – a war that was deliberately 'planned'. Fischer's main evidence is a War Council of German army and navy chiefs on 8 December 1912. At this meeting Moltke announced that Germany should go to war at the first suitable opportunity and Wilhelm called for increased armaments and talked of a 'racial struggle' with Russia.

Most historians are not convinced by this 'evidence'. In truth, the meeting was a typical piece of theatrical posing and blustering, suggesting a lack of direction at the top rather than a clear indication that Germany was actually planning to unleash a war in 1914. Chancellor Bethmann did not even attend the 8 December meeting.

German rearmament

In 1911–12 Bethmann, anxious to reduce naval expenditure, made another attempt to end the naval race with Britain. The negotiations soon stalled: each side felt the other asked too much and offered too little. The German naval bill of 1912, however, was more modest than Tirpitz had proposed. By 1912 the German army had become the main priority in the face of the perceived threat from France and Russia.

Key question
Was Germany planning a war after 1911?

Figure 6.2: The build-up of armies 1900–14.

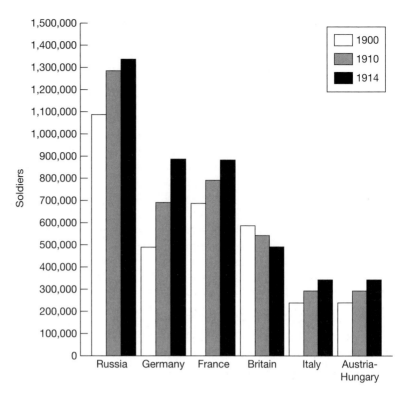

The Balkans 1912–13

In October 1912 the small Balkan states – Serbia, Greece, Bulgaria and Montenegro – attacked Turkey and easily defeated it. This was a severe blow to Austria: it was widely believed in Vienna that the Habsburg Empire could not survive the fall of the Ottomans. The dramatic expansion of Serbia, particularly the fear that it might obtain Albania and a foothold on the Adriatic Sea, aroused the gravest alarm. Hotzendorf advocated war to crush Serbia once and for all.

However, Berchtold, who succeeded Aehrenthal as foreign minister in 1912, opposed military action at this stage. Germany supported his cautious stance. The Great Powers met in London in 1913 to set the seal of approval on the territorial changes in the Balkans. Germany and Russia actually worked together, the former restraining the Austrians and the latter the Serbs.

However, German policy hardened when the victorious Balkan states fell out and went to war in the summer of 1913. Austria, alarmed by Serbian incursions into Albania, determined to force the Serbs out. Berchtold was assured by Wilhelm that Germany would stand by Austria. Faced with the prospect of war with Austria, and lacking Russian support, the Serbs pulled out of Albania.

The situation by 1914

In early 1914 Bethmann still saw hopeful signs in Germany's international position. He was encouraged by the extent of Anglo-German co-operation during the Balkan Wars and by the peaceful settlement of several colonial disputes.

However, tension continued to grow. In 1913 Germany increased its peacetime strength from 663,000 to 800,000. France and Russia followed suit, the latter launching a vast rearmament programme. Rearmament was accompanied in all countries by propaganda campaigns to persuade the ordinary citizen that the growing risk of war justified additional military spending. Most Germans believed they were surrounded by enemies. Russia's growing military power was a source of nightmare apprehensions. Many influential Germans saw war as an almost inevitable struggle for existence between nations and races. German right-wing groups favoured a war of expansion. Moreover, Germany's leaders were more inclined towards warlike solutions than the leaders of other countries. The German General Staff realised that 1914–15 represented the best time for war from the German standpoint. Thereafter Russia's rearmament programme would make war a more dangerous option.

July 1914

The assassination of Franz Ferdinand

The assassination of Austrian Archduke Franz Ferdinand, heir to the Habsburg throne, by Bosnian terrorists at Sarajevo on 28 June 1914 sparked the crisis that led to war. Austrian leaders, aware that the murders had been planned by a secret society that had links with the Serbian government, called for stern measures against Serbia. They believed the time had come to settle accounts with Serbia. Germany agreed. Wilhelm pledged full support for Austria, whatever the consequences, to the Austrian ambassador over lunch on 5 July. Bethmann confirmed Wilhelm's assurance on 6 July: 'Austria must judge what is to be done to clear up her relations with Serbia. But whatever Austria's decision, she could count with certainty upon it that Germany would stand behind her as an ally.'

Bethmann urged Austria to attack swiftly, hoping that it might destroy Serbia without the crisis developing into a general war. Even so, he recognised the very real danger of a general war breaking out over Serbia. While not necessarily wanting war, he was ready to risk it. He remarked to the Austrian ambassador: "If war must break out, better now than in 1 or 2 years' time, when the Entente will be stronger.'

Had Austria acted quickly, war between itself and Serbia might well have been localised. In early July, most European governments were horrified by the Sarajevo assassination. There was some sympathy for Austria, even in Russia. Unfortunately, Austrian reaction was not swift. When it finally came on 23 July, it was in the form of an ultimatum to Serbia. The terms of the ultimatum were so severe that Serbia, emboldened by promises of Russian support, refused to accept them, inserting reservations in the reply. When Austria received the reply on 25 July, it broke off diplomatic relations with Serbia.

Key question
Why did Germany go to war?

Key dates

Assassination of Franz Ferdinand: 28 June 1914

Germany gave Austria the 'blank cheque': 5–6 July 1914

Austrian ultimatum to Serbia: 23 July 1914

German declaration of war on Russia: 1 August 1914

German declaration of war on France: 3 August 1914

British declaration of war on Germany: 4 August 1914

Crisis

Europe's powers were now faced with a terrible crisis. Britain tried to mediate by calling for an international conference. Significantly Germany ignored such proposals and privately urged Austria to take military action. Until 27 July there was a reasonable degree of unanimity among German leaders. Thereafter doubts began to emerge amongst some key figures. Wilhelm returned from a Norwegian cruise on 28 July and decided that the Serbian reply was highly satisfactory and ought to be accepted by Austria, who must abandon plans for war and only occupy part of Serbia temporarily as a guarantee of good behaviour. The German foreign office was thoroughly alarmed by Wilhelm's change of heart. Bethmann simply passed the proposal to Vienna on 28 July without comment, taking care to suppress the fact that it emanated from the Kaiser. Bethmann's overriding concern was Russian mobilisation. If Russia mobilised first, all Germans would unite in (what would be perceived as) a defensive war against the threat of Tsarist aggression. Moreover, Britain might be persuaded to remain neutral.

Mobilisation and war

The Austrian declaration of war on Serbia on 28 July was followed by a Russian decision to order partial mobilisation. Moltke knew that once Russia began mobilising, Germany was committed to fight. This was the result of the Schlieffen Plan. Drawn up by Moltke's predecessor, it aimed to counteract the threat of a two-front war by launching a rapid all-out assault in the west in order to defeat France before turning east to face Russia. Thus, as soon as Russia began to mobilise Germany had to mobilise its own forces. On 30 July Bethmann stated 'that things are out of control and the stone has started to roll'. Military matters now took precedence over diplomatic considerations.

Bethmann informed Russia that unless partial mobilisation was cancelled, Germany would be obliged to order full mobilisation. Russia's partial mobilisation, aimed at bringing diplomatic pressure to bear on Austria, had not been intended as a prelude to war. But in view of Germany's warning Russia had either to suffer humiliation by cancelling that order or to order full mobilisation to defend itself against a possible German attack. On 31 July Russia opted for full mobilisation.

News of Russia's decision reached Berlin just before noon. The German war machine now swung into action. Full mobilisation was ordered and an ultimatum dispatched to Russia demanding cessation of all measures within 12 hours. When Russia refused to comply, Germany declared war on Russia on 1 August. War had to be declared on France as quickly as possible. After staging several clumsy border incidents, Germany declared war on France on 3 August. **German violation of Belgium's neutrality** brought Britain into the war on 4 August.

Key term

German violation of Belgium's neutrality
German troops, in order to get round French defences along the German frontier, invaded Belgium. Britain had pledged itself to protect Belgium's neutrality in 1839.

Summary diagram: Foreign policy

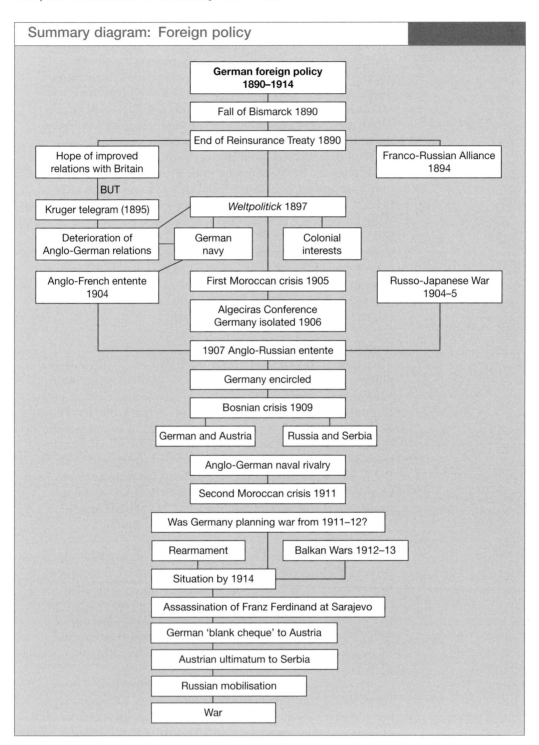

6 | Key Debate

To what extent was Germany responsible for the First World War?

In 1919 Germany was forced to accept responsibility for causing the First World War. By the mid-twentieth century, however, few historians believed that Germany alone was to blame for starting the war. Many, like A.J.P. Taylor, believed that the Great Powers accidentally stumbled into war in 1914. Others thought that the war was largely the result of the international system.

However, in 1961 Fritz Fischer (in his book *Germany's Aims in the First World War*) claimed that the German government bore the decisive share of responsibility for the start of the war because of its clear desire to achieve a German hegemony over Europe. In 1969 Fischer published *War of Illusions*, in which he suggested German leaders deliberately planned a war of expansion from 1911. Fischer suggested that the reasons for this aggressive expansionism were to be found less in Germany's international position than in the social, economic and political situation at home. A successful war, the government hoped, 'would resolve the growing social tensions' and consolidate the position of the ruling classes.

Fischer's views generated huge controversy and continue to divide historians. Fischer's critics claim:

- There is little evidence to support the view that German leaders were actively planning an offensive war policy from 1911 onwards.
- The élites did not pursue war as a means of deflecting political opposition and thereby preserving their own threatened position. There was no major domestic crisis in Germany in 1913–14.

It seems fair to say that Germany was by no means the only country to blame for the First World War. Other powers contributed to the general deterioration in the international situation and committed major errors in July 1914. Nevertheless, German leaders must shoulder the major responsibility both for the worsening international atmosphere in the years before 1914 and for the escalation of the July 1914 crisis.

- *Weltpolitik* and the ham-fisted diplomacy that accompanied it had contributed to a marked increase in international tension and to a dangerous deterioration in Germany's strategic position by 1907.
- After 1907 German foreign policy was typified by bluster and brinkmanship.
- From early July 1914, Bethmann adopted a strategy of calculated risk in the hope of winning a diplomatic victory that would weaken the Entente. To achieve this end the July crisis was deliberately escalated and attempts at constructive

mediation were torpedoed. The calculated risk was a badly miscalculated risk – another failed exercise in brinkmanship.

- When Russia mobilised in 1914 German leaders had little option, given the Schlieffen Plan, but to accept the challenge. They did so willingly. Many accepted the nationalist rhetoric about an inevitable showdown between Slavs and Germans and the need for *lebensraum*.

Thus, German leaders, especially Bethmann and Wilhelm, failed to do what they might have done to prevent war. This was because they were convinced that war was probably inevitable, and that it was in Germany's interest to wage it at a time, and on terms, most favourable to itself. In truth, it was Germany's ill-considered actions that made war inevitable.

Study Guide: AS Questions

In the style of AQA

(a) Explain why the traditional élites had such an impact on German politics in the years 1890–1914. (12 marks)

(b) How important was the position and authority of Kaiser Wilhelm II in shaping German politics in the years 1890–1914? (24 marks)

Exam tips

The cross-references are intended to take you straight to the material that will help you to answer the questions.

(a) You will need to provide a range of factors and should also try to show how these interlink. Consider the following ideas and before you begin writing, try to decide which you will argue to be the most important and what overall conclusions you will draw.

The élites were influential for a number of reasons:

- The Prussian constitution meant that they dominated Prussia (page 144).
- The power of industrialists like Krupp was considerable. Some industrialists (not least Krupp) pressed for an expanded navy and for German overseas colonies (page 161).
- They had influence over Wilhelm II, who usually agreed with their conservative views.
- They had considerable influence within the army – and the army had considerable influence within Germany (page 144).
- Influential pressure groups (for example, the Navy League) were given huge financial support by industrialists, etc. (page 143).
- The élites generally controlled the *Bundesrat* (page 141).
- The *Reichstag* had limited influence (page 142).

Note:
- You might argue that the Kaiser's personal support was crucial in ensuring the élites retained their power (page 140).
- You might well disagree with the question's assumption and argue that the élites were losing power and that their influence was not decisive (page 145).

(b) Your answer should examine the Kaiser's theoretical position as provided by the constitution (pages 102–3), and his practical position – the need to work through a chancellor and through ministers, who in turn had to have (some) authority within the *Reichstag*. This posed some limitations on his actions (page 158). The extent to which Wilhelm used his authority may be discussed with relation to the following:

- His interference in government, especially his choice of chancellors (page 140).

- His influence over the direction of policy (for example, *Weltpolitik*, page 153).
- His intervention in politics (for example, the *Daily Telegraph* affair, page 155).
- His attitude to the army (for example, the Zabern incident, page 157).

You might argue that Wilhelm was only a 'shadow Emperor' (Wehler's view) rather than being decisive in shaping German policy. However, you might also argue that he was decisive in shaping Germany policy. You must decide!

7 War and Revolution 1914–19

POINTS TO CONSIDER

The outbreak of war in 1914 was greeted with enthusiasm in Germany. Virtually everyone thought the war would be short and victorious. However, the conflict degenerated into a war of attrition on a scale without precedent. Millions of men were killed or badly wounded. In 1918, in the wake of military defeat, Wilhelm II abdicated and the Second Empire gave way to the Weimar Republic. Why did Germany fail to achieve victory? In what way did the war affect the country? How revolutionary were the events in 1918–19? These questions will be examined by looking at the following themes:

- Germany at war 1914–16
- Germany defeated 1917–18
- The German Revolution 1918–19
- The establishment of the Weimar Republic

Key dates

1914	August	German troops invaded Belgium
	September	Battle of the Marne
1915	February	Unrestricted submarine warfare introduced by Germany
1916	February– August	Battle of Verdun
	July– November	Battle of the Somme
	August	Establishment of 'silent dictatorship' under Hindenburg and Ludendorff
1917	February	Unrestricted submarine warfare re-introduced
	April	USA entered the war
1918	March	Treaty of Brest-Litovsk
	March–July	German offensive on the Western Front
	July– November	Allied counter-offensive
	October	Prince Max of Baden appointed Chancellor
		Introduction of constitutional reforms

	October– November	Mutiny of German sailors
	November 9	Abdication of Wilhelm II: declaration of republic
	November 11	Armistice between Allies and Germany
1919	January	Spartacist revolt
	January 19	Election of National Assembly
	June 28	Treaty of Versailles
	July 31	Weimar constitution adopted

1 | Germany at War 1914–16

In 1914 political differences in Germany were submerged in the
wave of patriotic fervour. All the parties, including the SPD,
promised their support for the war. SPD leaders, who tended
towards **pacifism**, could not ignore the fact that most of their
supporters wanted to defend the Fatherland against perceived
Allied aggression. On 4 August 1914 Wilhelm, addressing the
Reichstag, insisted that Germany had done all it could to avoid war
and now drew its sword with a clear conscience. 'I know no parties
any more, only Germans', he declared. All the party leaders,
including the SPD, agreed to a political truce for the duration of
the war. The *Reichstag* unanimously passed **war credits** and then
adjourned, leaving the conduct of the war to the government.

The failure of the Schlieffen Plan

Germany's military leaders had long recognised the danger of
fighting a two-front war. The Schlieffen Plan had been devised as
a way to counter the threat (see Map 7.2). Although attractive in
theory, the final draft of the plan was flawed in several ways:

- The invasion of Belgium brought Britain into the war.
- The plan assumed (incorrectly) that it would take Russia many
  weeks to mobilise its forces. As the bulk of its army moved west,
  Germany was largely unprotected from Russian attack.

Nevertheless, the Schlieffen Plan came close to success. In August
1914 French troops, hoping to recover Alsace-Lorraine, were
mown down by German machine guns and artillery in the Battle
of the Frontiers. Meanwhile 1.5 million German troops pushed
through Belgium.

However, not everything went well for the Germans:

- The Belgians and the 160,000-strong British Expeditionary
  Force (BEF) slowed down the German advance.
- The First Army under Kluck lost contact with the Second Army
  and a gap appeared between them. Instead of moving around
  Paris to the west, Kluck veered south-east to regain contact.
  Meanwhile French troops from Lorraine were rushed to defend
  Paris.

Key question
Why did Germany not
win the war in 1914?

Key terms

Pacifism
Opposition to war.

War credits
Financial bills,
enabling the war to
be funded.

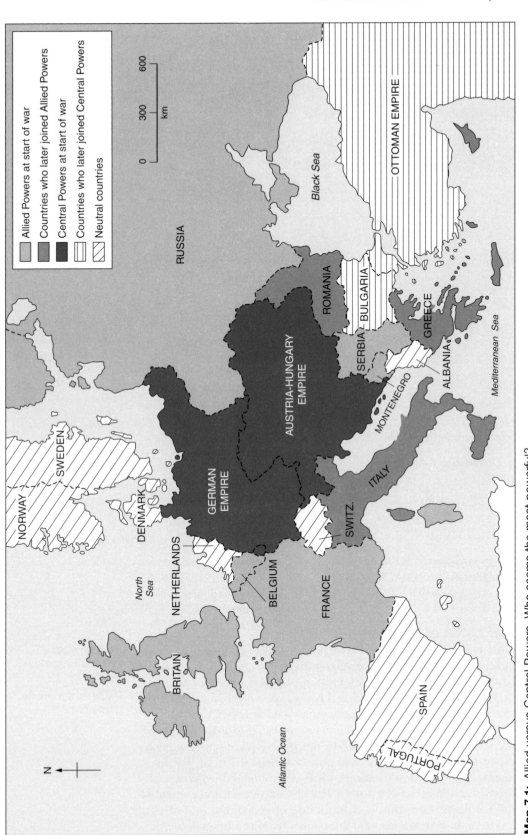

Map 7.1: Allied versus Central Powers. Who seems the most powerful?

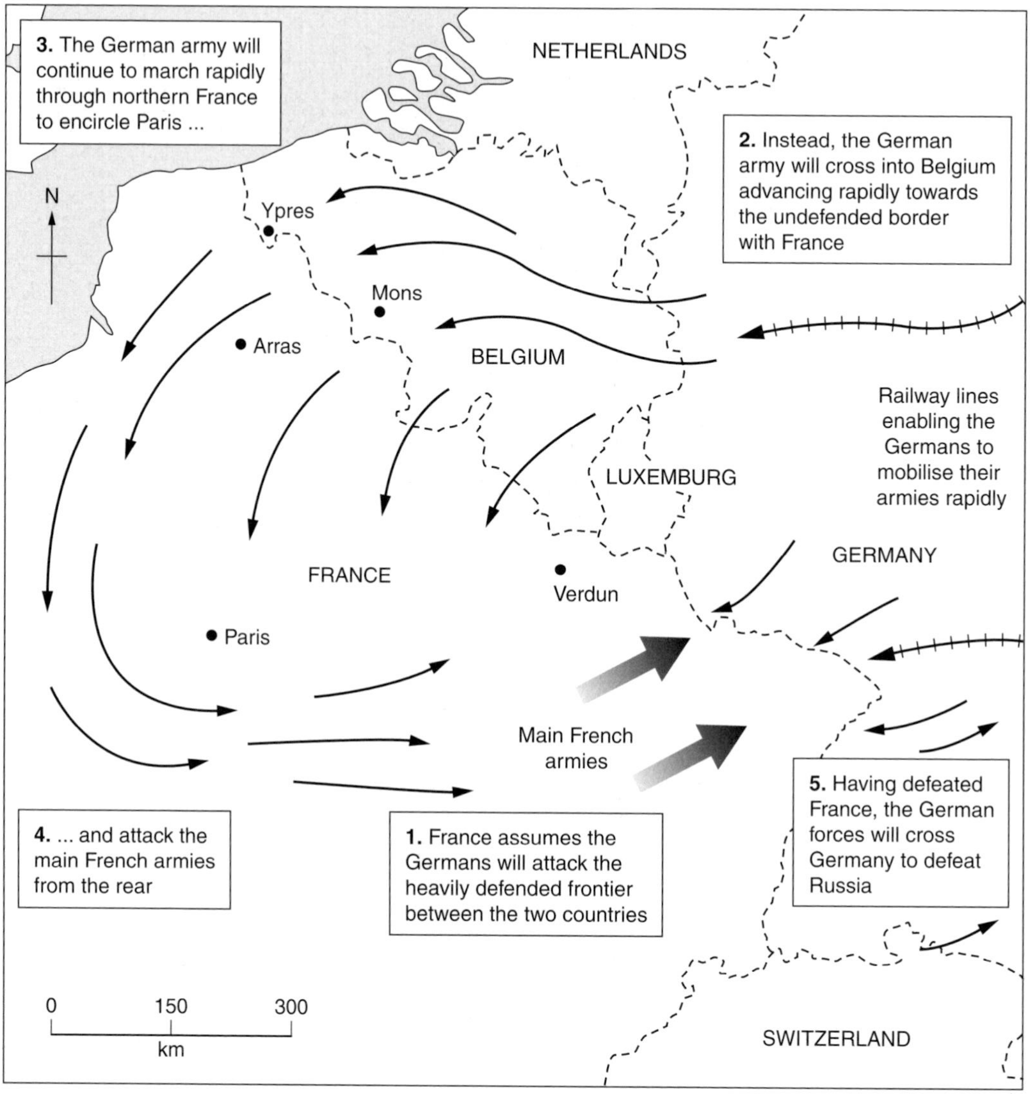

3. The German army will continue to march rapidly through northern France to encircle Paris ...

NETHERLANDS

2. Instead, the German army will cross into Belgium advancing rapidly towards the undefended border with France

N

Ypres

Mons

Arras

BELGIUM

Railway lines enabling the Germans to mobilise their armies rapidly

LUXEMBURG

GERMANY

FRANCE

Verdun

Paris

Main French armies

5. Having defeated France, the German forces will cross Germany to defeat Russia

4. ... and attack the main French armies from the rear

1. France assumes the Germans will attack the heavily defended frontier between the two countries

```
0        150       300
|         |          |
        km
```

SWITZERLAND

Map 7.2: The Schlieffen Plan.

The battle of the Marne

On 5 September, the French struck at Kluck's exposed flank. The fighting, which involved over two million men, is known as the battle of the Marne. The German Supreme Commander Moltke finally lost his nerve and ordered his troops to retreat to the Aisne river. Although the French had won a vital battle, they were unable to exploit it. Erich Falkenhayn replaced Moltke as chief of the German General Staff. Both sides now tried to outflank each other in a race for the Channel ports – crucial if Britain was to maintain easy communication with France. Dogged resistance at the first battle of Ypres ensured that the Allies retained control of the key ports. After this, both sides dug in and by the end of 1914 a system of trenches ran 600 kilometres from the English Channel to Switzerland.

German troops invaded Belgium: August 1914

Battle of the Marne: September 1914

Key dates

German troops 'digging in' in 1914.

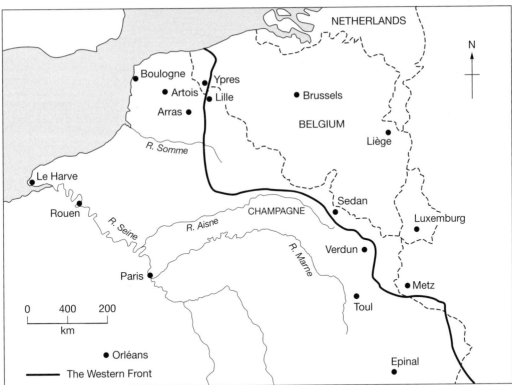

Map 7.3: The Western Front: December 1914.

The Eastern Front in 1914

In late August Russian forces invaded East Prussia. Wilhelm, deeply disturbed by the invasion, persuaded Moltke to send two divisions from France to the east. This was a mistake: the move weakened the armies in the west at a crucial moment, and the troops arrived too late to have any influence on the outcome in East Prussia.

German forces in the east, commanded by the aged General Paul Hindenburg and his Chief of Staff Erich Ludendorff, were able to deal with the Russian threat. At the end of August one Russian army was defeated at Tannenburg and a few days later the other army was beaten at the Masurian Lakes. East Prussia was now cleared of Russian troops. These victories made Hindenburg and Ludendorff popular heroes.

Table 7.1: Material resources in 1913

	Germany	Austria-Hungary	Central Powers	France	Russia	Britain	Entente	USA	Entente and USA
Population (in millions)	66.9	52.1	119.0	39.7	175.1	44.4	259.2	97.3	356.5
Iron and steel production (millions of tonnes)	17.6	2.6	20.2	4.6	4.8	7.7	17.1	31.8	48.9
Per cent of world manufacturing output	14.8	4.4	19.2	6.1	8.2	13.6	27.9	32.0	59.9

Source: Paul Kennedy, *Rise and Fall of the Great Powers: Economic Change and Military Conflict from 1500 to 2000* (New York, 1987).

Equal strength

Military strength:

- The Allies had more men.
- The Russian army was the largest in Europe.
- Britain possessed the world's strongest navy.

However:

- Germany had Europe's finest army.
- Germany had the world's second largest navy.
- The Central Powers had the advantage of interior lines of communication. Using their railway system, they could move men from one front to another.
- Although the Allies had more men, Russian forces were poorly equipped.

Economic strength:

- The British fleet was able to blockade Germany.
- The Allies were able to acquire resources world-wide. German overseas possessions, with the exception of East Africa, were quickly gobbled up.

However:

- Germany was Europe's strongest industrial power. By 1914 Germany produced two-thirds of continental Europe's steel and half of its coal.
- As a result of the German advance in 1914, France lost its main industrial area.

Key question
Why did the war last so long?

Map 7.4: The war in eastern Europe.

The nature of the war

The war on land

By the end of 1914 it was clear that the increased range, volume and accuracy of fire-power provided by the magazine rifle, the machine gun and heavy artillery made defence stronger than ever before. On all fronts, but especially on the Western Front, both sides dug in. The trench systems became more elaborate as the war progressed. In general, the Germans adapted better to trench warfare. They made better use of barbed wire, developed better machine guns, and built huge bunkers deep enough to withstand the heaviest artillery pounding.

The war at sea

Given that Britain and Germany had spent millions constructing powerful navies, a great naval battle seemed inevitable in 1914. It did not happen. The Germans were unwilling to risk their High Seas fleet against the (larger) British Grand Fleet. Britain, therefore, dominated the seas, imposing a tight blockade on German ports.

The U-boat

The main German naval threat came from the U-boat. This had not been envisaged before 1914. (Germany had only 30 U-boats in 1914.) German U-boats concentrated on sinking merchant ships, hoping to starve Britain into surrender. In February 1915 Germany declared the waters around Britain a war zone and announced that all shipping would be sunk without warning.

Key date: Unrestricted submarine warfare introduced by Germany: February 1915

While the U-boats inflicted serious damage on Allied shipping, they also sank neutral ships. The USA, Britain's greatest trading partner, protested. The sinking of the liner *Lusitania* in May 1915, resulting in the loss of over 1100 lives (including 128 Americans), led President Woodrow Wilson to issue an ultimatum to Germany. Rather than risk war with the USA, Bethmann agreed to abandon unrestricted submarine warfare. Tirpitz resigned in protest. However, Germany continued building more U-boats so that, if needs be, it could conduct a more deadly campaign in the future.

The domestic impact of the war

Key question: What impact did the war have on Germany?

Despite the failure to secure a quick victory and the onset of military stalemate, dissident views were few during the first half of the war. Lulled into a false sense of security by official propaganda, most Germans remained confident of eventual victory. Until mid-1916 Bethmann faced little opposition from the public or the *Reichstag*. He did his best to keep the SPD loyal, fearing social and political chaos if he failed to do so. This meant keeping secret his expansionist war aims: he knew that the SPD opposed 'wars of conquest'.

Military rule

As the war progressed Germany's military leaders were able to interfere in political and economic affairs, with only a limited degree of accountability. This occurred for several reasons:

- Army leaders justified intervention on the grounds of military necessity.
- Wilhelm II exerted little control. His self-confidence seemed to desert him with the onset of war. Despite being supreme warlord he was kept in the dark about military developments.

Mobilisation

The German government tried to ensure that all its citizens contributed to the war effort:

- Thirteen million men in total were called up to serve in the German army – nearly 20 per cent of Germany's 1914 population.
- Armies demanded men, but so did industry and agriculture. Substitute workers, particularly young women, helped industries to cope with the labour shortage.

The economic front

The German government, faced with the consequences of the British blockade, tried to organise its economic production. Although economically strong, Germany was far from self-sufficient. It lacked cotton, rubber, nitrates, petroleum, copper, nickel and tin. It was also dependent on imported fertilisers, fats and oils – all essential if Germany's population was to be adequately fed. As early as August 1914 Germany established a War Raw Materials Department. This soon exercised vast power – directing labour, controlling the railways, introducing rationing and price controls, and allocating resources to various industries competing for scarce raw materials. Scientists tried to produce substitute materials for goods of which Germany was short.

In the short term the measures taken to regulate Germany's war economy were reasonably successful. However, two crucial economic weaknesses continued to erode Germany's capacity to fight in the long term:

Key term

Inflation
An excessive increase in money supply that results in a decline in the purchasing power of money.

- Germany was running a huge financial deficit pre-1914 and once war started it soared. Bethmann's government, rather than raise taxes, simply printed money. This fuelled **inflation**.
- The blockade, a series of poor harvests, problems of transportation, a lack of chemicals for fertilisers and mass conscription led to a serious decline in grain production. In January 1915 bread rationing started, to be followed by the rationing of virtually every foodstuff.

Stalemate: 1915

For the most part, the Germans remained on the defensive on the Western Front. France and Britain launched a series of unsuccessful assaults.

In 1915 Germany and Austria launched a major offensive in the east. Breaking through the Russian lines, they forced the Russians into headlong retreat. By September German forces occupied Poland, Lithuania and Latvia. German success in the east ensured that the reputations of Hindenburg and Ludendorff remained sky-high.

The stalemate continues: 1916

Verdun

Falkenhayn was well aware that the growing power of the Allies would tip the scales against Germany. Believing that the war could only be won in the west, he decided to attack Verdun, the pivotal point in the French defence system. Gambling on French determination to defend the place at any cost, Falkenhayn, hoped to suck French forces into Verdun, bleed the French army 'white' and break France's will to resist. The German attack was launched in February: 1400 guns fired over 100,000 shells an hour on French positions. France rose to the bait, pouring forces into Verdun. German artillery wreaked terrible damage: some 315,000 French soldiers died in 5 months. However, more and more German troops were sucked into the fighting and they too suffered heavy casualties – 281,000 men.

The Somme

In an effort to help the French at Verdun, Britain launched a great assault on the River Somme. On the first day of the battle (1 July) Britain had 60,000 casualties. The fighting continued for another 5 months. Hundreds of thousands of men died on both sides. Allied forces advanced a maximum of 10 kilometres.

The Brusilov offensive

In June 1916 Russian commander Brusilov launched a major offensive. His forces broke through the Austrian lines and made great advances. However, Russian attacks against the Germans were less successful. Romania joined the war on the Allied side but was swiftly defeated and forced to surrender.

Key question
Why was 1916 a terrible year for the Central Powers and the Allies?

Key dates

Battle of Verdun: February–August 1916

Battle of the Somme: July–November 1916

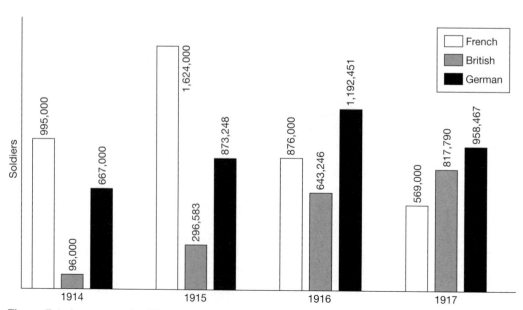

Figure 7.1: Losses on the Western Front 1914–17.

The battle of Jutland

In 1916 the German High Fleet ventured out of port and met the British Grand Fleet in the battle of Jutland. Some 250 ships were involved. Although the German fleet sank more British ships (14 to 11) and killed more British sailors (6000 to 2500), it retreated back to port where it stayed until 1918.

Hindenburg and Ludendorff

Key date

Establishment of 'silent dictatorship' under Hindenburg and Ludendorff: August 1916

Bethmann, keen to shore up his own position by winning popular support, decided to ditch Falkenhayn. On 29 August 1916 Hindenburg and Ludendorff were appointed Chief of the General Staff and Quartermaster-General, respectively, and given joint responsibility for the conduct of military operations. Far from strengthening his position, Bethmann soon found that his and Wilhelm's authority had been decisively weakened, since neither of them enjoyed the popular backing of Hindenburg and Ludendorff. By the simple expedient of threatening resignation, the two generals were able to exert a powerful influence over events – political, economic and military.

The Auxiliary Service Act

Hindenburg and Ludendorff tried to mobilise German resources more thoroughly than before:

Wilhelm (centre) studying maps alongside Hindenburg (left) and Ludendorff (right).

- Ludendorff ordered a systematic economic exploitation of the areas of France, Belgium and east-central Europe occupied by German troops.
- In December 1916 the Auxiliary Service Act enabled the government to control the labour of all males between 17 and 60. A Supreme War Office was set up and given wide powers over industry and labour.

The measures did not prevent serious shortages of coal and transport over the winter of 1916–17. Nevertheless there was a substantial recovery in iron and steel output and a huge increase in munitions production.

Summary diagram: Germany at war 1914–16

	The Western Front	The Home Front	The Naval War	The Eastern Front
1914	Schlieffen Plan Battle of the Marne Stalemate	German unity War Raw Materials Department Economic mobilisation		Battle of Tannenburg Battle of Masurian Lakes
1915		Effect of blockade Financial deficit Inflation	Unrestricted submarine warfare *Lusitania* US ultimatum Germany backed down	German success: occupation of Poland, Latvia and Lithuania
1916	Verdun The Somme	 Hindenburg and Ludendorff become 'the silent dictators' The Auxiliary Services Act	*Sussex* sunk US ultimatum Germany backed down Battle of Jutland	 Brusilov offensive

Key question
Why were events in
Russia in 1917–18
important for
Germany?

2 | Germany Defeated 1917–18

Table 7.2: Material and human resources 1917

	Central Powers	*Allied Powers*
Actives and reserves	10,610,000	17,312,000
Field artillery	14,730	19,465
Heavy artillery	9,130	11,476
Machine guns	20,042	67,276
Airplanes	1,500	3,163

Source: Fritz Klein *et al., Deutschland im Ersten Weltkrieg* (Berlin, 1968–9).

Revolution in Russia

Inflation, food shortages and high casualties led to revolution in Russia in March 1917, forcing Tsar Nicholas II to abdicate. The liberal politicians who led the new provisional government proved no more capable than the Tsar in terms of waging war and Russia quickly disintegrated into anarchy. The chief beneficiary of this situation was the only political group in Russia that had consistently opposed the war: the Bolshevik Party, an extreme Marxist group, led by Lenin. Hindenburg and Ludendorff, while hating Lenin's Marxist ideals, arranged for him to travel back to Russia from Switzerland across Germany. He lived up to German expectations, overthrowing the provisional government in November and taking Russia out of the war.

Key question
Why did the USA join
the war?

The USA joins the war

Key dates

Unrestricted
submarine warfare
re-introduced:
February 1917

USA entered the war:
April 1917

At the start of 1917 Hindenburg and Ludendorff, unaware that Russia was on the point of revolution, believed that Germany was losing the war. It seemed that German civilians were being slowly starved into surrender while German armies were worn down by attrition. Germany's military leaders decided that the U-boat was the last hope of victory. Aware that the re-introduction of unrestricted submarine warfare might well bring the USA into the war, they gambled that the U-boats would starve Britain into surrender before significant US military aid reached Europe.

On 1 February 1917, therefore, Germany commenced unrestricted U-boat warfare. It would again sink without warning all ships in Allied waters. President Wilson immediately severed diplomatic relations with Germany. US politicians and newspapers urged a declaration of war. Wilson, still anxious to avoid war, hesitated. Then, in March a telegram from the German Foreign Secretary Zimmermann to the German minister in Mexico was intercepted by British intelligence and published in the USA. Hoping to persuade Mexico to ally with Germany against the USA, Zimmermann promised Mexico the US states of Texas, New Mexico and Arizona. The telegram caused a wave of anti-German sentiment in the USA. The March Revolution in Russia removed a further obstacle to US entry into the war: the war now did seem like a struggle between autocracy and democracy. On 2 April, Wilson asked Congress to declare war on Germany. On 6 April Congress obliged.

The USA entered the war as an 'associated power', not as an ally of Britain and France. This separate status in part reflected Wilson's determination to distance the USA from what he saw as the selfish ambitions of the European powers. In Wilson's view the war was a war of principle – a crusade for democracy and freedom – not a sordid struggle for land and colonies. Despite this difference of emphasis, US entry into the war gave the Allies a huge morale boost. The resources of the world's greatest economic power would now be mobilised in the interests of the Allies. However, it would take many months before the USA was able to mobilise its forces. This gave the Central Powers some hope of victory.

Allied problems in 1917

The war on the Western Front went disastrously for the Allies:

- In April–May, a large part of the French army mutinied. Order was restored but the French army now adopted a defensive policy.
- In July British forces launched the battle of Passchendaele. In a 4-month offensive, British casualties numbered over 500,000.
- Russia no longer posed a serious military threat. Germany was thus able to transfer thousands of men to the west.
- In October German and Austrian forces defeated the Italians at Caporetto, forcing the Italians into a headlong retreat.
- The U-boat gamble came close to success. In April one out of four ships leaving British ports was sunk. Britain was threatened with starvation.

Central Power problems in late 1917

- Greece joined the Allies.
- The Turks faced a serious Arab revolt.
- At sea, Britain adopted the convoy system. Fewer ships were sunk.

German civilian morale

On the domestic front the impact of war slowly, but remorselessly affected the lives of ordinary Germans, weakening civilian morale. Cold weather and a poor potato crop led to a disastrous food and fuel crisis during the winter of 1917–18. Severe malnutrition and infectious diseases made life, for most, truly miserable. Many workers resented being forced to work even longer hours as a result of the Auxiliary Service Law. The result was that social discontent grew markedly. Considerable anger was harboured against big industrialists who were making vast profits from the war. In 1917 the 'left' organised an increasing number of strikes. The 'right' blamed Jews and socialists for all Germany's problems.

Key question
Why were Germans divided on the issue of making peace?

Table 7.3: Percentage indices of real wages 1913–18

Year	Railwaymen	Printers	Miners	Civil servants
1913	100.0	100.0	100.0	100.0
1914	97.2	97.2	93.3	97.2
1915	79.7	77.3	81.3	77.3
1916	69.2	60.6	74.4	58.9
1917	63.9	49.4	62.7	48.6
1918	83.9	54.1	63.7	55.0

Table 7.4: Strikes and lockouts 1915–19

Year	No. of strikes	No. of workers (millions)	Working days lost (millions)
1915	141	0.015	0.04
1917	562	0.668	1.86
1919	3719	2.132	33.08

The July 1917 crisis

As popular disillusionment with the conduct of the war increased, so did dissent in the *Reichstag*. Socialists, with National Liberal support, succeeded in establishing a *Reichstag* committee to consider constitutional reform. Bethmann, hoping to maintain unity, persuaded Wilhelm to promise reform of the Prussian franchise system, to the consternation of conservatives.

By 1917 it was impossible to overlook the widening gulf between those who sought a 'peace without victory' and those who believed that only a 'victorious peace' would legitimate the sacrifices already made. In June 1917 left-wing parties made it clear that they would vote against war credits if Bethmann did not support 'peace without victory'. He refused, thus losing the support of the *Reichstag* majority, which he had enjoyed since 1914.

Ludendorff refused to work any longer with a man who supported political change and who had lost control of the *Reichstag*. To spare Wilhelm embarrassment, Bethmann resigned on 14 July. Bethmann's resignation was not a victory for the *Reichstag*. *Reichstag* deputies did not appoint his successor or use the crisis to force negotiations for peace. Most felt that it was unpatriotic to divide the nation. The July crisis simply gave the Supreme Command an opportunity to assert its superiority. George Michaelis, an insignificant Prussian administrator who had impressed Ludendorff during a brief interview, became the new chancellor. He had no intention of sharing power with the *Reichstag*.

On 19 July the *Reichstag* passed a peace resolution by 212 votes to 126. 'The *Reichstag* strives for a peace of understanding and permanent reconciliation of peoples. Forced territorial acquisition and political, economic and financial oppressions are irreconcilable with such a peace.' The resolution, supported by SPD, Radical and Centre Party deputies, had no influence on German policy. Germany's military leaders remained committed to winning a victorious peace.

Michaelis and Hertling

On 1 November 1917 Michaelis was dismissed for his inept handling of a naval mutiny. Significantly, the *Reichstag* played a key role in his dismissal. Wilhelm, without consulting Hindenburg and Ludendorff, chose Count Hertling, an elderly Bavarian aristocrat, as his successor. Hertling disliked parliamentary government, but appreciated the need for consulting the parties. He promised to support the peace resolution and to reform the Prussian franchise. However, the decisive factor was the attitude of the Supreme Command. Ludendorff, busy with preparations for the 1918 offensive, hoped that Hertling's conciliatory measures could keep the home front quiet long enough for Germany to win the war.

The right

Radical nationalists, alarmed by the peace resolution, founded the Fatherland Party in September 1917. Heavily subsidised by industrialists, the party was opposed to political change, demanded annexations east and west, and supported military rule. It soon claimed it had over one million members. (It probably had fewer than 500,000.)

The left

By 1917 German socialists were seriously divided. Most SPD deputies, unwilling to damage the war effort, were prepared to work with the other parties. However, a number of radical socialists opposed collaboration with the capitalist German state. In April 1917, 42 SPD deputies formed a new party, the Independent Social Democratic Party (USPD). The USPD was committed to an immediate peace without annexations. The remaining 68 SPD deputies reconstituted themselves as the Majority Socialist Party with Friedrich Ebert as chairman.

The USPD was loosely associated with two other groups, the Spartacus League and the **revolutionary shop stewards**. The League, founded by a small group of socialist intellectuals and led by Karl Liebknecht and Rosa Luxemburg, had no mass following. The Revolutionary Shop Stewards, by contrast, had considerable grass roots influence. The League and the Shop Stewards believed that working people must use the war to destroy capitalism and inaugurate world revolution.

In January 1918 400,000 Berlin workers went on strike. The strike spread quickly to other cities. The strikers' demands, influenced by the revolutionary shop stewards, were political as well as economic: they included democratic government and a 'peace without victory'. The authorities acted firmly, placing the largest plants under military control, prohibiting public meetings and arresting a number of socialist leaders. Significantly, the Majority Socialists and most official trade union leaders opposed the strike. The shop stewards quickly backed down and called off the strike.

The Treaty of Brest-Litovsk, March 1918

By the terms of the Treaty of Brest-Litovsk, Russia lost its Polish territories, Lithuania, Courland, the Ukraine, Estonia, Latvia and Finland – a third of its population and agricultural land. Russia

Key term

Revolutionary shop stewards
Working-class activists who tried to organise mass action in the factories of Berlin in an attempt to end the war.

Key dates

Treaty of Brest-Litovsk: March 1918

German offensive on the Western Front: March–July 1918

Allied counter-offensive: July–November 1918

Key term

Fourteen Points
These were
President Wilson's
main war aims.
Wilson hoped to
prevent future wars
by eliminating
secret alliances and
frustrated
nationalism, and by
establishing a
League of Nations.

also had to pay three billion roubles in reparations. The *Reichstag* approved the Treaty by a large majority, even though it was a clear repudiation of the 1917 peace resolution. Only the USPD voted against it. Success in the east made Germany deaf to President Wilson's proposals for peace in January 1918 – his **Fourteen Points**.

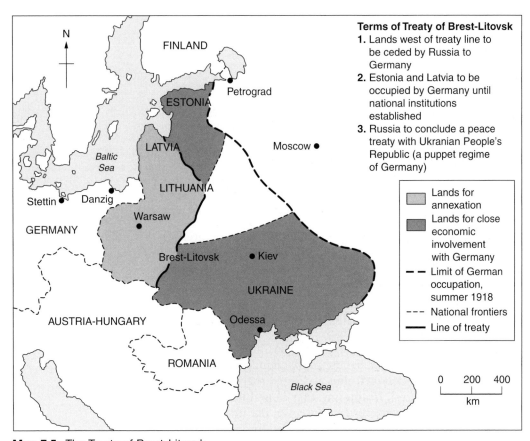

Map 7.5: The Treaty of Brest-Litovsk.

Key question
Why was Germany
defeated in 1918?

The German spring offensive: 1918

The war's outcome was still uncertain in early 1918. Germany's main advantage was that it no longer had to fight a two-front war. But Germany's allies were a source of concern and huge US forces would soon help the Allies. The German High Command therefore determined to launch a great spring offensive.

In late March German troops smashed through British lines on the Somme, driving the British forces back 65 kilometres. Further German offensives followed and by June German forces were within 60 kilometres of Paris. However, the German army did not possess sufficient manpower to exploit the breakthrough and the advance ground to a halt. Ironically, the Supreme Command had decided to keep 1.5 million men in the east controlling vast territories from the Baltic to the Black Sea. These men might have made all the difference.

The Allied counter-attack came in July and was brilliantly successful. On 8 August (Ludendorff later termed it the German army's 'black day'), British forces broke through the German lines at Amiens. Morale in the German army began to crumble and there were large numbers of desertions. The Allied advance continued through early September, ensuring that Germany lost all the gains made in the spring offensive.

The defeat of Germany's allies

Germany's allies suffered a number of defeats:

- On 30 September 1918 Bulgaria surrendered.
- On 30 October 1918 Turkey agreed to an armistice.
- In October 1918 the Italians smashed the Austrians at Vittorio Veneto. In late October Czech leaders took over Prague, Serb and Croat leaders proclaimed the establishment of a Yugoslav state, and Hungary asserted its independence. The Austrian government signed an armistice on 3 November.

Germany defeated

By the autumn of 1918 Germany's situation was desperate. German troops were being pushed back towards the Rhine while fresh US troops were arriving in Europe at the rate of 300,000 a month. On 29 September Ludendorff informed Wilhelm and Hertling that the war was lost. Consequently Hertling must approach Woodrow Wilson and ask for an immediate armistice and a peace based on his Fourteen Points.

On 30 September, Wilhelm accepted Hertling's resignation and issued a proclamation establishing parliamentary government. Hindenburg and Ludendorff thus abdicated their power, leaving the *Reichstag* in control. In this way, they hoped that Germany might obtain better peace terms. Moreover, the new government (and not the army leaders) would be blamed for Germany's defeat.

Table 7.5: Material resources, early 1918

	Germany (Western forces)	Western Allies
Machine guns (per infantry division)	324	1,084
Artillery	c. 14,000	c. 18,500
Airplanes	c. 3,670	c. 4,500
Trucks	23,000	c. 100,000
Tanks	10	800

Source: Fritz Klein *et al., Deutschland im Weltkrieg* (Berlin, 1968–9).

Summary diagram: German defeated 1917–18

	The Western Front	The Home Front	The Naval War	The Eastern Front
1917	French mutiny Battle of Passchendaele	'Turnip' Winter Hardship July Crisis Peace Resolution Bethmann resigned Chancellor Michaelis Chancellor Hertling	Unrestructed submarine warfare US entered war U-boat success Convoy system established	March Revolution Bolsheviks seize power Peace negotiations
1918	German spring offensive US troops arriving German offensive stalled Allied advance	Left-wing unrest Strikes Hertling resigned Parliamentary democracy established	Britain not starved into surrender	Treaty of Brest-Litovsk German troops moved to Western Front

September–October: Bulgaria, Turkey and Austria-Hungary surrendered

3 | The German Revolution 1918–19

Key question
How important were the constitutional reforms introduced in October 1918?

The 6 months from October 1918 to March 1919 witnessed turbulent revolutionary activity across Germany. There were several different revolutions, each with its own aims and agenda.

Constitutional reform

Key date

Prince Max of Baden appointed as Chancellor: October 1918

On 1 October Wilhelm asked Prince Max of Baden, a moderate conservative, to form a government. Max's government, which included representatives from the Majority Socialists and the Left Liberals, was stunned when told the seriousness of Germany's position. When Max raised objections to an immediate request for an armistice, Wilhelm told him: 'You have not been brought here to make things difficult for the Supreme Command'.

Thus, Max (on 3 October) wrote formally to President Wilson asking for an armistice and a peace based on the Fourteen Points. Wilson, who took a harder line than he would have done in January 1918, insisted on immediate evacuation of all occupied territory, the end of submarine warfare and firm guarantees that the new German government was truly democratic. Several weeks of secret negotiation followed. The main obstacle to peace now was the Kaiser, whose removal from power Wilson insisted on as a precondition for an armistice.

Meanwhile Max's government introduced a series of reforms that turned Germany into a parliamentary monarchy:

- The three-class franchise was abolished in Prussia.
- The Kaiser's powers over the army were severely curtailed.
- The Chancellor and the government were made accountable to the *Reichstag*.

At this point, Ludendorff recovered his nerve. Morale among front-line soldiers had not collapsed and the Allied advance seemed to have run out of steam. He thus issued an order to army commanders calling on all ranks to resist a humiliating surrender. Max was appalled. Further military resistance would only lead to more suffering. Moreover, Ludendorff had issued his order without consulting Max. Max told Wilhelm that he must choose between Ludendorff and the cabinet. On 26 October, after a heated exchange with Wilhelm, Ludendorff resigned and fled, disguised in a false beard, to Sweden. The next day Max reiterated Germany's wish for an armistice, emphasising that the military authorities were at last subject to the civilian government.

How important was the *Reichstag*?

In a 3-week period, power had been transferred peaceably from the Kaiser to the *Reichstag*. The changes have usually been portrayed as a 'revolution from above'. However, much of what occurred resulted from the influence of the *Reichstag*. The day Ludendorff recommended an armistice an inter-party *Reichstag* committee called for amendments to the constitution to permit the creation of a government responsible to the *Reichstag*. Thus, while Germany's first parliamentary government came into being partly by order of the Supreme Command, it is also clear that mounting pressure from the *Reichstag* for political change could not have been resisted for much longer.

Most Germans paid little heed to the hugely important (but ill-publicised) reforms. After all, Wilhelm remained Kaiser, a prince was still chancellor, and the war continued. Nor did the *Reichstag* behave as if the changes represented a turning point in German history. It adjourned on 5 October and did not meet until 22 October, when it again adjourned until 9 November. These were hardly the actions of an institution that wished to shape events decisively.

The revolutionary situation

Key question
Why did the November revolution occur?

By late October a revolutionary situation existed in Germany. Four years of privation had eroded the old relationship between ruler and subject. The shock of looming military defeat, after years of optimistic propaganda, radicalised popular attitudes. The stunned people were only too ready to blame Wilhelm for Germany's misfortunes. Once the public was aware that Wilson regarded Wilhelm as an obstacle to peace, popular pressure for his abdication grew rapidly. Many south Germans blamed Prussia and Prussian militarism for Germany's misfortunes. Some Bavarians pressed for independence.

The birth of the republic

Key dates
Mutiny of German sailors: October–November 1918

Abdication of Wilhelm II: 9 November 1918

Key term
Soviet
A council of workers, peasants and soldiers.

On 29 October rumours that the German High Seas Fleet was going to be sent out on a last do-or-die mission against the Royal Navy led to a mutiny among the sailors at Wilhelmshaven. The mutiny rapidly spread to Kiel and other ports. On 4 November dockworkers and soldiers in Kiel joined the mutinous sailors and set up workers' and soldiers' councils, on the 1917 Russian **soviet** model. Although Independent Socialists were in close touch with some mutineers, this was more a spontaneous protest movement than a politically motivated mutiny. The sailors' councils were not disloyal to the government. On the contrary, they asked for representatives to come and listen to their grievances. The government sent a Majority Socialist who promised better conditions and reassured the sailors that there would be no 'suicide offensive'.

However, news of the Kiel mutiny fanned the flames of discontent across Germany. By 8 November workers' and soldiers' councils had been established in most of the major cities. The councils demanded peace and assumed control of local food supplies and services. In Bavaria the Wittelsbach dynasty was deposed and an independent socialist republic was proclaimed by Kurt Eisner. There was little resistance. The time seemed ripe for a remodelling of society and a clean break with the imperial past.

Divisions among the revolutionaries

Key question
How serious was the revolutionary threat?

The revolutionary wave which swept Germany was not a united force:

- The Majority Socialists upheld democracy and favoured moderate reforms. They totally rejected Bolshevik-style communism.
- The Spartacists and shop stewards, intoxicated by events in Russia, believed that Germany should follow a similar road. They campaigned for a socialist republic, based on the workers' and soldiers' councils, which would smash the institutions of imperial Germany.

- The USPD was between the two extremes. It demanded radical social and economic change to complement political reform. Its influence was seriously curtailed by factional squabbles.

Left-wing socialists tried to drive forward the workers' revolution by organising strikes and demonstrations by workers. The situation appeared menacing to many Germans, who were alarmed by what they perceived as 'Russian solutions' being put forward for German problems. However, many of the councils were controlled by moderate socialists who were anxious to maintain law and order and ensure the smooth functioning of local services at a time of crisis. In most cases the councils co-existed uneasily with pre-revolutionary bodies.

The abdication of Wilhelm II

On 7 November, Majority Socialist leaders threatened to withdraw support from the government unless Wilhelm abdicated and the socialists were given greater representation in the cabinet. When Max failed to persuade Wilhelm to abdicate, the socialist ministers Scheidemann and Bauer resigned and the party agreed to call a general strike. Majority Socialist leaders took this step reluctantly. Their hand was forced by the revolutionary shop stewards who had already called a strike for 9 November in protest against the arrest of some of their leaders.

Thus on 9 November most workers went on strike. A deputation of socialists, headed by Ebert and Scheidemann, called on Max. They informed him that the local garrison in Berlin was on their side and that a new democratic government must be formed at once. Max hesitated no longer. At noon he announced the abdication of Wilhelm. By now even Hindenburg and Groener (Ludendorff's successor) realised that the Kaiser must go. Abandoned by his generals, Wilhelm finally accepted the reality of the situation and fled to the Netherlands. Later on 9 November, Max resigned and announced the formation of a new government, to be led by Ebert.

The German Republic

Ebert issued his first proclamation on 9 November, signing himself 'imperial chancellor', a title chosen to emphasise continuity between his government and that of Max. This device conferred some semblance of legitimacy on the new government and helped to rally the officer corps and the civil service behind it. So did the fact that the new government confirmed the old officials in power. Ebert declared that the goal of the government was to bring peace. He hoped to stabilise the political situation sufficiently to enable elections to take place as soon as possible for a National Assembly. This body would then draw up a new constitution. His main worry was that the extreme left would gain the upper hand. He was determined to prevent the descent into civil strife.

Ebert was under no illusions about the weak position of the new government. Its authority did not extend with certainty beyond

Key question
What were Ebert's aims?

Profile: Friedrich Ebert 1871–1925

1871	– Born, the son of a tailor. He became a saddler and entered politics through his trade union activities
1905	– Elected secretary to the SPD's central committee
1912	– Elected to the *Reichstag*. His hard work behind the scenes was partly responsible for the SPD's success in the elections
1913	– On the death of August Bebel, he was elected joint leader of the SPD alongside the more radical Hugo Haase
1918–19	– Effective leader of Germany. Ensured the defeat of the left-wing socialists and elections to a Constituent Assembly
1919	– Became the first President of the Weimar Republic
1925	– Died of a ruptured appendix

Ebert was not a great orator or charismatic leader. He was a calm, patient and subtle negotiator – more concerned with improving the lot of the working class by evolutionary rather than revolutionary change. During the war, he worked with other left-wing parties, hoping to push the Kaiser's administration towards an acceptance of parliamentary democracy. As well as a democrat, Ebert was a patriotic German who lost two sons during the war.

Berlin, and it was not even accepted in all parts of the capital. Furthermore he knew that the revolutionary shop stewards were planning to set up a provisional government, based on the workers' and soldiers' councils. To forestall this, Ebert decided to offer the USPD seats in the new government.

The USPD was deeply divided. While its right-wing favoured acceptance, the left bitterly opposed collaboration with Ebert and demanded instead that the workers' and soldiers' councils assume full power. By 21 votes to 19 the Independents finally decided to accept Ebert's offer. As a sop to their left-wing members they insisted on a number of concessions:

• Only socialists must be included in the government – not other parties as Ebert had hoped.
• The government must declare that all power resided in the councils.
• Elections to the National Assembly must be delayed until the revolution was consolidated.

Reluctantly Ebert accepted the conditions. Therefore, on 10 November, a new government, the Council of Peoples' Commissars was formed. It consisted of three SPD members and three USPD members: Ebert and Haase acted as co-chairmen.

The workers' and soldiers' councils

On 10 November elections to form workers' and soldiers' councils were held in all the factories and garrisons in Berlin. At a mass meeting of the councils, the delegates approved the composition of the new government by a huge majority. An executive committee was elected to manage the affairs of the Berlin councils. This committee, which consisted of seven Majority Socialists, seven Independents and 14 soldiers (many of whom were not socialists at all), began negotiations with the government to define the precise relationship between the two bodies.

The armistice

The change in government did not change the Allied attitude to Germany. In November 1918 German troops still controlled most of Belgium and huge areas of eastern Europe. Allied leaders feared that Germany intended to use the armistice as a breathing space before resuming the war. The armistice terms were designed to remove Germany's ability to fight:

Armistice between Allies and Germany: 11 November 1918 — Key date

- German troops had to withdraw beyond the Rhine. German territory on the left bank of the river was to be occupied.
- Germany had to surrender its U-boats, much of its surface fleet and its air force.
- Germany had to repudiate the Treaty of Brest-Litovsk.
- The blockade of Germany would continue until a final peace treaty had been signed.

The armistice terms were hugely resented in Germany. Nevertheless, the political situation made continuation of the war impossible. On 11 November the socialist government agreed to the terms and the First World War ended.

Table 7.6: Some costs of the war

	Britain	France	Germany	Austria-Hungary	Russia (–1917)
Population, 1910–11	40,460,000	39,192,000	64,296,000	51,356,000	160,700,000
Male population, 1910–11	19,638,000	19,254,000	32,040,000	25,374,000	78,790,000
Men mobilised	6,211,427	8,660,000	13,250,000	8,000,000	13,700,000
Percentage of men mobilised	31.6	45.0	41.4	31.5	17.4
Military casualties	2,437,964	3,100,000	6,193,058	6,400,000	5,409,000
dead	744,702	1,400,000	2,044,900	1,100,000	1,660,000
wounded	1,693,262	1,700,000	4,148,158	5,300,000	3,749,000
casualties per 1000 pre-war male population	124	161	193	252	69
Civilian deaths due to war	292,000	500,000	624,000	2,320,000	5,050,000

Germany: November 1918–January 1919

Relations between the Majority Socialists and Independents remained tense. A key issue was the authority of the workers' and soldiers' councils. Ebert viewed the councils with grave suspicion as a possible rival to parliamentary government. He therefore did his utmost to speed up the calling of the National Assembly.

Key question
Did Ebert betray the revolution?

The Independents were not opposed to this: most believed in parliamentary democracy. But whereas the Majority Socialists maintained that the revolution was over, the Independents believed that the gains of the revolution must be consolidated before the assembly met. They believed that the councils, the embodiment of the revolutionary will of the people, should supervise the implementation of a crash programme of socialism. Independents called for the nationalisation of key industries, the breaking-up of the great landed estates and the democratisation of the civil service, the judiciary and the army.

As the weeks passed Ebert's position grew stronger. Permanent officials co-operated willingly enough with him, regarding him as the legitimate successor of Max. They would not work with the executive committee of the councils.

The Ebert–Groener pact

On 10 November General Groener telephoned Ebert. Groener, afraid that the revolution would destroy the authority of the officer corps, agreed to support the government in return for Ebert's promise to resist Bolshevism and to preserve the officers' authority against the councils. Ebert's critics, both at the time and since, have claimed that this 'pact' was proof that he had betrayed the revolution. However, Ebert never made any secret of his distaste of Bolshevik revolution. His understanding with Groener was a reasonable precaution to protect his government against violence from the extreme left.

The Stinnes–Legien agreement

On 15 November the Stinnes–Legien agreement strengthened Ebert's position. (Hugo Stinnes was an industrialist and Carl Legien a trade union leader.)

- The trade unions agreed not to interfere with private ownership.
- Employers guaranteed full legal recognition to trade unions.
- Workers' councils (which were to be introduced into all large factories) could help to regulate wages and working conditions.
- An 8-hour working day was introduced.

This agreement, quickly endorsed by the government, went a good way to satisfying workers' grievances.

The All-German Congress of Workers' and Soldiers' Councils

The Congress met in Berlin from 16 to 21 December. Over 300 of the 500 delegates supported the Majority Socialists and only 90 the USPD. The Congress was more radically inclined than the government. Delegates passed resolutions demanding the nationalisation of key industries and the **democratisation of the army**.

Nevertheless, most delegates wanted Germany to be a parliamentary democracy. On 19 December Congress approved by a huge majority the government decision to hold elections to the National Assembly on 19 January. In the meantime, it agreed that all power should be vested in the government.

The resignation of the Independent Socialists

On 23 December the sailors' division, which had come from Kiel to defend the government, was ordered to evacuate its quarters in the former royal palace. The disgruntled sailors barricaded themselves in the palace. Faced with a direct challenge to its authority, the government – on Christmas Eve – ordered a regular army division to attack the palace. Having failed to dislodge the sailors, the troops were withdrawn. Violence quickly spread to other parts of Berlin. Fortunately for Ebert the sailors agreed to leave the building once the question of their back pay – the real cause of the action – was settled.

The Independents were incensed by Ebert's action, undertaken without their knowledge. Their three ministers were already frustrated by the slow progress towards socialism and highly suspicious of the ties between Ebert and the army. On 29 December the Independent ministers resigned. Ebert now had a freer hand in the government. However, he also faced growing opposition from the streets.

The Spartacist rising

On 1 January 1919, the Spartacists broke with the USPD and founded the German Communist Party, led by Liebknecht and Luxemburg. The communists dismissed Ebert's government as the 'enemy of the working class'. They declared that the National Assembly would be an organ of counter-revolution and called instead for government by workers' and soldiers' councils. On 6 January a revolutionary committee of 53 communists and shop stewards was set up. It issued a proclamation deposing Ebert and announcing the establishment of a new revolutionary government. At the same time armed communists occupied newspaper offices and various public buildings in Berlin.

Faced with this challenge, the government first tried to negotiate with the Spartacist leaders, to no effect. It thus had little option but to turn to the army. Groener, in addition to using regular units, recruited hundreds of right-wing ex-soldiers, organised into Free Corps units. The Free Corps, who bitterly resented the outbreak of revolution, were only too willing to suppress communist activity. By 15 January the Spartacist revolt was crushed after savage street fighting. Liebknecht and Luxemburg were shot while in police custody.

The events of January 1919, especially the murder of Liebknecht and Luxemburg, ensured the implacable hostility of the Marxist left towards the Majority Socialists (who again called themselves the SPD) and the new parliamentary republic. In March 1919 the USPD rejected parliamentary democracy entirely and came out in favour of government by workers' councils. Many Independents agreed with the Communist Party that Ebert had sold his soul to the conservative forces of imperial Germany.

Key question
How serious was the Spartacist threat?

Key date
Spartacist revolution defeated by Free Corps: January 1919

Barricades in Berlin during the Spartacist rising in 1919.

Further bloodshed

In February widespread strikes were organised by communists and in some towns there was sporadic street fighting. In Berlin, in March, the communists called for a general strike. Again Berlin became the scene of street fighting: again the Free Corps were sent in. By mid-March 1919 order had been restored at the cost of over 1000 dead.

Bavaria

The elections to the Bavarian parliament in mid-January 1919 resulted in an overwhelming defeat for Eisner's Independents: they won only three seats. On the way to opening the first session of the new parliament in February Eisner was murdered by a right-wing fanatic. Disorder broke out and the new coalition government, led by Majority Socialists, fled from Munich, leaving the city in the hands of Independents and communists. On 9 April, the communists, brushing aside the Independents, set up a soviet republic. The coalition government called on a local Free Corps unit for help. The army and Free Corps restored order in Munich after some days of savage fighting. Hundreds of communists were shot.

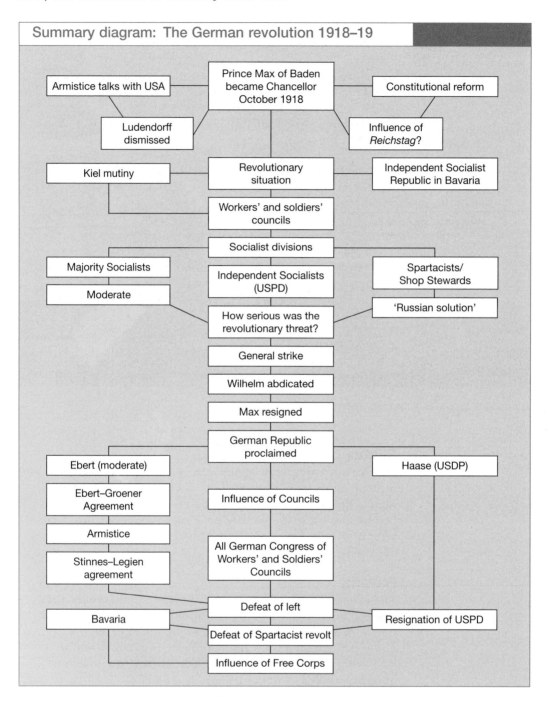

Summary diagram: The German revolution 1918–19

4 | The Establishment of the Weimar Republic

The elections for the National Assembly took place on 19 January 1919. Most political parties took the opportunity to re-form themselves. New names did not hide the fact that there was considerable continuity in the structure of the party system. The Nationalists were essentially an amalgamation of the old

Election of National Assembly: 19 January 1919

Key date

Conservative parties. The liberals remained divided between left (the Democrats) and right (the People's Party).

There was a turnout of 83 per cent of those eligible to vote (including women). Contrary to expectations, the socialists failed to secure an absolute majority. The SPD won 165 seats (38 per cent of the vote) and the USPD 22. The Centre won 91 seats, the Democrats 75, the Nationalists 44 and the Populists 19.

On 10 February Ebert was elected first president of the Republic by 277 votes to 51. He immediately asked the SPD, as the largest party, to form a government. The SPD found allies in the Centre and Democrat parties. Over 75 per cent of the electorate had voted for these three parties, all of which were committed to the new republic. The election, a clear repudiation of the extreme right and left, seemed a promising start to a new chapter in German history. The new government was headed by Chancellor Scheidemann and consisted of six Social Democrats, three Centrists and three Democrats. The new Assembly met in the picturesque town of Weimar: conditions in Berlin were too unsettled to risk meeting there.

The Weimar constitution

The Assembly's main task was to draw up a constitution. Largely the work of Hugo Preuss (a Democrat), it attempted a careful balance of political forces:

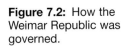

Key question
What were the weaknesses of the Weimar constitution?

Figure 7.2: How the Weimar Republic was governed.

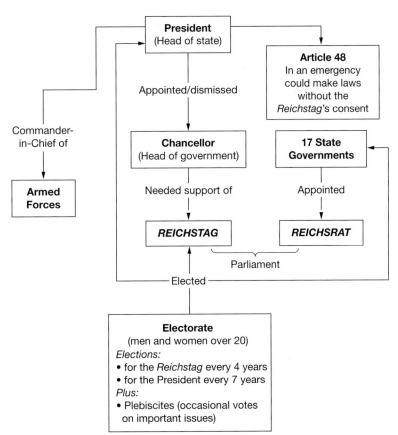

- Germany was to be a republic, its sovereignty based on the people.
- It remained a federal rather than a unitary state.
- The central government would control direct taxation, foreign affairs, the armed forces and communications.
- The states retained their powers over education, police and the churches.

At national level Germany was to be governed by a president, a *Reichstag* and a *Reichsrat*. *Reichstag* deputies were to be elected every 4 years by all men and women over the age of 20. A system of **proportional representation** was introduced, ensuring that all German views would be represented in the new *Reichstag*. The chancellor and his ministers had to possess the confidence of the *Reichstag* and were obliged to resign when they forfeited it. The *Reichstag* was to initiate and approve legislation.

The *Reichsrat* was to be composed of delegates from the German states. Each state was represented according to its population, except that no state was allowed to have more than two-fifths of the seats: this was designed to prevent Prussian preponderance. The *Reichsrat* could veto *Reichstag* legislation: its veto, in turn, could be over-ridden by a two-thirds vote of the Reichstag.

The president was directly elected by the people for 7 years:

- He was supreme commander of the armed forces.
- He convened and dissolved the *Reichstag*.
- He appointed the chancellor and the *Reich* government.

Proportional representation This system of voting ensures that a party receives the same percentage of seats as votes received.

The creation of a presidency, intended to act as a political counter-balance to the *Reichstag*, created a somewhat ambiguous system. Was the ultimate source of authority in the republic vested in the *Reichstag* or the presidency? The situation was further exacerbated by the powers conferred on the president by Article 48. This provided the president with the authority to suspend civil rights in an emergency and to take whatever action was required to restore law and order by the issue of presidential decrees. Although the intention was to create the means by which government could continue to function in a temporary crisis, Article 48 gave the president considerable potential power.

The Weimar constitution guaranteed German people personal liberty, equality before the law, freedom of movement, expression, and conscience, and the right of association.

On 31 July 1919 the new constitution was passed by 262 votes to 75. Only the USPD and the right were in opposition. The adoption by the new republic of the black, red and gold revolutionary flag of 1848 enraged right-wing nationalists.

Weimar constitution adopted: 31 July 1919

The peace settlement

In January 1919 the leaders of 32 countries assembled in Paris to make peace with the defeated Central Powers. The main decisions were taken by the 'Big Three': Wilson, Lloyd George and Clemenceau. The peacemakers faced huge problems:

Key question How harsh was the Treaty of Versailles?

The Big Three at Versailles: Clemenceau, Wilson and Lloyd George.

- The map of Europe as it had existed in 1914 had been swept away. There was political and economic chaos across much of central and eastern Europe.
- There was the fear that Bolshevism might spread westwards from Russia.
- The Big Three held different views about how to ensure a durable peace settlement. Clemenceau, like most French people, wanted Germany punished and its power permanently reduced. Wilson was primarily concerned with establishing a just and lasting system of international relations. Lloyd George, not wanting to leave an embittered Germany, was inclined to leniency. Thus, while he 'talked hard' for home consumption, he often did all he could to ease some of the harsher terms that Clemenceau was intent on imposing.

Germany was not allowed to participate in the peace negotiations. On 7 May German delegates were handed a document consisting of 440 articles. They were told that they had 3 weeks to consider it and to formulate counter-proposals.

The Treaty of Versailles
On 12 May, Chancellor Scheidemann described the Treaty as unacceptable. (Figure 7.3 shows the main terms.) Virtually every German agreed with him. Germany lodged its objections at considerable length but to little effect. On 19 June the German cabinet rejected the Treaty and Scheidemann resigned. The new government, led by Gustav Bauer, knew that rejection of the

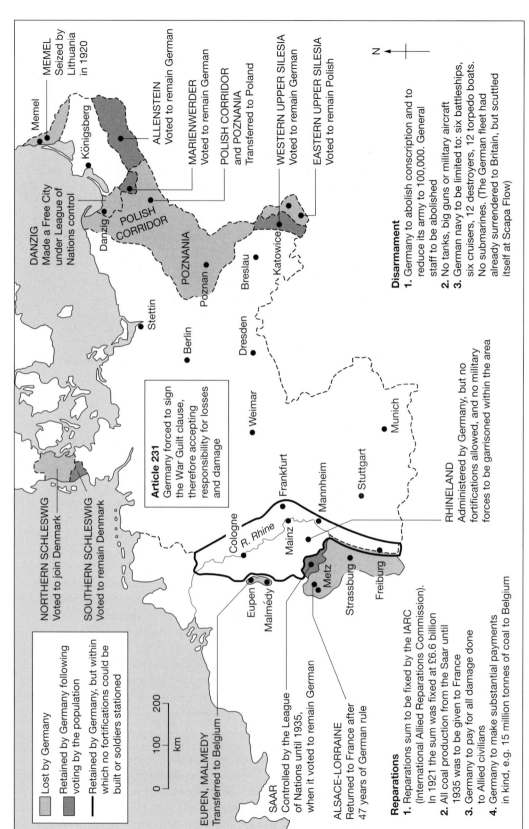

Figure 7.3: The Treaty of Versailles.

Key date

Treaty of Versailles:
28 June 1919

Key terms

Diktat
A dictated
settlement allowing
for no negotiations.

Self-determination
The right of people
to decide their own
form of
government.

Treaty was not really an option. Germany was in no state to fight a new war, a war which might result in Germany being dismembered. Accordingly the *Reichstag* sanctioned the signing of the Treaty. Foreign Minister Muller and Minister of Justice Bell signed the Treaty on 28 June 1919 in the Hall of Mirrors at Versailles – the same place in which the German Empire had been proclaimed in 1871.

Criticisms of Versailles

The Versailles settlement provoked furious controversy. France thought the treaty far too soft. This was not the view in Germany. On no other political issue were Germans so united as in the condemnation of the Treaty. It was seen as a humiliating **diktat** – at variance with the Fourteen Points. If **self-determination** was the guiding principle, Germans found it incomprehensible that Germans in Austria, Danzig, Posen and West Prussia, Memel, Upper Silesia, the Sudetenland and the Saar were all excluded from Germany and placed under foreign rule. Germans, convinced they had fought a war of self-defence, found it impossible to accept the War Guilt clause and regarded reparations as totally unfair.

Historians today are not convinced that Germany was treated over-harshly. The application of self-determination was not as unfair as many Germans believed. Virtually all of the German territory lost (with the exception of Danzig and the Polish Corridor) was justified on the grounds of nationality. More Poles were left under German rule than Germans under Polish rule. The only outright violation of self-determination was the refusal of the Allies to permit the union of Austria and Germany. Had they done so, Germany would have ended the war with more territory and six million more people. Despite German claims to the contrary, the treaty was not radically different from the Fourteen Points (in so far as they applied to Germany).

The Treaty's territorial provisions were mild compared with the Treaty of Brest-Litovsk (see page 193). Germany lost 13.5 per cent of its territory and ten per cent of its population. Yet Germany remained a formidably strong economic power. Reparations – fixed in 1921 at £6600 million – were a significant, but not impossibly heavy burden. The sum was not unreasonable given the destruction visited on Belgium and France by German armies.

Arguably the Treaty was the worst of all worlds – too severe to be permanently acceptable to most Germans, and too lenient to constrain Germany. After June 1919 every German government would do its best to overthrow the Treaty. The peace settlement would last only as long as the victorious powers were in a position to enforce it on the resentful Germans. However, in fairness to the peacemakers, it is hard to conceive of any peace treaty acceptable to the Allied powers and to their electorates in 1919 which the Germans would not have found humiliating. In the circumstances it may be that Versailles was a reasonable attempt at marrying principle and pragmatism in a dramatically altered world.

Economic problems

- The First World War impoverished Germany. Between 1913 and 1919 the national debt had risen from 5000 million marks to 144,000 million marks.
- In 1919 real national income was only two-thirds of what it had been in 1913.
- Manufacturing output was 30 per cent lower in 1919 than in 1914.
- A large trade deficit and the difficulties of re-adjusting a war economy to the requirements of peace were not helped by Allied demands for reparations and the loss of important industrial regions.
- The Allied blockade, which did not end until the signing of the Treaty of Versailles, worsened an already dire food supply situation.

Key question
How serious were the economic and political problems facing Germany in 1919?

Financial problems

Germany's finances were a total mess. Rather than increase taxation, Germany had financed the war through short-term loans and by printing money. Between 1914 and 1919 the value of the mark against the dollar had fallen from 4.20 marks to 14.00 marks and the prices of basic goods had increased three- to four-fold. The situation did not improve with the coming of peace. By early 1920 a dollar was worth 100 marks. Narrowing the massive gap between government income and expenditure and thereby bringing about the control of inflation could only be achieved by increasing taxation and/or by cutting expenditure. Neither of these options was attractive.

Political problems

The fact that there were so many political parties, all obtaining a percentage of seats in the *Reichstag*, meant that German cabinets were dependent on coalitions. Most parties were fairly narrowly based, on a class, religious or regional basis. Political activists were often too closely tied to their particular political ideology to find it easy to co-operate with other parties. Between 13 February 1919 and 30 January 1933 there were no fewer than 20 different cabinets, each lasting on average 239 days. This made for weak government.

The threat from the left

The suppression of workers' uprisings in 1919 was neither forgotten nor forgiven by the extreme left. After 1919 the SPD and the Communists competed for working-class support.

The threat from the right

Ebert's willingness to compromise with the old order did not endear him to those who regretted its passing. Right-wing political forces totally rejected the Weimar system and democratic principles. They demanded strong government. Right-wing parties vied with each other to attack the Versailles settlement and to blame all Germany's problems on the 'shameful peace'. The right also had considerable success in propagating the notion that the German army had been 'stabbed in the back' in 1918 by the 'November Criminals': pacifists, socialists, communists and Jews.

The right was divided between conservatives and radicals. Many of the conservative supporters of the Nationalist party hoped to bring back the Kaiser. Conservatives continued to exert influence in a number of key institutions, not least the army, civil service, the judiciary and the education system, all of which were preserved in much their old form. Large numbers of army officers, bureaucrats, judges and professors were lukewarm or indeed actively hostile to the new republic.

After 1918 there were numerous radical right-wing groups, which often had little sympathy with the conservatives. These groups – nationalistic, anti-democratic, anti-socialist and anti-Jewish – wanted to smash the new Republic. Ex-soldiers, some of whom belonged to Free Corps units, were particularly attracted to the radical right. In September 1919 an obscure corporal joined the small right-wing German Workers' Party, founded in Munich by Anton Drexler. The obscure corporal was Adolf Hitler.

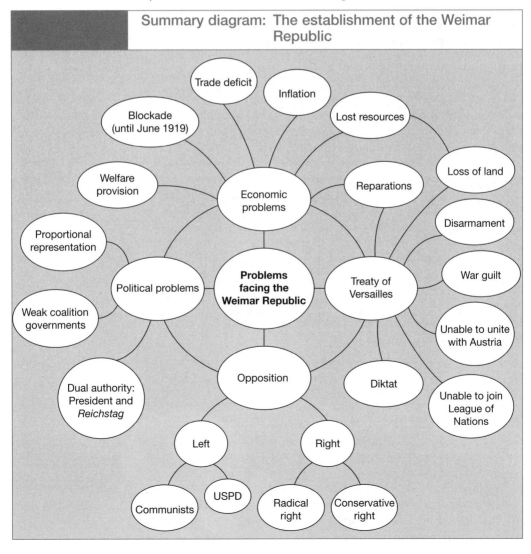

Summary diagram: The establishment of the Weimar Republic

5 | Key Debate

How successful was Ebert in achieving his aims?

Radical critics at the time and since have accused Ebert of betraying the interests of workers and of ensuring the failure of the revolution by allying with forces of conservatism. In the eyes of the left, the new Germany looked remarkably like the old. The Kaiser was gone but the imperial institutions, run by men with imperial mentalities, remained. The structure of German society was hardly affected by the revolution. The old élites – industrial barons, great landowners, the civil service, army officers – retained their power. In truth, however, the radical socialists had little support and little to offer Germany in 1918–19. Nationalisation of industry or massive land redistribution would have led to economic chaos. Any attempt to extend the power of the workers' councils might well have led to civil war.

Ebert had no wish to preside over chaos. Like most SPD leaders, he was suspicious of the extreme left. Given the left-wing threat, he had little option but to rely on the forces of reaction. In the context of 1918–19, Ebert had a sensible set of political and economic goals. He aimed to end the war, to maintain law and order, and (most importantly) to establish parliamentary democracy. In the event, he achieved most of his goals.

There could surely not have been a worse time for the establishment of a new democratic republic. The war, and its immediate aftermath, had dislocated the economy, helped to initiate run-away inflation, and polarised divisions between right and left. Massive recriminations about where the responsibility for Germany's defeat should lie deepened political bitterness.

Ebert's moderation did not inevitably doom the new republic to political failure. Right- and left-wing extremists were a minority in 1919. Most German parties were committed to parliamentary democracy and to social reform. Unfortunately, the years after 1919 were ones of almost continuous crisis. Only after 1923 was there a period of relative calm. This lasted until 1929 and the onset of the Great Depression. With the rise of unemployment came the rise of the National Socialist Party, led by Adolf Hitler. However, it would be unfair to blame Ebert for Hitler's accession to power in 1933.

Study Guide: AS Questions

In the style of AQA

(a) Explain why the Kaiser abdicated in November 1918.

(12 marks)

(b) How important was the Ebert–Groener pact of November 1918 for the survival of the new German state, 1918–23?

(24 marks)

Exam tips

The cross-references are intended to take you straight to the material that will help you to answer the questions.

(a) You should be able to provide a variety of both long- and short-term factors to explain why the Kaiser abdicated. For the short-term factors re-read pages 195–8. For the long-term factors you will need to reflect on Germany's experience of war and the effect that this had on the political situation. You may even wish to allude briefly to the pre-war situation and revisit some of the material given in Chapter 6. The important requirement is that you assemble a list of factors and show some linkage between them. Try to single out those factors that were crucial to the abdication and prioritise them in your answer. You will also need to provide a short conclusion.

(b) To answer this question you will need to consider the positive and negative contributions of the Ebert–Groener pact to the new German state in 1918–23 (pages 201–3).

Obviously the pact was important in enabling the new state to survive attacks from the left, but you should also consider the disadvantages it brought. Did it weaken the revolution? Did it tie Ebert's hands so that he was unable to fulfil his ideals? Did it associate the new Weimar Republic too closely with the right and right-wing attitudes? Did it encourage those on the right who sought to destroy the new state?

When you have made up your mind about such issues, you should plan your answer so that you can advance an argument, providing a balanced assessment which leads to a well-supported conclusion.

Glossary

Absolute rule   A state where a single person has total power.

Anarchist   A person whose ideal society is one without government of any kind. Late nineteenth-century anarchists often sought to bring about such a condition by terrorism.

Anti-Semitic   Someone who is anti-Jewish.

Armistice   Ceasefire.

Aryan   The Germanic or Teutonic race.

Austrian Empire   The Austrian Empire included much of what is today Austria, Hungary, Poland, the Czech Republic, Slovakia, Croatia and northern Italy.

Boer War   The conflict in South Africa (1899–1902) between Britain and the Boer republics of the Transvaal and the Orange Free State. Britain eventually triumphed.

Bonapartist   Supportive of the Bonaparte family. Although Napoleon Bonaparte had been defeated in 1815, many French people regarded his rule with great nostalgia. They hoped that a member of his family might again rule France.

Bourgeoisie   The upper and middle classes who owned the capital and the means of production (factories, mills, mines, etc.), who (Marx claimed) exploited the workers.

Breech-loading needle gun   This gun, which loaded at the breech rather than the barrel, could fire seven shots a minute.

Bundesrat   The Federal Council, comprising 58 members nominated by state assemblies. Its consent was required in the passing of new laws.

Bureaucracies   Systems of administration.

Cartel   An association of manufacturers who come to a contractual agreement about the level of production and the scale of prices and maintain a monopoly.

***Chassepot* rifle**   A breech-loading rifle, named after the man who invented it.

Civic Guard   A military force composed of ordinary people, not professional soldiers.

Civil disobedience   Refusal to obey state laws and regulation.

Client state   A country that is friendly with, and dependent on, a stronger country.

The Communist Manifesto   This book, written by Karl Marx, supported the idea of class revolution. It encouraged workers everywhere to unite.

Constitution   A set of rules by which a state is governed.

Constitutional monarch   A king or queen whose powers are limited by a constitution and who usually rules in co-operation with an elected parliament.

Cortes   The Spanish Parliament.

Counter-revolution   A subsequent revolution (usually by conservative forces) counteracting the effect of a previous one.

Crimean War   This was a war fought by Britain, France and Turkey against Russia. Most of the fighting was in the Crimea – a southern part of Russia. The war, lasting from 1854 to 1856, ended with Russia's defeat.

Democratisation of the army   Officers would be elected by the men and the standing army would be replaced by a people's militia.

Deutschland über Alles   This means 'Germany above the others'. It eventually became Germany's national anthem, the words being set to a popular melody by the eighteenth-century composer Joseph Haydn.

Diet   An assembly or parliament.

Diktat   A dictated settlement allowing for no negotiations.

Divine right of kings   The notion that kings are God's representatives on earth and thus entitled to full obedience from their subjects.

Duchies   States ruled by a duke.

Dynastic   States ruled by the same family.

Entente   A friendly agreement.

Executive   The power or authority in government that carries the laws into effect.

Federal   A government in which several states, while independent in domestic affairs, combine for general purposes.

Federation   A group of states joined together in some form of union.

Feudal restrictions   The feudal system was a system of social organisation prevalent in much of Europe in the Middle Ages. Powerful landowning lords limited the freedom of the people who worked on their estates.

Fourteen Points   These were President Wilson's main war aims. Wilson hoped to prevent future wars by eliminating secret alliances and frustrated nationalism, and by establishing a League of Nations.

Franchise   The right to vote.

Free trade   Unrestricted trade without protective import duties.

German violation of Belgium's neutrality   German troops, in order to get round French defences along the German frontier, invaded Belgium. Britain had pledged itself to protect Belgium's neutrality in 1839.

Gross national product   The total value of all good and services produced within a country.

Grossdeutschland   A greater Germany that would include the German-speaking provinces of the Austrian Empire.

Habsburg   The ruling family of the Austrian Empire.

Hanseatic towns   A league of German commercial cities on the Baltic Sea coast.

Holy Roman Empire   Formed in the ninth century, the Empire had little power or meaning by 1800. The French philosopher Voltaire said it was not holy, Roman or an empire.

Hottentot election   This election was named after native rebels in South-West Africa.

Indirect taxes   Taxes placed on the sale of goods rather than those collected directly from the taxpayer (like income tax).

Inflation   An excessive increase in money supply that results in a decline in the purchasing power of money.

Jameson Raid   In December 1895 Dr Jameson, administrator for the British South African Company, led a force of 470 men into the Transvaal, hoping to spark a revolt which would overthrow President Kruger's Boer government. The raid was a total failure.

Jesuit order   A Catholic order of priests (the Society of Jesus), founded in 1534 by Ignatius Loyola.

July Revolution in Paris   In 1830 the reactionary King Charles X of France was overthrown and replaced by the more liberal Louis Philippe.

Junkers   The conservative landed aristocracy of Prussia.

Kleindeutschland   A little Germany that would exclude Austria.

Kulturkampf A struggle for culture or the struggle for civilisation. In Germany, the struggle was between the state and the Catholic Church.

Landtag The Prussian state Parliament.

Landwehr A middle-class reserve force that could be called up for service in an emergency. Many of its officers were old and poorly trained.

Lebensraum Living space.

Lobby groups People who campaign to persuade politicians to pass legislation favouring particular interests.

Martial law The exercise of military power by a government in time of emergency with the temporary suspension of ordinary administration and policing.

Martin Luther's stand against the Pope In 1517 German religious leader Martin Luther protested against a number of practices within the Catholic Church. His move led to a bitter religious divide. Luther's followers became known as Protestants.

Marxist historians Historians who accept the ideas of Karl Marx and believe that history is essentially about class conflict.

Marxist programme The plan of those who supported the ideas of Karl Marx. Marxists believed that the leaders of the proletariat must work to overthrow the capitalist system by (violent) revolution.

Military service The requirement for young men to serve in the army.

Multinational Austrian Empire The Austrian Empire contained people of many different nationalities. Although a relatively small minority, the Germans were the dominant ethnic group within the Empire.

National guard A national guard had first appeared in France during the French Revolution. It was supposed to be a force of the people and thus less under the control of the monarch.

Nationalisation Government ownership.

Nationalism The belief in – and support for – a national identity.

North Italian War In 1859 French Emperor Napoleon III supported Piedmont against Austria. Piedmont was seeking to increase its influence in northern Italy, at Austria's expense. Austria was defeated.

Orthodox Church The Greek or Eastern Christian Church.

The Ottoman Empire The Turkish Empire, which was ruled by the Ottoman family.

Pacifism Opposition to war.

The Pan-German League Formed in 1893, the League was a right-wing nationalist movement. It supported German expansion both in Europe and world-wide. Many of its members were anti-democratic, anti-socialist and anti-Semitic. Although never having more than 50,000 members, its propaganda influenced middle-class Germans.

Pan-Slavist Someone who supported the union of all Slav peoples.

Potato blight A destructive disease of the potato caused by a parasitic fungus.

Principalities States ruled by a prince.

Proletariat The exploited industrial workers who (Marx claimed) would triumph in the last great class struggle.

Proportional representation This system of voting ensures that a party receives the same percentage of seats as votes received.

Protectionist Favouring the protection of trade by having duties on imports.

Reactionary Opposing political or social change and wanting to revert to past conditions.

Realpolitik The term is used to describe the ruthless and cynical policies of politicians, like Bismarck, whose main aim was to increase the power of a state.

Regent   A ruler invested with authority on behalf of another.

Reich   The German for empire.

Reichsbank   A national German bank (like the Bank of England).

Reichstag   The National Parliament, elected by all males over 25 years of age.

Republican   Of, or favouring, a government without a monarch.

Revolutionary shop stewards   Working-class activists who tried to organise mass action in the factories of Berlin in an attempt to end the war.

Russo-Japanese War   This conflict, caused by the conflicting imperial ambitions of Japan and Russia in Asia, was fought in 1904–5. Japan won.

Second German Empire   The first Empire was the Holy Roman Empire, established by Charlemagne. The second Empire was the one established by Bismarck.

Secular   Non-religious and non-spiritual: civil, not ecclesiastical.

Self-determination   The right of people to decide their own form of government.

Septennates   The arrangement whereby military spending was agreed for 7 years.

Slavs   People who regard themselves to be of the same ethnic group and whose language is Slavonic. Slavs include Russians, Czechs, Serbs and Bulgarians.

Sovereignty   Supreme power.

Soviet   A council of workers, peasants and soldiers.

Splendid isolation   For much of the late nineteenth century, Britain had not allied with any major power. Its great naval strength meant that it seemed to be in no danger of invasion. However, by 1900 Britain faced challenges from France, Russia and Germany. Suddenly its isolation seemed far from splendid.

Standing army   A state's main military force. The army usually supported the government against revolutionary activity.

Status quo   The existing condition or situation.

The Straits   The Bosphorus and Dardanelles, which link the Black Sea with the Mediterranean Sea.

Tariffs   Import duties, intended to raise money or protect domestic industry and agriculture from foreign competition.

Tenant farmers   Farmers who rented their land from a landowner.

Triple Entente powers   Britain, France and Russia.

Vormärz   The period from 1815 to 1848.

Vorparlament   This is usually translated as 'pre-parliament', but it is better thought of as 'preparatory parliament', which was preparing the way for the real parliament.

War credits   Financial bills, enabling the war to be funded.

Wilhelmine Germany   The period from 1888 to 1918 when Wilhelm II was Kaiser.

Zollverein   The Prussian Customs Union.

Index